Edexcel

foundation

GCSE Modular Mathematics

unit 3

Keith Pledger

Gareth Cole

Peter Jolly

Graham Newman

Joe Petran

www.heinemann.co.uk
✓ Free online support
✓ Useful weblinks
✓ 24 hour online ordering

01865 888058

Inspiring generations

Heinemann is an imprint of Pearson Education Limited, a company incorporated in England and Wales, having its registered office at Edinburgh Gate, Harlow, Essex, CM20 2JE. Registered company number: 872828

www.heinemann.co.uk

Heinemann is a registered trademark of Pearson Education Limited

Text © Harcourt Education Limited, 2007

First published 2008

12 11 10 09
10 9 8 7 6 5 4 3 2

British Library Cataloguing in Publication Data is available from the British Library on request.

ISBN 978 0 435585 29 7

Typeset by Tech-Set Ltd
Cover design by mccdesign
Cover photo: © Photolibrary
Printed in China (SWTC/02)

Acknowledgements

The author and publisher would like to thank the following individuals and organisations for permission to reproduce photographs: Corbis pp**3**, **9** bottom, **18**, **39** middle, **43**, **52** top, **52** bottom, **93**, **118**, **127**; Alamy Images/Brand X Pictures p**5**; Photos.com pp**6**, **20** top, **21**, **41** bottom, **44**, **73**, **107** top, **107** bottom, **211**; MorgueFile/Chris Trott p**9** top; Alamy Images/ ImageSource p**13** top; Harcourt Ltd/Jules Selmes pp**13** bottom, **30** bottom, **96**; Getty Images/ PhotoDisc pp**20** bottom, **24**, **25**, **26**, **36** bottom, **42**, **125**, **144**; iStockPhoto/Rob Sylvan p**28** top; Harcourt Ltd/Mark Bassett p**28** bottom; iStockPhoto/Melissa Carroll p**29**; Brand X Pictures p**30** top; Dreamstime/Violet Star p**36** top; Dreamstime/Caroline Hedges p**38**; iStockPhoto/ Greg Nicholas p**39** top; Dreamstime; Harcourt Ltd/Gareth Boden pp**39** bottom, **115** top; iStockPhoto/April Turner p**41** top; Harcourt Ltd/Tudor Photography pp**41** middle, **115** bottom; Dreamstime/Ian Francis p**47**; iStockPhoto/Paul Hill p**49** top; Harcourt Ltd/Jill Birschbach p**49** bottom; Harcourt Ltd/Malcolm Harris p**53**; Dreamstime/Juan Nel p**113**; Digital Vision p**129**; iStockPhoto/Dan Mason p**196**

Every effort has been made to contact copyright holders of material reproduced in this book. Any omissions will be rectified in subsequent printings if notice is given to the publishers.

Quick reference to chapters

Contents

1 Working with number

2 Fractions

3 Percentage, ratio and proportion

4 Elements of algebra

5 Equations and inequalities

6 Graphs

7 Formulae

8 Symmetry and transformations

9 Angles, bearings, drawings and constructions

10 Mensuration and Pythagoras' theorem

About this book

This book has been carefully matched to the new two-tier modular specification for Edexcel GCSE Maths. It covers everything you need to know to achieve success in Unit 3. The author team is made up of the Chief Examiner, the Chair of Examiners, Principal Examiners and Senior Moderators, all experienced teachers with an excellent understanding of the Edexcel specification.

Key features

Chapters are divided into **sections**. In each section you will find:
• **key points**, highlighted throughout like this

> • When working out a decimal addition or subtraction, always write the decimal points under each other.

• **examples** that show you how to tackle questions
• an **exercise** to help develop your understanding.

Each chapter ends with a **mixed exercise** and a **summary of key points**. Mixed exercises, which include past exam questions marked with an [E], are designed to test your understanding across the chapter.

Hint boxes are used to make explanations clearer. They may also remind you of previously learned facts or tell you where in the book to find more information.

> Keep the digits in their columns then add each column.

An examination practice paper is included to help you prepare for the exam at the end of the unit.

Answers are provided at the back of the book to use as your teacher directs.

Quick reference and detailed Contents pages

Use the thumb spots on the **Quick reference page** to turn to the right chapter quickly.

Use the detailed **Contents** to help you find a section on a particular topic. The summary and reference codes on the right show your teacher the part(s) of the specification covered by each section of the book. (For example, NA5a refers to Number and algebra, section 5 Use of symbols, subsection a.)

Teaching and learning software

References to the Heinemann Edexcel GCSE Mathematics **Teaching and Learning Software** are included for you and your teacher. (The number refers to the relevant chapter from the linear course on which the software is based.)

> **8** Calculating with fractions

Use of a calculator

 These symbols show where you must, or must not, use a calculator.

1 Working with number

1.1 Long multiplication and long division

In Foundation Unit 3 you learned to multiply and divide numbers.
Here is some further practice.

In the exam you may be asked to add, subtract, multiply or divide any numbers.

You can also use the grid method as demonstrated on page 5.

Example 1

Work out 278×42.

$$
\begin{array}{r}
2\,7\,8 \\
\times\ \ 4\,2 \\
\hline
5_1 5_1 6 \\
+\ 1\ 1_3 1_3 2\ 0 \\
\hline
1\ 1\ 6\ 7\ 6 \\
\hline
\end{array}
$$

$5_1 5_1 6$ —— This is 278×2

$+\ 1\ 1_3 1_3 2\ 0$ —— This is 278×40, which is $278 \times 10 \times 4$

$1\ 1\ 6\ 7\ 6$ —— This is $278 \times 2 + 278 \times 40$

Example 2

Work out $901 \div 17$.

Method 1

17 divides into 90
5 times remainder 5

17 divides into 51
3 times exactly

$$17\overline{)9\,0\,1}$$

$$
\begin{array}{r}
5 \\
17\overline{)9\,0\,1} \\
-\ 8\,5 \\
\hline
5
\end{array}
$$

$$
\begin{array}{r}
5\,3 \\
17\overline{)9\,0\,1} \\
8\,5\ \downarrow \\
\hline
5\,1 \\
5\,1 \\
\hline
0\,0
\end{array}
$$

Method 2

This is a shorter way of setting out the steps in Method 1.

$$
\begin{array}{r}
5\,3 \\
17\overline{)9\,0^5 1}
\end{array}
$$

Exercise 1A

1 Work out

   (a) 582×13 (b) 681×43 (c) 479×37

   (d) 892×17 (e) 634×72 (f) 726×43

   (g) 307×25 (h) 809×20 (i) 912×59

2 Work out

   (a) $386 \div 16$ (b) $952 \div 17$ (c) $828 \div 18$

   (d) $903 \div 21$ (e) $782 \div 22$ (f) $782 \div 34$

   (g) $968 \div 14$ (h) $876 \div 19$ (i) $570 \div 15$

1.2 Negative numbers

In Foundation Unit 3 you learned to add, subtract, multiply and divide negative integers.
Here is some further practice.

- You can use **negative numbers** to describe quantities such as temperatures less than $0\,°C$.
  You can also use negative numbers in calculations.

- Subtracting a positive number is the same as adding the negative number.
  Subtracting a negative number is the same as adding the positive number.

- This table shows the signs you get when you multiply or divide two numbers together.

+	×/÷	+	=	+
+	×/÷	−	=	−
−	×/÷	+	=	−
−	×/÷	−	=	+

Example 3

Work out

(a) $4 - +5$ (b) $-2 - -3$

(c) $3 + -4$ (d) $-2 + +2$

(a) $4 - +5$ is the same as $4 + -5$.

    $4 - +5 = -1$

Start at 4:
go down 5
to get to -1.

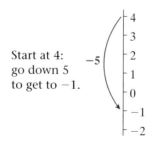

(b) $-2 - -3$ is the same as $-2 + +3$.

$$-2 - -3 = +1$$

Start at -2 and go up 3 to get to $+1$.

(c) $3 + -4$

$$3 + -4 = -1$$

Start at 3 and go down 4 to get to -1.

(d) $-2 + +2$

$$-2 + +2 = 0$$

Start at -2 and go up 2 to get to 0.

Example 4

Work out
(a) $-25 \times +2$ **(b)** $-9 \div -3$
(c) -12×-4 **(d)** $-20 \div +10$

(a) $-25 \times +2 = -50$ **(b)** $-9 \div -3 = +3$
(c) $-12 \times -4 = +48$ **(d)** $-20 \div +10 = -2$

 Exercise 1B

1 Work out
  (a) $-5 + -2$ **(b)** $7 - +3$ **(c)** $6 - -4$ **(d)** $4 + +5$
  (e) $-9 - -8$ **(f)** $-4 + +6$ **(g)** $4 + -6$ **(h)** $-4 - +6$

2 Work out
  (a) -4×-6 **(b)** $-3 \times +5$ **(c)** $32 \div -4$ **(d)** $-30 \div -10$
  (e) $-10 \times +4$ **(f)** $-36 \div +6$ **(g)** 5×-6 **(h)** $-100 \div -50$

3 A submarine dives to a depth of -47 metres, surfaces and then dives to a depth of -36 metres.
What is the difference in the depths of the dives?

4 The temperature in the Antarctic is recorded as $-24\,°C$ one night. The following day it rises by $6\,°C$.
What is the temperature during the day?

5 Copy and complete these tables.

(a)

		1st number	
×	−3	5	−8
2nd number 2		10	
−7			
4	−12		

(b)

		1st number	
−	3	−5	7
2nd number −2			
4		−9	
−3			

(c)

		1st number	
+	−1	−3	6
2nd number 4	3		
7			
−2			

(d)

		1st number	
÷	8	−16	−24
2nd number −2		8	
4			
−8			

1.3 Adding and subtracting decimals

- When working out a decimal addition or subtraction, always write the decimal points under each other.

Example 5

Two adults weigh 64.5 kg and 75.85 kg.
What is their combined weight?

Write the decimal points under each other.

$$
\begin{array}{r}
6\,4.5 \\
+\ 7\,5.8\,5 \\
\hline
1\,4\,0.3\,5 \\
\scriptstyle 1
\end{array}
$$

Answer: 140.35 kg

> Keep the digits in their columns then add each column.

Example 6

Mary buys an iron costing £17.85.
She pays with a £20 note.
How much change should she receive?

£20 − £17.85 is

$$
\begin{array}{r}
\overset{1}{\cancel{2}}\,\overset{9}{\cancel{0}}\,\overset{9}{.}\overset{}{\cancel{0}}\,{}^{1}0 \\
-\ 1\,7.8\,5 \\
\hline
2.1\,5
\end{array}
$$

Write £20 as 20.00

Change: £2.15

> Shops often give change by counting on:
>
> £17.85 + (5p) = £17.90
> £17.90 + (10p) = £18.00
> £18.00 + (£2) = £20.00
> (5p) + (10p) + (£2) = £2.15

Exercise 1C

Work out these calculations.
Show all your working.

1 2.5 + 3.7

2 5 + 0.45

3 0.9 − 0.1

4 16.23 + 3.79

5 0.004 + 2.949

6 5.84 − 2.60

7 27.49 − 9.52

8 11.01 + 5.2 + 23.17

9 8 + 0.31 + 1.117

10 205.8 − 46.92

11 118 − 11.8

12 5.06 + 15 − 11.38

13 4.49 + 1.6 − 2.79

14 421.605 − 35.1 + 2.05

1.4 Multiplying decimals

- When multiplying decimals, the answer must have the same number of decimal places as the total number of decimal places in the numbers being multiplied.

Example 7

Find the total cost of 35 CDs at £8.45 each.

Method 1 Long multiplication

```
      8 4 5
  ×     3 5
    4 2 2 5  —— 845 × 5
  2 5 3 5 0  —— 845 × 30
  2 9 5 7 5
```

8.45 has 2 d.p.
35 has 0 d.p.
Total: 2 decimal places

Answer: £295.75

This method is also called Napier's Bones.

Method 2 Grid method

8 × 3 = 24

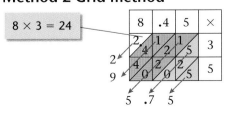

Write the products 8 × 3, 8 × 5, 4 × 3, 4 × 5, 5 × 3, 5 × 5 in the grid.
Add along the diagonals from right to left.

Answer: £295.75

Method 3 Adding method

```
        £ 8.4 5
    +   £ 8.4 5
      £ 1 6.9 0    2 lots
      £ 1 6.9 0    2 lots
        £ 8.4 5    1 lot
      £ 4 2.2 5    5 lots
      £ 8 4.9 0    10 lots
      £ 8 4.9 0    10 lots
      £ 8 4.9 0    10 lots
    £ 2 9 5.7 5
```

Exercise 1D

1 Work out these calculations.
Show all your working.

    (a) 8.6 × 4   **(b)** 0.57 × 14   **(c)** 0.57 × 0.14

    (d) 3.35 × 6   **(e)** 4.23 × 0.04   **(f)** 42.3 × 0.04

    (g) 0.423 × 0.4   **(h)** 3.16 × 0.02   **(i)** 4.35 × 2.6

2 Work out the total cost of

    (a) 6 tins of paint at £2.73 each

    (b) 4 magazines at £1.95 each

    (c) 4.5 kg of potatoes at £0.45 per kg

    (d) 9 melons at £1.45 each.

3 A full jug holds 2.4 pints of liquid.
How much liquid is there in

    (a) 16 full jugs   **(b)** 26 full jugs   **(c)** 56 full jugs?

4 A book costs £4.85.
Work out the cost of

    (a) 19 books   **(b)** 33 books   **(c)** 65 books.

5 An adult's cinema ticket costs £5.95.
What is the total cost of tickets for

    (a) 12 adults   **(b)** 28 adults   **(c)** 37 adults?

6 A can of paint contains 2.55 litres.
How much paint is there in

    (a) 15 cans   **(b)** 25 cans   **(c)** 55 cans?

1.5 Dividing with decimals

Example 8

Work out $66 \div 8$.

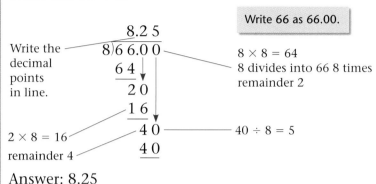

Write 66 as 66.00.

$$
\begin{array}{r}
8.2\,5 \\
8\,)\overline{6\,6.0\,0} \\
6\,4 \\
\hline
2\,0 \\
1\,6 \\
\hline
4\,0 \\
4\,0 \\
\hline
\end{array}
$$

Write the decimal points in line.

$8 \times 8 = 64$
8 divides into 66 8 times remainder 2

$2 \times 8 = 16$
remainder 4

$40 \div 8 = 5$

Answer: 8.25

- When dividing decimals by decimals, make sure you always divide by a whole number. You do this by multiplying both numbers by 10 or 100 or 1000 etc.

Example 9

1.8 m of fabric cost £10.08.
Work out the cost per metre of the fabric.

$10.08 \div 1.8$

1.8 is not a whole number.

To change 1.8 to a whole number, multiply by 10:
$1.8 \times 10 = 18$

Do the same to 10.08: $10.08 \times 10 = 100.8$
So $10.08 \div 1.8 = 100.8 \div 18$

$$
\begin{array}{r}
5.6 \\
18\,)\overline{1\,0\,0.8} \\
9\,0 \\
\hline
1\,0\,8 \\
1\,0\,8 \\
\hline
\end{array}
$$

Always write amounts of money with 2 decimal places.

The fabric costs £5.60 per metre.

Exercise 1E

Work out the calculations in questions **1–6**.

1 $7.2 \div 4$	**2** $22.2 \div 6$	**3** $4.125 \div 5$
4 $30.204 \div 9$	**5** $152.4 \div 6$	**6** $37.2 \div 8$

7   Five people raise £62.50 at a car boot sale.
They share the money equally.
How much is each person's share?

8   How many 5 litre oil cans are needed for 62.5 litres
of oil?

9   Work out
   (a) $7.2 \div 2.4$ (b) $9.66 \div 2.3$
   (c) $2.37 \div 0.3$ (d) $4.7 \div 0.1$
   (e) $23.535 \div 4.5$ (f) $9.8 \div 3.5$

10   Share £500 equally between 8 people.

1.6 Problems involving speed and units of measure

Example 10

A train travels at 100 km per hour.
How far will it travel in 4 hours?

The train travels 100 km in 1 hour.
So it will travel 100×4 km $= 400$ km in 4 hours.

Remember:
100 km per hour means
100 km each hour.

Example 11

A 3 km race is split into 5 equal stages.
How many metres is each stage?

3 km $= 3 \times 1000$ m $= 3000$ m

Each stage $= \dfrac{3000}{5} = 600$ m

Example 12

A kilogram is approximately 2.2 pounds.
A baby weighs 8 pounds at birth.
Approximately how many kilograms is this?

The baby weighs 8 pounds.
1 kg $\approx$ 2.2 pounds

So the baby weighs about $\dfrac{8}{2.2} = 3.636$ kg   (to 3 d.p.)

$\approx$ means 'is approximately
equal to'.

Exercise 1F

1 A runner can run 300 m per minute.
How far can he run in 5 minutes?

2 A car travels at an average speed of 50 mph (miles per hour).
How far will the car travel in
(a) 3 hours **(b)** 8 hours?

3 In sailing, one knot equals one nautical mile per hour.
A boat can sail at an average speed of 5 knots.
How long will it take the boat to travel
(a) 50 nautical miles **(b)** 80 nautical miles
(c) 35 nautical miles?

4 A snail moves at 3 mm per second.
How long will it take the snail to move
(a) 12 mm **(b)** 21 mm **(c)** 150 mm?

5 A 2 litre bottle of cola is shared between 8 children.
How many millilitres of cola does each child receive?

Remember:
1 litre = 1000 millilitres

6 A portion of chips weighs 300 g.
How many kilograms will 12 portions weigh?

7 A fence is made from six similar fence panels.
Each panel is 150 cm long.
How many metres long is the fence?

8 A pile of 30 exercise books is 12 cm high.
How thick is each exercise book in mm?

9 A pencil is 6 inches long.
Approximately how long is the pencil in cm?

1 inch ≈ 2.5 cm

10 Tom puts 8 gallons of petrol into his car.
Approximately how many litres of petrol does Tom put
into his car?

1 gallon ≈ 4.5 l

11 Samina is 165 cm tall.
Approximately how tall is Samina in feet?

30 cm ≈ 1 foot

12 Harry weighs 198 pounds.
Approximately how much does Harry weigh in kg?

1 kg ≈ 2.2 lb

13 The distance from Manchester to London is 200 miles.
Write down the approximate distance from London to
Manchester in km.

5 miles ≈ 8 km

14 The speed limit in a town is 30 mph.
Approximately what is the speed limit in km per hour?

5 miles ≈ 8 km

1.7 Index laws

- The ^{2} in 5^2 is called an **index** or a **power**. It tells you how many times the number must be multiplied by itself.
  For example: $5^2 \times 4^3 = 5 \times 5 \times 4 \times 4 \times 4$

- Any number (apart from zero) raised to the power zero is 1.

You used index notation in Foundation Unit 3.

For example
$5^2 \times 4^3 = 5 \times 5 \times 4 \times 4 \times 4$

$5^0 = 1$

Example 13

(a) Find the value of x if $5^x = 25$
(b) Find the value of n if $3^n = 81$

(a) $5 \times 5 = 25$, so $5^2 = 25$ and $x = 2$
(b) $3 \times 3 \times 3 \times 3 = 81$, so $3^4 = 81$ and $n = 4$

'Indices' is the plural of index.

- To multiply powers of the same number, add the indices.
  In general: $x^n \times x^m = x^{n+m}$

- To divide powers of the same number, subtract the indices.
  In general: $x^n \div x^m = x^{n-m}$

- To raise a power of a number to a **further power**, multiply the indices.
  For example: $(10^2)^3 = 10^{2 \times 3} = 10^6$

Example 14

Simplify
(a) $2^2 \times 2^4$ (b) $3^3 \times 3^6$ (c) $7^5 \div 7^3$

(d) $3^4 \div 3$ (e) $\dfrac{5^6 \times 5^3}{5^4}$ (f) $y^3 \times y^2$

(a) $2^2 \times 2^4 = 2^{2+4} = 2^6$ (b) $3^3 \times 3^6 = 3^{3+6} = 3^9$
(c) $7^5 \div 7^3 = 7^{5-3} = 7^2$ (d) $3^4 \div 3 = 3^{4-1} = 3^3$
(e) $\dfrac{5^6 \times 5^3}{5^4} = \dfrac{5^{6+3}}{5^4} = \dfrac{5^9}{5^4} = 5^{9-4} = 5^5$
(f) $y^3 \times y^2 = y^{3+2} = y^5$

$3 = 3^1$

Exercise 1G

1 Rewrite these expressions using index notation.

(a) $4 \times 4 \times 4$

(b) $2 \times 2 \times 2 \times 2 \times 2 \times 2$

(c) $5 \times 5 \times 5 \times 7 \times 7$

(d) $3 \times 5 \times 5 \times 11 \times 11 \times 11$

2 Evaluate

(a) 3^3

(b) $2^3 \times 3^4$

(c) $5^0 \times 7^2$

(d) $\dfrac{2^9}{2^5}$

3 (a) Find x when $5^x = 625$

(b) Find n when $2^n = 128$

(c) Find m when $9^m = 1$

4 Simplify

(a) $6^2 \times 6^4$

(b) $5^4 \times 5^2$

(c) $7^6 \times 7^3$

(d) 10×10^2

(e) $8^4 \div 8$

(f) $10^4 \div 10^2$

(g) $4^5 \div 4^3$

(h) $3^5 \div 3^2$

(i) $2^2 \times 2^3 \times 2^4$

(j) $5^3 \times 5^5 \times 5$

(k) $3^3 \times 3 \times 3^0$

(l) $\dfrac{4^3 \times 4^2}{4^3}$

(m) $\dfrac{3^9 \div 3^2}{3^4}$

(n) $\dfrac{5^8 \times 5^4}{5^2}$

(o) $\dfrac{7^4 \div 7^2}{7}$

(p) $\dfrac{2^6 \div 2^2}{2^4}$

(q) $x^3 \times x^4$

(r) $z^4 \div z^2$

(s) $\dfrac{c^3 \times c^4}{c^2}$

(t) $\dfrac{y^4 \times y}{y^2}$

(u) $(4^2)^3$

(v) $(3^3)^2$

1.8 Reciprocals

- Multiplying a number by its **reciprocal** gives 1.

Example 15

Find the reciprocal of

(a) 6

(b) 0.2

(c) $\frac{2}{5}$

(a) 6 times its reciprocal = 1

$$6 \times x = 1$$

$$x = \tfrac{1}{6}$$

The reciprocal of 6 is $\frac{1}{6}$

The reciprocal of 6 is $\frac{1}{6}$
$\frac{1}{6}$ is also the multiplicative inverse of 6, because
$6 \times \frac{1}{6} = 1$

(b) 0.2 times its reciprocal = 1

$$0.2 \times x = 1$$

$$x = \frac{1}{0.2}, \quad 1 \div 0.2 = 5$$

$$x = 5$$

The reciprocal of 0.2 is 5

(c) $\frac{2}{5} \times x = 1$

$$x = 1 \div \frac{2}{5}$$

$$= 1 \times \frac{5}{2}$$

$$= \frac{5}{2}$$

The reciprocal of $\frac{2}{5}$ is $\frac{5}{2} = 2\frac{1}{2}$

- The reciprocal of any number is 1 divided by that number.
- Zero has no reciprocal because you cannot divide by zero.

The reciprocal of 5 is $\frac{1}{5}$; the reciprocal of x is $\frac{1}{x}$

 Exercise 1H

1 Find the reciprocal of
   (a) 6   (b) 3   (c) 2
   (d) 7   (e) 9   (f) 20

2 Find the reciprocal of
   (a) 0.1   (b) 0.5   (c) 0.25
   (d) 0.4   (e) 0.3   (f) 0.125

3 Find the reciprocal, in its simplest form, of
   (a) $\frac{3}{5}$ (b) $\frac{2}{7}$ (c) $\frac{1}{4}$
   (d) $\frac{1}{8}$ (e) $\frac{3}{16}$ (f) $\frac{5}{8}$

4 Find the reciprocal of
   (a) m (b) y (c) $\frac{1}{x}$ (d) y^3

 Mixed exercise 1

1 Work out
   (a) 623×17 (b) 563×42
   (c) $744 \div 24$ (d) $954 \div 18$

2 Work out
   (a) $-6 + -3$ (b) $7 - -3$
   (c) $8 - +4$ (d) $-3 + +5$

3 Work out
   (a) $-8 \times +2$ (b) $-10 \div -5$
   (c) $6 \div -3$ (d) -7×-5

4 Work out
   (a) $7.3 + 5.2$ (b) $50.2 - 37.9$
   (c) $109 - 15.3$ (d) $4.56 - 9.13 + 15.2$

5 Work out the total cost of 25 litres of fuel at £1.06
   per litre.

6 Find the value of
   (a) 65.6×0.6 (b) 8.25×2.6
   (c) $37.5 \div 50$ (d) $44.5 \div 0.5$

7 Jack travels 4.85 miles to work.
   In one month he goes to work on 22 days.
   How far does he travel?

8 Sally wrote down the temperature at different times on
   1st January 2003.

Time	Temperature
midnight	$-6\,°C$
4 am	$-10\,°C$
8 am	$-4\,°C$
noon	$7\,°C$
3 pm	$6\,°C$
7 pm	$-2\,°C$

   (a) Write down
       (i) the **highest** temperature
       (ii) the **lowest** temperature.

   (b) Work out the difference in the temperature between
       (i) 4 am and 8 am   (ii) 3 pm and 7 pm.
   At 11 pm that day the temperature had fallen by $5\,°C$ from
   its value at 7 pm.

   (c) Work out the temperature at 11 pm.   [E]

9 Fatima bought 48 teddy bears at £9.55 each.
   (a) Work out the total amount she paid.
   Fatima sold all the teddy bears for a total of £696.
   She sold each teddy bear for the same price.
   (b) Work out the price at which Fatima sold each teddy
       bear.   [E]

10 1€ = £0.62
   (a) How many pounds sterling would be exchanged for €55?
   (b) How many euros would be exchanged for £485?

11 A train travels at an average speed of 70 km per hour.
   (a) How far will the train travel in
       (i) 4 hours   (ii) 10 hours?
   (b) How long will it take the train to travel
       (i) 210 km   (ii) 385 km?

12 A brick wall is 1.2 m high.
   The wall is made from 20 layers of bricks.
   How high is each layer of bricks?

13 A bag of potatoes weighs 11 pounds.
   Write down the approximate weight of the bag of potatoes
   in kilograms.

   > 1 kg ≈ 2.2 pounds

14 Rewrite the following expressions using index notation.
   (a) $3 \times 3 \times 3$ (b) $5 \times 5 \times 5 \times 5$
   (c) $5 \times 5 \times 7 \times 7 \times 9$ (d) $3 \times 3 \times 5 \times 5$

15 Evaluate
   (a) 7^3 (b) 6^4 (c) 9^0
   (d) $2^4 \times 3^3$ (e) $3^2 \times 2^3$ (f) $\dfrac{7^5}{7^2}$

16 Find x if
   (a) $9^x = 729$ (b) $2^x = 32$ (c) $10^x = 10\,000$

17 Simplify
   (a) $2^4 \times 2^5$ (b) $5^4 \times 5^5$ (c) $3^2 \times 3^3$ (d) $7^4 \div 7^3$
   (e) $9^6 \div 9^3$ (f) $7^3 \div 7$ (g) $\dfrac{4^2 \times 4^4}{4^3}$ (h) $\dfrac{3^4 \div 3}{3^3}$

18 Find the reciprocal of
   (a) 9   (b) 6   (c) 0.5   (d) 0.625
   (e) $\frac{4}{5}$ (f) $\frac{3}{7}$ (g) x (h) $\frac{1}{y}$

19 A Large tub of popcorn costs £3.80 and holds 200 g.
A Regular tub of popcorn costs £3.50 and holds 175 g.

Rob says that the 200 g Large tub is the better value
for money.
Linda says that the 175 g Regular tub is the better value
for money.

Who is correct?

Explain the reasons for your answer.
You must show all your working.   [E]

Summary of key points

1 You can use **negative numbers** to describe quantities such
as temperatures less than 0 °C.
You can also use negative numbers in calculations.

2 Subtracting a positive number is the same as adding the
negative number.
Subtracting a negative number is the same as adding the
positive number.

3 This table shows the signs you get when you multiply or
divide two numbers together.

+	×/÷	+	=	+
+	×/÷	−	=	−
−	×/÷	+	=	−
−	×/÷	−	=	+

4 When working out a decimal addition or subtraction,
always write the decimal points under each other.

5 When multiplying decimals, the answer must have the
same number of decimal places as the total number of
decimal places in the numbers being multiplied.

6 When dividing decimals by decimals, make sure you always
divide by a whole number. You do this by multiplying both
numbers by 10 or 100 or 1000 etc.

7 The ^{2} in 5^2 is called an **index** or a **power**. It tells you how many times the number must be multiplied by itself.

8 Any number (apart from zero) raised to the power zero is 1.

$$5^0 = 1$$

9 To multiply powers of the same number, add the indices.
In general: $x^n \times x^m = x^{n+m}$

10 To divide powers of the same number, subtract the indices.
In general: $x^n \div x^m = x^{n-m}$

11 To raise a power of a number to a **further power**, multiply the indices.

12 Multiplying a number by its **reciprocal** gives 1.

13 The reciprocal of any number is 1 divided by that number.

14 Zero has no reciprocal because you cannot divide by zero.

2 Fractions

2.1 Multiplying fractions

8 Calculating with fractions

- To multiply two fractions:

Multiply the numerators.

Multiply the denominators.

- To multiply a fraction by a whole number:

Multiply the numerator by the whole number.

The denominator stays the same.

- After multiplying fractions you should simplify the answer if you can.

Example 1

Work out

(a) $\frac{2}{3} \times \frac{3}{5}$ (b) $\frac{1}{2} \times \frac{3}{7}$ (c) $\frac{2}{3} \times 4$ (d) $\frac{1}{6} \times 3$

(a) $\frac{2}{3} \times \frac{3}{5} = \frac{2 \times 3}{3 \times 5} = \frac{6}{15} = \frac{2}{5}$ (b) $\frac{1}{2} \times \frac{3}{7} = \frac{1 \times 3}{2 \times 7} = \frac{3}{14}$

(c) $\frac{2}{3} \times 4 = \frac{2 \times 4}{3} = \frac{8}{3} = 2\frac{2}{3}$ (d) $\frac{1}{6} \times 3 = \frac{1 \times 3}{6} = \frac{3}{6} = \frac{1}{2}$

Exercise 2A

1 Work out

(a) $\frac{2}{5} \times \frac{3}{4}$ (b) $\frac{1}{2} \times \frac{2}{7}$ (c) $\frac{1}{3} \times \frac{3}{7}$ (d) $\frac{3}{7} \times \frac{1}{5}$

(e) $\frac{2}{3} \times \frac{2}{5}$ (f) $\frac{3}{8} \times \frac{1}{4}$ (g) $\frac{5}{9} \times \frac{1}{4}$ (h) $\frac{2}{11} \times \frac{1}{2}$

(i) $\frac{5}{8} \times \frac{2}{3}$ (j) $\frac{4}{5} \times \frac{1}{6}$

2 Work out

(a) $\frac{2}{3} \times 4$ (b) $\frac{3}{5} \times 2$ (c) $\frac{5}{8} \times 6$ (d) $\frac{1}{2} \times 7$

(e) $4 \times \frac{2}{7}$ (f) $5 \times \frac{3}{10}$ (g) $3 \times \frac{2}{5}$ (h) $4 \times \frac{4}{7}$

3 One centimetre is about $\frac{1}{2}$ an inch.
How many inches are there in 7 cm?

4 A bottle of water contains $\frac{7}{10}$ of a litre of water.
How many litres of water are there in 6 bottles?

5 A can holds $\frac{1}{3}$ of a litre of lemonade.
How much lemonade is there in 10 cans?

6 Samina's Maths lesson is $\frac{3}{4}$ of an hour long.
She has 3 lessons a week.
How long does Samina spend in Maths lessons
during 1 week?

2.2 Finding a fraction of a quantity

- To find a fraction of a quantity, multiply the quantity by the fraction.

Example 2

(a) Find $\frac{2}{3}$ of 9.
(b) A cake weighs 300 g.
How much does $\frac{1}{5}$ of the cake weigh?

(a) $\frac{2}{3}$ of $9 = \frac{2}{3} \times 9 = \frac{18}{3} = 6$
(b) $\frac{1}{5}$ of $300\,\text{g} = \frac{1}{5} \times 300 = \frac{300}{5} = 60\,\text{g}$

Multiplying by $\frac{1}{5}$ is the same as dividing by 5.

 Exercise 2B

1 Work out
  (a) $\frac{3}{4}$ of 12   (b) $\frac{2}{5}$ of 10   (c) $\frac{2}{3}$ of 15   (d) $\frac{5}{7}$ of 28
  (e) $\frac{3}{8}$ of 32   (f) $\frac{4}{11}$ of 22   (g) $\frac{5}{9}$ of 36   (h) $\frac{2}{3}$ of 60
  (i) $\frac{3}{4}$ of £18   (j) $\frac{3}{4}$ of 6 m   (k) $\frac{1}{5}$ of £4.50 (l) $\frac{2}{3}$ of 24 kg

2 A pizza weighs 400 g.
How much does $\frac{1}{8}$ of a pizza weigh?

3 There are 24 houses in Lancaster Place.
$\frac{3}{4}$ of the houses have garages.
How many houses have garages?

4 Liverpool played 48 matches last season.
They won $\frac{5}{6}$ of these matches.
How many matches did they win?

5 The normal price of a computer game is £36.
In a sale the game is sold for $\frac{2}{3}$ of its normal price.
How much does the game cost in the sale?

6 28 students took a Maths test.
$\frac{3}{4}$ of the students passed the test.
How many passed the test?

7 A car costs £2500.
To buy the car, Shona needs to pay a deposit of $\frac{1}{4}$ of the price.
How much is the deposit?

2.3 Fractions and decimals

- To change a fraction into a decimal, divide the numerator by the denominator.

Example 3

Write as a decimal
(a) $\frac{2}{5}$ (b) $\frac{3}{8}$

(a) $\frac{2}{5} = 2 \div 5 = 0.4$ (b) $\frac{3}{8} = 3 \div 8 = 0.375$

- To change a decimal into a fraction, you can use a place value table.

Example 4

Write as a fraction
(a) 0.3   (b) 0.281   (c) 0.25

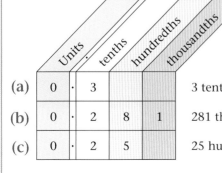

(a) | 0 | · | 3 | | | 3 tenths $= \frac{3}{10}$

(b) | 0 | · | 2 | 8 | 1 | 281 thousandths $= \frac{281}{1000}$

(c) | 0 | · | 2 | 5 | | 25 hundredths $= \frac{25}{100} = \frac{1}{4}$

Simplify the fraction.

Simplifying fractions was covered in Chapter 2 of Foundation Unit 3.

Exercise 2C

1 Change these fractions into decimals.

(a) $\frac{1}{2}$ (b) $\frac{1}{4}$ (c) $\frac{3}{4}$ (d) $\frac{3}{5}$ (e) $\frac{7}{10}$

(f) $\frac{11}{20}$ (g) $\frac{5}{8}$ (h) $\frac{17}{100}$ (i) $\frac{7}{8}$ (j) $\frac{4}{5}$

2 Change these decimals into fractions.

(a) 0.3   (b) 0.6   (c) 0.21   (d) 0.36   (e) 0.789

(f) 0.623   (g) 0.02   (h) 0.031   (i) 0.008   (j) 0.203

2.4 Writing one number as a fraction of another

Example 5

A library has 1000 books. Of these books, 648 are fiction.
The others are non-fiction.
What fraction of the books are

(a) fiction   (b) non-fiction?

(a) 648 out of 1000 are fiction.

The fraction is $\frac{648}{1000}$

which is $\frac{81}{125}$ in its simplest form.

(b) $1000 - 648 = 352$ books are non-fiction.

The fraction is $\frac{352}{1000} = \frac{44}{125}$

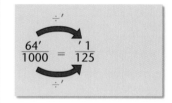

$$\frac{64\cancel{8}}{1000} = \frac{\cancel{8}1}{125}$$

Exercise 2D

1 There are 30 staff in an office. 16 are women.
What fraction of the staff are

(a) women   (b) men?

2 40 flowers are grown from a packet of seeds.
15 are yellow and 20 are red. The rest are white.
What fraction of the flowers are

(a) blue   (b) red   (c) white?

3 Fozia earns £360 a week.
She spends £30 on travel, £50 on food and £120 on
household bills.
What fraction of her earnings does Fozia spend on

(a) travel   (b) food   (c) bills?

(d) What fraction of her earnings is left?

4 Alex wins £1000. He saves £400 and spends the rest.
   What fraction of the prize does Alex spend?

5 Write 60 cm as a fraction of 2 m.

6 Write 55 out of 77 as a fraction in its simplest form.

7 Samina travels from her home to her friend's home.
   The total length of the journey is 275 km, including
   165 km on a motorway.
   What fraction of Samina's journey is
   (a) on a motorway   (b) not on a motorway?

8 Out of 150 employees, 30 walk to work.
   Write this as a fraction in its simplest form.

9 Five light bulbs in a box of 100 are broken.
   What fraction of the bulbs are not broken?

10 Jules has £5.
   She spends £2.40 on a magazine and £2 on sandwiches.
   What fraction of her money does Jules
   (a) spend on sandwiches
   (b) spend on a magazine
   (c) have left?

2.5 Adding and subtracting fractions

> **8** Calculating with fractions

- To add fractions with the same denominator (bottom),
  add the numerators (tops) then write the answer over the
  denominator.

Example 6

Work out

(a) $\frac{2}{5} + \frac{1}{5}$ (b) $\frac{3}{7} + \frac{2}{7}$

Add the numerators.

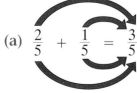

(a) $\frac{2}{5} + \frac{1}{5} = \frac{3}{5}$ (b) $\frac{3}{7} + \frac{2}{7} = \frac{5}{7}$

Same denominator

- To add fractions that have different denominators (bottoms), first find equivalent fractions that have the same denominator.

Example 7

Work out $\frac{1}{6} + \frac{2}{5}$

Find equivalent fractions that have the same denominator:

$$\frac{1}{6} = \frac{2}{12} = \frac{3}{18} = \frac{4}{24} = \frac{5}{30} \qquad\qquad \frac{2}{5} = \frac{4}{10} = \frac{8}{20} = \frac{12}{30}$$

$$\frac{1}{6} + \frac{2}{5} = \frac{5}{30} + \frac{12}{30} = \frac{17}{30}$$

> Equivalent fractions are covered in Chapter 2 of Foundation Unit 3.

Example 8

Work out $\frac{3}{8} + \frac{4}{5}$

An easy way to find equivalent fractions with the same denominator is

$$\frac{3}{8} \qquad + \qquad \frac{4}{5}$$

$$\frac{3 \times 5}{8 \times 5} = \frac{15}{40} \qquad \frac{4 \times 8}{5 \times 8} = \frac{32}{40}$$

$$\frac{3}{8} + \frac{4}{5} = \frac{15}{40} + \frac{32}{40} = \frac{47}{40}$$

$$\frac{47}{40} = 1\frac{7}{40}$$

> Give the answer in its simplest form.

Example 9

Work out $\frac{3}{4} + \frac{5}{12}$

$$\frac{3}{4} + \frac{5}{12} \quad\text{—}\quad 12 = 4 \times 3$$

$$\frac{3 \times 3}{4 \times 3} = \frac{9}{12}$$

$$\frac{3}{4} + \frac{5}{12} = \frac{9}{12} + \frac{5}{12} = \frac{14}{12}$$

$$\frac{14}{12} = 1\frac{2}{12} = 1\frac{1}{6}$$

> Write $\frac{14}{12}$ in its simplest form.

> Notice that 4 is a factor of 12. So you can write $\frac{3}{4}$ as an equivalent fraction with denominator 12.

- To add mixed numbers, first add the whole numbers then add the fractions.

Example 10

Work out $2\frac{3}{4} + 1\frac{1}{5}$

First add the whole numbers.   Then add the fractions.

$2 + 1 = ③$ $\frac{3}{4} + \frac{1}{5} = \frac{15}{20} + \frac{4}{20} = \overgroup{\frac{19}{20}}$

$2\frac{3}{4} + 1\frac{1}{5} = 3 + \frac{19}{20} = 3\frac{19}{20}$

Put the two parts back together.

$\frac{3 \times 5}{4 \times 5} = \frac{15}{20}$

$\frac{1 \times 4}{5 \times 4} = \frac{4}{20}$

- To subtract fractions with the same denominator, subtract the numerators, then write the answer over the denominator.
- To subtract fractions that have different denominators, first find equivalent fractions that have the same denominator.

Example 11

Work out

(a) $\frac{4}{7} - \frac{2}{7}$ (b) $\frac{3}{4} - \frac{2}{5}$ (c) $\frac{5}{8} - \frac{7}{16}$

(a) $\frac{4}{7} - \frac{2}{7} = \frac{2}{7}$

Denominators are the same.

(b) $\frac{3}{4} - \frac{2}{5}$

Denominators are different, so find equivalent fractions with the same denominator.

$\frac{3 \times 5}{4 \times 5} - \frac{2 \times 4}{5 \times 4}$

$= \frac{15}{20} - \frac{8}{20} = \frac{7}{20}$

(c) $\frac{5}{8} - \frac{7}{16}$

Denominators are different, so find equivalent fractions with the same denominator.

$= \frac{10}{16} - \frac{7}{16} = \frac{3}{16}$

Notice that $16 = 8 \times 2$

$\frac{5 \times 2}{8 \times 2} = \frac{10}{16}$

- To subtract mixed numbers, first subtract the whole numbers then subtract the fractions.

Example 12

Work out $4\frac{5}{8} - 2\frac{1}{4}$

First subtract the whole numbers.

$4 - 2 = ②$

$4\frac{5}{8} - 2\frac{1}{4} = 2\frac{3}{8}$ ◄

Then subtract the fractions.

$\frac{5}{8} - \frac{1}{4} = \frac{5}{8} - \frac{2}{8} = \boxed{\frac{3}{8}}$

Put the two parts back together.

$\frac{1 \times 2}{4 \times 2} = \frac{2}{8}$

Exercise 2E

1 Work out

(a) $\frac{2}{5} + \frac{3}{5}$ (b) $\frac{4}{7} + \frac{2}{7}$ (c) $\frac{3}{12} + \frac{5}{12}$ (d) $\frac{5}{8} - \frac{3}{8}$

(e) $\frac{7}{10} - \frac{3}{10}$ (f) $\frac{5}{9} - \frac{2}{9}$ (g) $\frac{4}{5} + \frac{2}{5}$ (h) $\frac{5}{6} + \frac{5}{6}$

(i) $\frac{7}{10} + \frac{5}{10}$ (j) $\frac{3}{4} + \frac{1}{4}$

2 Work out

(a) $\frac{3}{4} + \frac{1}{2}$ (b) $\frac{5}{8} + \frac{3}{4}$ (c) $\frac{5}{7} + \frac{11}{14}$ (d) $\frac{3}{4} - \frac{1}{2}$

(e) $\frac{5}{7} - \frac{3}{14}$ (f) $\frac{13}{20} - \frac{2}{5}$ (g) $\frac{2}{3} + \frac{1}{4}$ (h) $\frac{3}{4} + \frac{2}{5}$

(i) $\frac{5}{8} + \frac{1}{3}$ (j) $\frac{2}{3} - \frac{1}{4}$ (k) $\frac{4}{5} - \frac{2}{3}$ (l) $\frac{7}{8} - \frac{1}{5}$

(m) $\frac{7}{20} + \frac{1}{3}$ (n) $\frac{2}{11} + \frac{5}{7}$ (o) $\frac{11}{13} + \frac{3}{4}$ (p) $\frac{6}{7} - \frac{4}{9}$

(q) $\frac{8}{13} - \frac{2}{5}$ (r) $\frac{13}{15} - \frac{3}{4}$

3 Work out

(a) $2\frac{1}{4} + 1\frac{3}{4}$ (b) $4\frac{1}{5} + 1\frac{3}{5}$ (c) $2\frac{4}{7} + 3\frac{1}{7}$ (d) $4\frac{5}{8} - 1\frac{3}{8}$

(e) $5\frac{3}{4} - 2\frac{1}{4}$ (f) $2\frac{5}{8} - 1\frac{3}{8}$ (g) $4\frac{1}{4} + 2\frac{1}{2}$ (h) $1\frac{2}{5} + 2\frac{3}{10}$

(i) $2\frac{5}{8} - 1\frac{1}{4}$ (j) $5\frac{1}{3} - 2\frac{4}{15}$ (k) $2\frac{3}{5} + 1\frac{1}{7}$ (l) $3\frac{2}{3} + 1\frac{2}{7}$

(m) $3\frac{6}{7} - 1\frac{2}{3}$ (n) $5\frac{7}{8} - 2\frac{2}{5}$

4 Megan buys $\frac{3}{4}$ kg of strawberries and $\frac{1}{2}$ kg of cherries.
Work out the total weight of the fruit Megan buys.

5 When Ryan gets up in the morning he spends $\frac{3}{10}$ hour in the shower, $\frac{1}{5}$ hour drying his hair and $\frac{1}{12}$ hour getting dressed. What fraction of an hour does it take Ryan to get ready?

6 A packet of dried fruit is $\frac{2}{5}$ sultanas and $\frac{1}{6}$ apricots.
(a) What fraction of the fruit is either sultanas or apricots?
(b) What fraction of the fruit is neither sultanas nor apricots?

7 A bag of flour weighs $1\frac{1}{2}$ kg.
Ted uses $\frac{3}{8}$ kg of flour to make some bread.
How much flour will be left?

8 A carpenter buys $2\frac{3}{4}$ metres of wood.
He uses $\frac{5}{8}$ metres for a job.
How many metres of wood does he have left?

9 Tristan watches three programmes on television.
The programmes are:

Quiz	$\frac{1}{2}$ hour
Film	$1\frac{3}{4}$ hour
News	$\frac{3}{4}$ hour

How long does Tristan spend watching the three programmes?

10 Callum is weeding a flower bed.
The bed is $4\frac{3}{4}$ metres long. He has weeded $2\frac{1}{2}$ m.
How much is left to weed?

2.6 Dividing mixed numbers and fractions by an integer

- To divide a fraction by an integer, multiply the fraction by the inverse of the integer.

- To divide a mixed number, first change it to an improper fraction.

> An integer is a whole number. To find the multiplicative inverse of an integer, turn it upside down. For example, the inverse of 5 is $\frac{1}{5}$.

> In an improper fraction, the numerator is larger than the denominator.

Example 13

Work out
(a) $\frac{2}{7} \div 5$ (b) $\frac{6}{7} \div 3$ (c) $1\frac{3}{4} \div 5$

(a) $\frac{2}{7} \div 5$

$= \frac{2}{7} \times \frac{1}{5} = \frac{2 \times 1}{7 \times 5} = \frac{2}{35}$ Invert the 5 and multiply.

(b) $\frac{6}{7} \div 3$

$= \frac{6}{7} \times \frac{1}{3} = \frac{6}{21}$ Inverse of $3 = \frac{1}{3}$

$= \frac{2}{7}$ Simplify the answer.

(c) $1\frac{3}{4} \div 5$

$= \frac{7}{4} \div 5$ Change the mixed number into an improper fraction.

$= \frac{7}{4} \times \frac{1}{5}$ Invert the 5 and multiply.

$= \frac{7}{20}$

Exercise 2F

1 Work out

(a) $\frac{3}{5} \div 3$ (b) $\frac{4}{7} \div 2$ (c) $\frac{5}{8} \div 2$ (d) $\frac{3}{7} \div 6$

(e) $\frac{3}{4} \div 5$ (f) $\frac{4}{5} \div 3$ (g) $\frac{7}{12} \div 8$ (h) $\frac{9}{10} \div 4$

(i) $\frac{4}{9} \div 12$ (j) $\frac{1}{2} \div 7$

2 After a party $\frac{3}{4}$ of a cake is left. 5 people share it.
What fraction of the cake does each person have?

3 $1\frac{1}{2}$ kg of fruit will make 6 smoothies.
How much fruit is needed for 1 smoothie?

4 A $1\frac{1}{4}$ hour film is shown in 5 equal parts.
How long is each part?

5 A piece of rope is $3\frac{1}{8}$ yards long. It is cut into 5 equal
lengths. How long is each length?

2.7 Working with fractions efficiently

- You can simplify or cancel fractions to make multiplying and
  dividing easier.

Example 14

Work out

(a) $\frac{3}{4} \times \frac{7}{15}$ (b) $\frac{5}{18} \times \frac{4}{15}$ (c) $\frac{6}{7} \div 3$

(a) $\frac{3}{4} \times \frac{7}{15}$ 3 divides into 15.

$= \frac{3 \div 3}{4} \times \frac{7}{15 \div 3}$ Divide top and bottom by 3.

$= \frac{1}{4} \times \frac{7}{5}$

$= \frac{1 \times 7}{4 \times 5} = \frac{7}{20}$

(b) $\frac{5}{18} \times \frac{4}{15}$ 5 divides into 15.
Also, 2 divides into 4 and 18.

$= \frac{5 \div 5}{18 \div 2} \times \frac{4 \div 2}{15 \div 5}$ Divide top and bottom by 5.
Divide top and bottom by 2.

$= \frac{1 \times 2}{9 \times 3}$

$= \frac{2}{27}$

(c) $\frac{6}{7} \div 3$ A denominator divides into a numerator.

$= \frac{6}{7} \times \frac{1}{3}$ 3 divides into 6.

$= \frac{6 \div 3}{7} \times \frac{1}{3 \div 3}$

$= \frac{2 \times 1}{7 \times 1} = \frac{2}{7}$

Simplifying fractions is
covered in Section 2.2 of
Foundation Unit 3.

Exercise 2G

Look for numbers to cancel as you do this exercise.

1 $\frac{1}{2} \times \frac{4}{5}$ **2** $\frac{3}{4} \times \frac{8}{15}$ **3** $\frac{2}{5} \times \frac{5}{8}$

4 $\frac{1}{7} \times \frac{21}{25}$ **5** $\frac{2}{3} \times \frac{9}{14}$ **6** $\frac{3}{4} \times \frac{12}{21}$

7 $\frac{3}{5} \times \frac{20}{27}$ **8** $\frac{4}{7} \times \frac{21}{24}$ **9** $\frac{8}{15} \div 4$

10 $\frac{6}{11} \div 3$ **11** $\frac{14}{25} \div 7$ **12** $\frac{15}{19} \div 5$

2.8 Multiplying and dividing fractions and mixed numbers

- To divide by a fraction, invert the dividing fraction (turn it upside down) and change the division sign to multiplication.
- To multiply or divide mixed numbers, first change them to improper fractions.

For more on improper fractions see Chapter 2 in Foundation Unit 3.

Example 15

Work out

(a) $\frac{3}{4} \div \frac{4}{5}$ (b) $1\frac{1}{2} \times 2\frac{3}{4}$ (c) $2\frac{1}{3} - 1\frac{1}{3}$

(a) $\frac{3}{4} \div \frac{4}{5}$

$= \frac{3}{4} \times \frac{5}{4}$ | Invert the dividing fraction and multiply.

$= \frac{15}{16}$

(b) $1\frac{1}{2} \times 2\frac{3}{4}$ | Change the mixed numbers into improper fractions.

$= \frac{3}{2} \times \frac{11}{4}$

$= \frac{3 \times 11}{2 \times 4}$ | $\frac{33}{8}$ is an improper fraction. Simplify by changing it to a mixed number.

$= \frac{33}{8}$

$= 4\frac{1}{8}$

(c) $2\frac{1}{3} \div 1\frac{1}{3}$ | Change the mixed numbers into improper fractions.

$= \frac{7}{3} \div \frac{4}{3}$ | Invert the dividing fraction and multiply.

$= \frac{7}{3} \times \frac{3}{4}$

$= \frac{7}{3 \div 3} \times \frac{3 \div 3}{4}$ | Divide top and bottom by 3.

$= \frac{7}{4}$ | $\frac{7}{4}$ is an improper fraction. Simplify by changing it to a mixed number.

$= 1\frac{3}{4}$

Exercise 2H

Write all your answers in this exercise in their simplest form.

1 Work out

(a) $\frac{1}{5} \times \frac{2}{3}$ (b) $\frac{1}{4} \div \frac{1}{2}$ (c) $\frac{2}{5} \times \frac{3}{4}$ (d) $\frac{3}{5} \times \frac{5}{6}$

(e) $\frac{5}{8} \div \frac{3}{4}$ (f) $\frac{11}{6} \div \frac{3}{8}$ (g) $\frac{2}{3} \times \frac{6}{11}$ (h) $\frac{5}{12} \times \frac{4}{15}$

(i) $\frac{3}{8} \div \frac{5}{16}$ (j) $\frac{9}{15} \div \frac{12}{25}$

2 Work out

(a) $1\frac{1}{2} \times \frac{3}{4}$ (b) $2\frac{1}{5} \times 1\frac{1}{4}$ (c) $3\frac{1}{6} \times 1\frac{2}{3}$

(d) $4\frac{1}{2} \times 3\frac{3}{5}$ (e) $2\frac{3}{4} \times 1\frac{2}{11}$ (f) $4\frac{2}{5} \times 2\frac{5}{11}$

(g) $5 \times \frac{3}{4}$ (h) $2 \times \frac{3}{8}$

3 Work out

(a) $1\frac{1}{2} \div 1\frac{3}{8}$ (b) $2\frac{2}{5} \div 1\frac{3}{10}$ (c) $3\frac{1}{3} \div 1\frac{5}{6}$

(d) $2\frac{1}{7} \div 1\frac{3}{14}$ (e) $5\frac{1}{2} \div 1\frac{3}{4}$ (f) $6\frac{1}{8} \div \frac{3}{4}$

(g) $3 \div \frac{1}{4}$ (h) $5 \div \frac{3}{8}$

4 A plank of wood is 6 m long. It is cut into lengths, each measuring $\frac{3}{4}$ m.
How many lengths can be cut from the plank?

5 A recipe for a fruit cake requires $2\frac{3}{8}$ kg of fruit.
How much fruit would be required for 3 cakes?

6 Jobinder spends $4\frac{1}{2}$ hours on his computer.
He spends $\frac{1}{3}$ of that time surfing the internet.
How much time does he spend on the internet?

7 Karen is writing a book. She writes for $10\frac{3}{4}$ hours during a weekend. She takes $3\frac{1}{2}$ hours to write a chapter.
How many chapters does she write during the weekend?

Mixed exercise 2

1 Work out

(a) $\frac{3}{7} \times \frac{2}{5}$ (b) $\frac{4}{5} \times \frac{2}{9}$ (c) $\frac{6}{7} \times \frac{5}{8}$

2 Work out

(a) $\frac{3}{11} \times 5$ (b) $\frac{4}{7} \times 3$ (c) $6 \times \frac{2}{3}$

3 An estate agent has 4 viewings booked.
Each viewing should take $\frac{3}{4}$ hour.
How long will they take in total?

4 Work out

(a) $\frac{3}{4}$ of 32   (b) $\frac{3}{5}$ of 15   (c) $\frac{2}{3}$ of 27

5 A coach holds 54 passengers. $\frac{2}{3}$ of the passengers are adults. How many passengers are adults?

6 Write as decimals

(a) $\frac{3}{4}$ (b) $\frac{1}{8}$ (c) $\frac{3}{10}$

(d) $\frac{13}{20}$ (e) $\frac{4}{5}$ (f) $\frac{27}{100}$

7 Write these decimal numbers as fractions.

(a) 0.7   (b) 0.381   (c) 0.27

(d) 0.03   (e) 0.036   (f) 0.002

8 Ameet plants 20 bushes. Four of the bushes die.
What fraction of the bushes

(a) die   (b) survive?

9 Jade is given £25 as a present. She saves £5, spends £12 on books and spends the rest on make-up.
What fraction of her present does she spend on

(a) books   (b) make-up?

10 Work out

(a) $\frac{3}{7} + \frac{2}{7}$ (b) $\frac{7}{11} - \frac{4}{11}$ (c) $\frac{5}{8} + \frac{7}{8}$ (d) $\frac{8}{15} - \frac{3}{15}$

11 Work out

(a) $\frac{4}{5} + \frac{2}{3}$ (b) $\frac{3}{4} - \frac{2}{5}$ (c) $\frac{5}{8} - \frac{1}{4}$ (d) $\frac{7}{10} + \frac{2}{5}$

12 Work out

(a) $2\frac{1}{4} + 3\frac{3}{8}$ (b) $5\frac{3}{4} - 2\frac{1}{5}$ (c) $1\frac{4}{5} + 2\frac{1}{10}$ (d) $3\frac{5}{6} - 1\frac{3}{5}$

13 Simon spent $\frac{1}{3}$ of his pocket money on a computer game.
He spent $\frac{1}{4}$ of his pocket money on a ticket for a football match.
Work out the fraction of his pocket money that he had left.   [E]

14 Fariah bought $2\frac{1}{4}$ kg of potatoes and $1\frac{1}{2}$ kg of carrots.
Work out the total weight of vegetables Fariah bought.

15 A length of material measures $1\frac{7}{8}$ yards.
$\frac{3}{4}$ yard is used to make a cushion.
How much material is left?

16 Work out

    (a) $\frac{2}{3} \div 3$ (b) $\frac{4}{5} \div 2$ (c) $\frac{7}{8} \div 4$ (d) $\frac{8}{15} \div 4$

17 $\frac{5}{8}$ of a pizza is shared equally between 3 people.
What fraction of the pizza does each person receive?

18 Work out

Simplify where possible.

    (a) $\frac{3}{4} \times \frac{2}{3}$ (b) $\frac{4}{5} \times \frac{15}{18}$ (c) $\frac{1}{6} \times \frac{15}{24}$ (d) $\frac{9}{15} \times \frac{5}{6}$

19 Rebecca buys $1\frac{1}{4}$ kg of apples, $\frac{1}{2}$ kg of grapes and $\frac{3}{4}$ kg of bananas.
How much fruit does she buy altogether?

20 Molly has $2\frac{1}{4}$ hours of free time one evening.
She watches TV for $1\frac{1}{2}$ hours and spends the rest of her time on the telephone.
How long does she spend on the telephone?

21 Work out

    (a) $\frac{4}{5} \times \frac{5}{8}$ (b) $\frac{2}{3} \div \frac{5}{6}$ (c) $2\frac{1}{4} \times 1\frac{2}{3}$

    (d) $1\frac{1}{2} \div 5\frac{1}{4}$ (e) $2\frac{2}{3} \div 1\frac{1}{8}$ (f) $1\frac{3}{5} \times 2\frac{3}{4}$

22 The total lesson time in 1 day in a particular secondary school is $4\frac{1}{2}$ hours. Each lesson lasts $\frac{3}{4}$ hour.
How many lessons are there in the school day?

23 A litre of water is about the same as $1\frac{3}{4}$ pints.
Approximately how many pints of water are there in $3\frac{1}{2}$ litres?

24 A train travels from London to Manchester.
It leaves London at 16:55.
It arrives in Manchester at 19:45.

    (a) Work out the number of minutes this train takes to travel from London to Manchester.

There are 800 people on the train at Manchester.
$\frac{1}{10}$ of these 800 people are children.

    (b) (i)   Work out $\frac{1}{10}$ of 800.

$\frac{3}{8}$ of those 800 people are women.

        (ii)   Work out $\frac{3}{8}$ of 800.

The rest of the 800 people are men.

        (iii) Work out the number of men on the train.

320 of the 800 people are under 21 years old.

    (c) Work out 320 out of 800 as a percentage.

Summary of key points

1 To multiply two fractions:

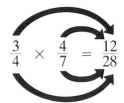

Multiply the numerators.

Multiply the denominators.

2 To multiply a fraction by a whole number:

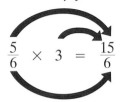

Multiply the numerator by the whole number.

The denominator stays the same.

3 After multiplying fractions you should simplify the answer if you can.

4 To find a fraction of a quantity, multiply the quantity by the fraction.

5 To change a fraction into a decimal, divide the numerator by the denominator.

6 To change a decimal into a fraction, you can use a place value table.

7 To add or subtract fractions with the same denominator (bottom), add or subtract the numerators (tops) then write the answer over the denominator.

8 To add or subtract fractions that have different denominators (bottoms), first find equivalent fractions that have the same denominator.

9 To add or subtract mixed numbers, first add or subtract the whole numbers then add or subtract the fractions.

10 To divide a fraction by an integer, multiply the fraction by the inverse of the integer.

11 You can simplify or cancel fractions to make multiplying and dividing easier.

12 To divide by a fraction, invert the dividing fraction (turn it upside down) and change the division sign to multiplication.

13 To multiply or divide mixed numbers, first change them to improper fractions.

3 Percentage, ratio and proportion

3.1 Converting between fractions, percentages and decimals

15 Converting percentages

15 Converting fractions to percentages and decimals

Converting fractions to decimals was covered in Chapter 2 of Foundation Unit 3.

- To write a percentage as a fraction, always use the denominator 100.
- To write a percentage as a decimal, write the percentage as a fraction and convert the fraction to a decimal *or* divide the percentage by 100%.

Example 1

(a) Write 65% as (i) a fraction (ii) a decimal.
(b) Write $17\frac{1}{2}$% as (i) a fraction (ii) a decimal.

(a) (i) $65\% = \frac{65}{100} = \frac{13}{20}$

    (ii) $65\% = \frac{65}{100} = 65 \div 100 = 0.65$

(b) (i) $17\frac{1}{2}\% = \dfrac{17\frac{1}{2}}{100} \overset{\times 2}{\underset{\times 2}{=}} \dfrac{35}{200} = \dfrac{7}{40}$

Multiply top and bottom by 2 to remove the $\frac{1}{2}$ in the numerator.

    (ii) $17\frac{1}{2}\% = \frac{35}{200} = 35 \div 200 = 0.175$

- To change a decimal to a percentage, multiply the decimal by 100%.
- To write a fraction as a percentage, change the fraction to a decimal and multiply the decimal by 100%.

Example 2

Change to a percentage

(a) 0.35   (b) 0.125   (c) $\frac{4}{20}$ (d) $\frac{18}{80}$

(a) $0.35 \times 100\% = 35\%$ (b) $0.125 \times 100\% = 12.5\%$

(c) $\frac{4}{20} = 4 \div 20 = 0.2$

   $0.2 \times 100\% = 20\%$

   so $\frac{4}{20} = 20\%$

(d) $\frac{18}{80} = 18 \div 80 = 0.225$

   $0.225 \times 100\% = 22.5\%$

   so $\frac{18}{80} = 22.5\%$

Example 3

Penny earns £960 a month.
Her rent is 45% of her income and she spends $\frac{1}{5}$ of her income on bills. The remainder is available to spend on what she chooses.

(a) How much does Penny spend on her rent and bills?

(b) Write this as a fraction of her income.

(a) £960 $\times$ 0.45 = £432

   $\frac{1}{5}$ = 0.20 and 0.20 $\times$ £960 = £192

   £432 + £192 = £624

(b) 45% + 20% = 65% = $\frac{65}{100} = \frac{13}{20}$

Example 4

In four class tests Sereen scored 8 out of 10 in English, 15 out of 20 in Maths, 78 out of 100 in Business Studies and 36 out of 50 in Science.
Which test did she do best in?

Sereen's scores as percentages are:

English: $\frac{8}{10} = 8 \div 10 = 0.8$ $0.8 \times 100\% = 80\%$ | Change to a decimal, then a percentage.

Maths: $\frac{15}{20} = 15 \div 20 = 0.75$ $0.75 \times 100\% = 75\%$

Business Studies: $\frac{78}{100} = 78\%$

Science: $\frac{36}{50}$ $\xrightarrow{\times 2}$ $\frac{72}{100} = 72\%$ | It is quicker to multiply by 2 than to work out $36 \div 50 = 0.72$

Sereen did best in English.

Exercise 3A

1 Write the following percentages as fractions.
  (a) 20%   (b) 50%   (c) 25%   (d) 75%
  (e) 32%   (f) 64%   (g) $37\frac{1}{2}$%   (h) $62\frac{1}{2}$%

2 Write the following percentages as decimals.
  (a) 30%   (b) 70%   (c) 45%   (d) 85%
  (e) 32%   (f) 51%   (g) $18\frac{1}{2}$%   (h) $72\frac{1}{2}$%

3 Write the following decimals as percentages.
  (a) 0.24   (b) 0.3   (c) 0.55   (d) 0.6
  (e) 0.37   (f) 0.235   (g) 0.175   (h) 0.425

4 Write the following fractions as percentages.
  (a) $\frac{9}{10}$ (b) $\frac{3}{10}$ (c) $\frac{3}{5}$ (d) $\frac{1}{5}$
  (e) $\frac{23}{40}$ (f) $\frac{4}{25}$ (g) $\frac{17}{50}$ (h) $\frac{37}{100}$

5 Kate and Tim took an English test. The test was out of 50. Kate scored 75%, and Tim scored $\frac{4}{5}$ of the marks.
  (a) Who scored the higher marks?
  (b) Explain your answer.

> Hint: write the marks as percentages.

6 The road tax for a car is £190.
Peter calculates that road tax represents $\frac{1}{8}$ of his annual costs of running the car, and buying petrol 50%.
The remainder of the costs are insurance and servicing.
  (a) How much does Peter spend on insurance and servicing his car?
  (b) Write this as a percentage of his total costs.

7 Which is the better mark, 90 out of 120 or 24 out of 30? Explain your answer.

3.2 Percentages in real-life situations

Percentages are used in many real-life situations, especially those involving money.

> Working out percentages is covered in Chapter 2 of Foundation Unit 3.

Example 5

  (a) Work out the cost, including VAT, of Flash trainers.
  (b) Work out the sale price of Streak trainers.
  (c) Which pair of trainers is the cheaper?

FLASH TRAINERS

£20 + **VAT**
(VAT = 17.5%)

STREAK TRAINERS

Normal price: £30 inc. VAT

SALE PRICE:
15% reduction

(a) The cost of Flash trainers is

$£20 + 17.5\%$ of $£20$

Work out 17.5% of £20: $\dfrac{17.5}{100} \times £20 = £3.50$

Total cost of Flash trainers $= £20 + £3.50$
$= £23.50$

> Working out $\dfrac{17.5}{100} \times £20$ on a calculator gives
>
> | 3.5 |
>
> You need to write this as £3.50 because the answer is in pounds.

(b) The sale price of Streak trainers is

$£30 - 15\%$ of $£30$

Work out 15% of £30: $\dfrac{15}{100} \times £30 = £4.50$

Sale price of Streak trainers $= £30 - £4.50$
$= £25.50$

(c) Flash trainers are cheaper by £2.

Example 6

Cameron's salary is £18 900. He is given a pay rise in line with the annual rate of inflation.
The annual rate of inflation is 2.4%.
(a) Work out the value of Cameron's pay rise.
(b) Work out Cameron's new salary.

(a) The pay rise is 2.4% of £18 900.

$\dfrac{2.4}{100} \times £18\,900 = £453.60$

(b) Cameron's new salary is
$£18\,900 + £453.60 = £19\,353.60$

Exercise 3B

1 Work out
  (a) 15% of £200
  (b) 20% of £28.50
  (c) 17.5% of £35
  (d) $33\frac{1}{3}\%$ of £90
  (e) 40% of £19 800
  (f) 25% of £18.50

2 Lucy earns £15 600. She is given a pay rise of 5%.
  (a) Work out the value of Lucy's pay rise.
  (b) Work out Lucy's new salary.

3 Karen buys a new car for £18 000. After 1 year the value of the car has depreciated by 7%.
  Calculate the value of Karen's car after 1 year.

> 'Depreciation' means that the value is reduced.

4 Addison's department store has a winter sale.
In their winter sale items in the furniture department are
reduced by 30%.

SOFA
£450

BED
£199

Coffee table
£30.50

Calculate the sale price of each item.

5 VAT is charged at a rate of 17.5%.
How much VAT is there to pay on
(a) a garage bill of £95.50
(b) a necklace costing £17.95
(c) a car costing £7850?

6 Asif buys a flat-screen TV for £375.
After 1 year its value has depreciated by 45%.
Calculate the value of Asif's TV after 1 year.

7 A bank charges 2% commission for changing currency.
How much commission would the bank charge for
changing €400?

8 Pensions are increased by the annual rate of inflation
every year.
In a particular year the annual rate of inflation is 1.8%.
(a) Calculate the increase for a pension of £51.50.
(b) Work out the new amount of the pension.

9 A holiday company offers a discount of 30% on any
holidays booked before January 31st.
Work out the discount on a holiday to Spain costing £379.

10 Louisa's salary is £24 000.
She does not have to pay tax on the first £4560.
She must pay 10% tax on the next £1880. She pays tax at
a rate of 22% on the rest.
(a) Calculate the amount of salary she must pay tax on.
(b) Work out 10% of £1880.
(c) On how much salary does she have to pay tax at a rate
of 22%?
(d) Calculate Louisa's total tax bill.

11 In a survey, some families were asked to name their favourite supermarket.
Some of the results are shown in the diagram.

Favourite Supermarkets for Families

| TRESCO | SALISBURY | BROADWAY | MONTROSE | GATESHEAD |
| 20% | 18% | 9% | 7% | 5% |

(a) Write as a **fraction** the percentage whose favourite supermarket was Montrose.

(b) Write as a **decimal** the percentage whose favourite supermarket was Salisbury.

200 families took part in the survey.

(c) Work out the number of families whose favourite supermarket was Tresco.　　　　　　[E}

3.3 Percentage increase and decrease

8 Finding percentage multipliers

- To increase a quantity by a percentage, use a multiplier *or* find the percentage of the quantity and add it to the original quantity.

Example 7

Phil earns £15 000 per year. He receives a 5% pay increase. Work out his new earnings.

Phil's new earnings are 100% + 5% = 105% of his old earnings.
105% as a decimal = 1.05
Phil's new earnings are 1.05 × £15 000 = £15 750

1.05 is the multiplier.

- To decrease a quantity by a percentage, use a multiplier *or* find the percentage of the quantity and subtract it from the original quantity.

Example 8

In the first year of ownership a car's value depreciates by 12%. Work out the value of a car after 1 year if it costs £8000 when new.

Depreciation means decrease.
Value after 1 year = 100% − 12% = 88% of value when new.
As a decimal, 88% = 0.88
The value after 1 year is 0.88 × £8000 = £7040

> 0.88 is the multiplier.

Example 9

At the start of 2000 Farouk and Sophie's house was valued at £50 000. During 2000 house prices rose by 15%, but during 2001 they fell by 10%. Calculate the value of Farouk and Sophie's house at the end of 2001.

At the end of 2000 house prices were (100 + 15)% of the original value. 115% as a decimal = 1.15

At the end of 2001 house prices were (100 − 10)% of the value at the end of 2000. 90% as a decimal = 0.9

So the value of the house at the end of 2001 was
£50 000 × 1.15 × 0.9 = £51 750

Exercise 3C

1 (a) Work out the sale price of the Leggit trainers.
   (b) Work out the sale price of the Strut tracksuit.

2 A discount warehouse advertises a sofa at £400 + VAT. The rate of VAT is $17\frac{1}{2}$%. Work out the total cost of the sofa.

3 Mohammed and Derya buy a flat for £40 000.
   Two years later they sell it, making a profit of 12%.
   How much do they sell their flat for?

4 Keith buys some slabs for a patio. The normal cost of the slabs is £330. Keith is offered a 10% discount if he pays in cash.
   How much will the slabs cost if Keith pays for them in cash?

5 The money in a savings account earns 6% interest per year. Rebecca puts £240 into the account at the start of the year. How much will Rebecca have in her savings account after 1 year?

SALE
25% off
normal prices

Leggit trainers
Normal price
£42

Strut tracksuit
Normal price
£68

6 Maria buys a new car. The car costs £14 000.
After 1 year the value of the car has depreciated by 18%.
What is the value of Maria's car after 1 year?

7 Emma's salary is £18 500. She is given a pay rise equal to
the annual rate of inflation for that year. The annual rate
of inflation for that year is $2\frac{1}{2}$%.
Calculate Emma's new salary.

8 Calculate the cost of a TV.

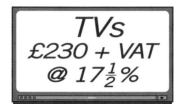

TVs
£230 + VAT
@ $17\frac{1}{2}$%

9 An electrical retailer decreases all its prices in a sale
by 12.5%.
Calculate the sale prices of the following items.
(a) PC: normal price £400
(b) games console: normal price £150
(c) DVD recorder: normal price £225

10 A company gives all its employees a 4% pay rise.
Calculate the new salary of the following employees.
(a) office junior: previously earning £13 500
(b) team administrator: previously earning £17 300
(c) manager: previously earning £24 700

11 VAT at the rate of $17\frac{1}{2}$% is added onto all items sold in a
builder's yard.
Calculate the cost of the following items including VAT.

Item	Price (excluding VAT)
Ladder	£82
Tin of paint	£6
Electric drill	£37.50

12 A frozen-food manufacturer has a '10% extra free' promotion.
Calculate the promotional weights of the following
packets of food.
(a) frozen peas: normal weight 400 g
(b) oven chips: normal weight 1.5 kg
(c) fish fingers: normal weight 225 g

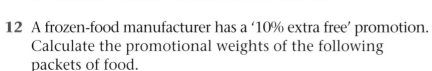

13 A company tries to increase its profits by reducing the expenditure of the following departments by 7.5%. Calculate the target expenditure for each department.
  (a) Administration: original expenditure £734 000
  (b) Marketing: original expenditure £1 430 000
  (c) Production: original expenditure £2 300 000
  (d) Calculate the overall target saving by these three departments.

14 Jackie bought £3000 worth of shares in a company at the end of August. During September the value of the shares fell by 3%, then it rose again by 5% in October. Calculate the value of Jackie's shares at the end of October.

3.4 Finding one quantity as a percentage of another

- To write one quantity as a percentage of another:
  - write one quantity as a fraction of the other;
  - change the fraction to a decimal;
  - multiply the decimal by 100%.

Example 10

In a box of 20 chocolates, 12 chocolates are soft-centred. What percentage of the chocolates are soft-centred?

Write the quantities as a fraction: $\frac{12}{20}$

Change the fraction to a decimal: $\frac{12}{20} = 12 \div 20 = 0.6$
Multiply the decimal by 100%: $0.6 \times 100\% = 60\%$

60% of the chocolates are soft-centred.

- When a quantity changes (increases or decreases), find the percentage change using

$$\text{Percentage change} = \frac{\text{actual change}}{\text{original quantity}} \times 100\%$$

Example 11

A shopkeeper buys apples at £1.50 per kilo.
He sells them for £1.62 per kilo.
Calculate his percentage profit.

$$\text{Percentage change (profit)} = \frac{\text{actual change}}{\text{original quantity}} \times 100\%$$

The original price is £1.50. The actual profit is £0.12.

$$\text{Percentage profit} = \frac{£0.12}{£1.50} \times 100\%$$

$$= 8\%$$

Actual profit =
£1.62 − £1.50 = £0.12

Exercise 3D

1 Oliver scored 36 out of 40 in a spelling test.
Write this as a percentage.

2 A pet food manufacturer claims that 8 out of 10 cats prefer
its cat food.
What percentage of cats is this?

3 In a village of 2500 people, there are 650 children, 960
men and 890 women.
What percentage of the people in the village are

(a) children   (b) men   (c) women?

4 Out of a flock of 150 sheep, 100 gave birth to twin lambs
and the rest gave birth to single lambs.
What percentage of the flock gave birth to

(a) twin lambs

(b) single lambs?

5 The weight of a particular sort of chocolate bar is
increased from 60 g to 72 g.
Calculate the percentage increase in the weight of the
chocolate bar.

6 The cost of a PC fell from £440 to £363.
Calculate the percentage decrease in the cost of the PC.

7 The normal price of a pair of trainers is £50.
In a sale they are sold for £37.50.
Calculate the percentage reduction in the price of the
trainers.

8 A carpenter makes kitchen tables.
They cost him £240 to make. He sells them for £288.
Calculate his percentage profit.

9 After Christmas a supermarket sells off its left-over Christmas cakes. The Christmas cakes were bought by the supermarket for £3.20, and sold off at £2.
Calculate the percentage loss.

10 In 2000 the cost of a skiing holiday was £450. In 2001 the same holiday cost £549.
Calculate the percentage increase in the cost of the holiday.

3.5 Simplifying ratios

- A **ratio** is a way of showing the relationship between two numbers.
- To simplify a ratio, divide its numbers by a common factor.

Example 12

There are 16 boys and 14 girls in a Year 11 tutor group.
Write down the ratio of boys to girls.
Give your answer in its simplest form.

Ratio of boys to girls is $\div 2 \left(\begin{array}{c} 16 : 14 \\ 8 : 7 \end{array} \right) \div 2$

2 is a common factor of 16 and 14.

The ratio is $8 : 7$ in its simplest form.

Exercise 3E

1 Write these ratios in their simplest form.
   (a) $8 : 4$ (b) $9 : 3$ (c) $12 : 4$
   (d) $9 : 6$ (e) $15 : 9$ (f) $24 : 16$
   (g) $35 : 21$ (h) $100 : 30$ (i) $150 : 100$
   (j) $500 : 250$ (k) $8 : 4 : 2$ (l) $10 : 8 : 2$
  (m) $25 : 15 : 5$

Write your answers to questions **2–7** in their simplest form.

2 A bunch of flowers contains 10 daffodils and 15 tulips.
Write down the ratio of daffodils to tulips.

3 Write down the ratio of grey squares to white squares.

4 36 adults and 16 children go on a trip to a theme park.
Write down the ratio of adults to children.

5 Write down the ratio of vowels to consonants in the alphabet.

> a, e, i, o and u are the vowels in the alphabet.

6 Write down the ratio of face cards to non-face cards in a normal pack of 52 playing cards.

> Face cards are King, Queen and Jack.

7 A box of chocolates contains 20 plain chocolates, 15 milk chocolates and 10 white chocolates.
Write down the ratio of the different types of chocolate.

3.6 Ratio, proportion and scale

- Two quantities are in **proportion** if their ratio stays the same when the quantities get larger or smaller.

Example 13

The ratio of boys to girls in a class is $2:3$.
There are 10 boys in the class.
How many girls are there?

Ratio of boys to girls is $2:3$.
There are 10 boys, so an equivalent ratio is

$$\times 5 \left(\begin{array}{c} 2:3 \\ 10:15 \end{array} \right) \times 5$$

There are 15 girls in the class.

- A **scale** is a ratio that shows the relationship between a measurement on a map and the real distance.

Example 14

A model of a car is made using a scale of $1:50$.
The model is 7 cm long.
How long is the real car?

The ratio $1:50$ means that 1 cm on the model represents 50 cm on the real car.
So the real car is 7×50 cm long or 350 cm.

$$\times 7 \left(\begin{array}{c} 1:50 \\ 7:350 \end{array} \right) \times 7$$

Exercise 3F

1 The ratio of flour to fat for pastry is $2:1$.
A baker makes some pastry using 300 g of flour.
How much fat should he use?

2 The instructions on a bottle of orange squash state:

> Dilute orange squash with water in the ratio $1:10$.

If a glass of orange drink is made using 30 m*l* of orange
squash, how much water should be used?

3 A car uses 5 litres of petrol to travel 30 miles.
Work out how much petrol it uses to travel 180 miles.

4 A cafe sells cups of tea and coffee in the ratio $4:5$.
The cafe sells 100 cups of tea one afternoon.
Work out the number of cups of coffee sold.

5 A recipe for 12 burgers requires 1200 g of minced beef.
Work out the amount of beef required for 30 burgers.

6 A map of a wood is drawn to a scale of $1:250$.
On the map the wood is 16 cm wide.
Work out the width of the real wood.

7 A scale drawing of a classroom is made using a scale
of $1:20$. On the drawing the whiteboard is 8 cm wide.
Work out the width of the real whiteboard.

8 (a) Write down the actual distance from the
lighthouse to the port.
   (b) Write down the actual distance from the
town centre to the port.

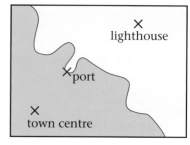

Scale 1 cm = 500 m

3.7 Writing ratios as fractions

- The ratio $a:b$ can be written as the fraction $\frac{a}{b}$.

Example 15

(a) The ratios $8:4$ and $2:x$ are equivalent. Find x.
(b) The ratio of milk chocolates to plain chocolates in a
box of chocolates is $2:3$.
There are 18 milk chocolates in the box.
How many plain chocolates are there in the box?

(a) Write the ratios as fractions:

$8:4$ is $\dfrac{8}{4}$ and

$2:x$ is $\dfrac{2}{x}$

So $\dfrac{8}{4}\left(=\dfrac{2}{1}\right)=\dfrac{2}{x}$

Therefore $x=1$

> Using equivalent fractions.

(b) The ratio of milk to plain chocolates is $2:3$.
Use m to represent the number of plain chocolates.
There are 18 milk chocolates, so the ratio of milk to plain chocolates is $18:m$.

$18:m$ is equivalent to $2:3$

so $\qquad \dfrac{18}{m}=\dfrac{2}{3}$

$\dfrac{2}{3}=\dfrac{18}{27}=\dfrac{18}{m}$

> Write the fractions with the same numerator.
> $\dfrac{2\times 9}{3\times 9}=\dfrac{18}{27}$

Therefore $m=27$

There are 27 plain chocolates.

Exercise 3G

1 Find x for each of these pairs of equivalent ratios.
- (a) $10:15$ and $2:x$
- (b) $12:3$ and $x:1$
- (c) $15:10$ and $3:x$
- (d) $8:x$ and $16:4$
- (e) $x:5$ and $21:35$
- (f) $x:42$ and $3:7$
- (g) $2:5$ and $x:30$
- (h) $4:5$ and $x:50$

2 The ratio of women to men in a company is $5:3$.
There are 15 women in the company.
How many men are there?

3 The ratio of two gears is $4:1$.
The smaller gear rotates
8 complete turns.
How many turns does the
larger gear rotate?

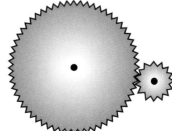

4 The ratio of the sides of a rectangle is $7:4$.
The length of a shorter side of the rectangle is 16 cm.
Calculate the length of a longer side of the rectangle.

5 The ratio of almonds to cashews in a packet of nuts is $4:5$.
There are 24 almonds in the packet.
How many cashews are there in the packet?

6 The ratio of the diameters of two circles is $5:2$.
The diameter of the larger circle is 24 cm.
Calculate the diameter of the smaller circle.

7 Rosie and Lewis are paid in the ratio $3:4$.
Rosie earns £162.60 per week.
How much does Lewis earn?

8 Four A5 sheets of paper can be cut from an A3 sheet.
   (a) Write this as a ratio.
   (b) How many sheets of A3 paper do you need to make
       100 A5 sheets?

3.8 Proportion

- A useful way of solving proportion problems is to find the
  value of 1 unit first. This is called the **unitary method**.

Example 16

5 CDs cost £52.50. How much will 3 CDs cost?

   5 CDs cost £52.50
   1 CD costs £52.50 ÷ 5 = £10.50
   So 3 CDs cost 3 × £10.50 = £31.50

> First work out the cost of 1 CD.

Example 17

6 men build a wall in 4 days.
How long will it take 8 men to build a similar wall?

   6 men take 4 days
   1 man takes 6 × 4 = 24 days

   8 men take $\dfrac{24}{8} = 3$ days

> First work out how long it takes 1 man.

Exercise 3H

1 6 books costs £36. How much will
  (a) 1 book cost
  (b) 3 books cost?

2 5 cinema tickets cost £20.
  How much will
  (a) 1 ticket cost
  (b) 8 tickets cost?

3 8 blank CDs cost £3.20. How much will
  (a) 3 CDs cost
  (b) 10 CDs cost?

4 A recipe for 10 buns uses
       200 g flour
       100 g sugar
       50 g butter
  Write down the amount of each ingredient needed for
  25 buns.

5 Veronica is going on holiday to France.
  She exchanges £100 and receives €161.66.
  (a) How many euros would she get for £250?
  (b) How much would she have to exchange to get €315?

6 Ross is paid £231.25 for working a 37-hour week.
  How much would he be paid if he worked
  (a) 40 hours
  (b) 30 hours?

7 Eight men can build a garage in 5 days.
  How long will it take ten men?

8 A bottle of shampoo lasts a family of five for 1 week.
  How long will the same bottle of shampoo last a family of
  seven?

9 Three gardeners can weed a large garden in 8 hours.
  How long would it take four gardeners to weed the same
  garden?

3.9 More proportion problems

Example 18

The distance a car travels is directly proportional to the amount of petrol it uses.
A car travels 59 km and uses 5 litres of petrol.
How far can the same car travel using 11 litres of petrol?

Method 1
The ratio of distance travelled to petrol used is $59:5$.

The distance travelled by the car on 11 litres of petrol is x.
The ratio of distance travelled to petrol used is $x:11$.

$59:5$ and $x:11$ are equivalent ratios.
Writing the ratios as fractions gives

$$\frac{59}{5} = \frac{x}{11}$$

$\times 2.2$

So x must be $59 \times 2.2 = 129.8$ km.

Method 2 (unitary method)
On 5 litres of petrol the car travels 59 km.

On 1 litre of petrol the car travels $59 \div 5 = 11.8$ km.

On 11 litres of petrol the car travels $11 \times 11.8 = 129.8$ km.

Example 19

18 pens cost £3.92.
How much will 30 pens cost?

Method 1
Proportion of pens to cost is $18:3.92$.
30 pens cost x, so the ratio is $30:x$.

$\times 1\frac{2}{3}$

$$\frac{18}{3.92} = \frac{30}{x}$$

The cost of 30 pens will be $£3.92 \times 1\frac{2}{3}$
$\qquad = £6.53\frac{1}{3} = £6.53$ to the nearest penny

| The answer £6.53$\frac{1}{3}$ isn't sensible, so round to the nearest penny. |

Method 2
18 pens cost £3.92
1 pen costs $3.92 \div 18 = £0.21\dot{7}$
30 pens cost $30 \times 0.21\dot{7}$
$\qquad = £6.5\dot{3} = £6.53$ to the nearest penny

| $0.21\dot{7}$ means $0.217\,777...$ |

Exercise 3I

1   A car travels at a steady speed of 50 km/h.
    How far will the car travel in
    (a) 2 hours   (b) 5 hours   (c) $\frac{1}{2}$ hour?

2   A train travels at a steady speed of 120 km/h.
    How long will it take the train to travel
    (a) 360 km   (b) 700 km   (c) 280 km?

3   8 gel pens cost £12. How much will
    (a) 1 gel pen cost   (b) 13 gel pens cost?

4   Climbing rope costs £18.70 for 5 metres.
    Work out the cost of
    (a) 1 metre of rope   (b) 11 metres of rope.

5   A data entry clerk can type 1000 words in $\frac{1}{4}$ hour.
    How many words can he type in
    (a) $1\frac{1}{2}$ hours   (b) 5 minutes   (c) 25 minutes?

6   The time taken for a microwave oven to heat up some
    soup is directly proportional to the amount of soup.
    A microwave oven can heat up 400 ml of soup in
    5 minutes.
    How long will it take the oven to heat up 750 ml of soup?

7   An 8 m-tall statue casts a shadow 6 m long. The length
    of the shadow is directly proportional to the height of
    the statue. Calculate the length of the shadow cast by a
    5 m-tall statue.

8   The voltage across a resistor is directly proportional to the
    current flowing through it.
    A current of 9.4 amperes produces a voltage of 16.5 volts.
    (a) Calculate the voltage produced by 5 amperes.
    (b) Calculate the current that produces a voltage of 10
         volts.

9   The distance travelled by a car is directly proportional to
    the amount of petrol used by the car.
    A car travels a distance of 200 miles and uses 18.6 litres
    of petrol.
    (a) How far will the car travel on 15 litres of petrol?
    (b) How much petrol will the car need to travel a distance
         of 60 miles?

10 The ingredients for 18 shortcake biscuits are as follows:

     8 oz flour, 4 oz butter and 2 oz sugar.

Calculate the amount of each ingredient needed to make 27 biscuits.

11 The ingredients for 12 potato pancakes are as follows:

     500 g potatoes, 200 g tomatoes, 50 g flour, 15 g butter.

Calculate the amount of each ingredient needed for 30 pancakes.

3.10 Dividing quantities in a given ratio

• Ratios can be used to share or divide quantities.

Example 20

(a) Divide £15 in the ratio 3 : 2.

(b) Jumana, Malik and Hala share £100 in the ratio 5 : 3 : 2. How much does each person receive?

(a) 3 : 2 means 3 parts to 2 parts.
So £15 needs to be divided into 5 parts altogether.
    1 part = £15 ÷ 5 = £3
so 3 parts = 3 × £3 = £9
    2 parts = 2 × £3 = £6

> 3 parts + 2 parts = 5 parts

(b) £100 is shared in the ratio 5 : 3 : 2.
            5 + 3 + 2 = 10 parts
      1 part = £100 ÷ 10 = £10
    Jumana receives 5 parts = 5 × £10 = £50
      Malik receives 3 parts = 3 × £10 = £30
       Hala receives 2 parts = 2 × £10 = £20

> Check:
> £50 + £30 + £20 = £100

Example 21

$\frac{1}{4}$ of a class are boys. What is the ratio of boys to girls?

$\frac{1}{4}$ of the class are boys, so the class has been divided into 4 parts.
1 part is boys, so the rest, 3 parts, are girls.
The ratio of boys to girls is
    1 part to 3 parts
    or 1 : 3

Exercise 3J

1 Divide the quantities in the ratios given.
  (a) 25 in the ratio $3:2$ **(b)** 100 in the ratio $7:3$
  (c) £30 in the ratio $4:1$ **(d)** £24.60 in the ratio $7:5$
  (e) 350 in the ratio $4:2:1$
  (f) 150 cm in the ratio $3:1:1$
  (g) £240 in the ratio $4:3:1$
  (h) £36.90 in the ratio $5:3:1$

2 Juan, Gabrielle and Kwame share £200 in the ratio of their ages, $12:8:5$.
   How much does each person receive?

3 The ratio of men, women and children in a village is $5:4:8$. The population of the village is 3400.
   How many women are there in the village?

4 The ratio of apple, orange and mango in a fruit drink is $4:2:1$.
   What fraction of the fruit drink is apple?

5 The sides of a triangle are in the ratio $3:4:5$.
   The perimeter of the triangle is 42 cm.
   Work out the length of the longest side of the triangle.

6 $\frac{1}{5}$ of the pages in a book are printed in colour.
   The rest are printed in black and white.
   What is the ratio of colour pages to black and white pages?

7 $\frac{3}{8}$ of a class of students catch a bus to school. The rest of the class walk.
   What is the ratio of students who catch the bus to those who walk?

Mixed exercise 3

1 Change the following percentages to
  (i) fractions   **(ii)** decimals.
  (a) 30%   **(b)** 90%   **(c)** 35%   **(d)** 85%
  (e) 18%   **(f)** 64%   **(g)** $17\frac{1}{2}\%$ **(h)** $42\frac{1}{2}\%$

2 Change the following fractions and decimals to percentages.
  (a) $\frac{1}{2}$ **(b)** 0.2   **(c)** $\frac{4}{5}$ **(d)** 0.65
  (e) $\frac{13}{20}$ **(f)** $\frac{14}{25}$ **(g)** $\frac{11}{40}$ **(h)** 0.275

3 Lucy and Jessica were both given £50.
Lucy put 76% of her money into the bank and Jessica put $\frac{3}{4}$ of her money into the bank.
Who saved the most? Explain your answer.

4 VAT is charged at a rate of 17.5%.
Calculate the cost of the following items including VAT.
(a) a dressmaker's bill of £25
(b) a pair of trainers costing £49.99
(c) a new car costing £8760

5 A holiday rep is paid 15% commission on any activities she sells.
Calculate the commission that she earns on the following activities.
(a) boat trip €30   (b) beach party €25
(c) flamenco night €16.50

6 80 girls enter a ballet examination. 85% of the girls pass the exam.
Write down the number of girls who
(a) pass the exam   (b) fail the exam.

7 A department store offers a 15% discount on all sports equipment on Bank Holiday Monday.
A pair of trainers normally costs £44.
Calculate the cost of the pair of trainers on Bank Holiday Monday.

8 Mary scores 28 out of 35 on her driving theory test.
What percentage is this?

9 Daniel earns £18 000. He is given a pay rise of 5%.
Work out how much his salary rises by.

10 In a sale a computer game costing £25 is reduced by 15%.
How much would a customer save by buying the game in the sale?

11 Douglas buys a computer for £500.
Two years later he sells it for £175.
Calculate his percentage loss.

12 The weight of a cereal bar is increased from 80 g to 90 g.
The manufacturers claim that this is a 15% increase.
Is the manufacturers' claim justified?
Give a reason for your answer.

13 A recipe for a cake requires 250 g of flour, 125 g of fat and 100 g of sugar.
Write down the ratio of flour to fat to sugar in its simplest form.

14 A doll's house is built to a scale of 1 : 50.
   (a) The bed in the doll's house is 4 cm long.
      How long would the real bed be?
   (b) A real washing machine is 90 cm high.
      How high would the one in the doll's house be?

15 Find x for these pairs of equivalent ratios.
   (a) 4 : 2 and x : 4   (b) x : 7 and 20 : 35

16 The ratio of two sides of a rectangle is 7 : 2.
The length of the longer side is 17.5 cm.
Calculate the length of the shorter side.

17 Three children share £250 in the ratio of their ages.
Their ages are

      Rebecca   15 years
      Pamela   7 years
      Philip   3 years.

How much does Pamela receive?

18 $\frac{3}{5}$ of a bag of bulbs are tulips; the remainder are daffodils.
What is the ratio of tulip bulbs to daffodil bulbs in the bag?

19 A bag of rabbit food lasts 4 rabbits for 9 days.
How long will the same bag of rabbit food last
   (a) 3 rabbits   (b) 8 rabbits?

20 Evan buys 5 packets of pasta for £3.
How much would 8 packets of the same pasta cost?

21 A 12 m-tall tree casts a shadow 9 m long. The length of the shadow is directly proportional to the height of the tree.
Calculate the length of the shadow cast by a 10 m-tall tree.

22 A kitten increases its weight by 12% each week during the first eight weeks of its life. A kitten weighs 400 g at birth.
How heavy will the kitten be after eight weeks?

23 A basketball is dropped from a height and bounces.
Each bounce is $\frac{2}{3}$ of the height of the previous bounce.
The height of the first bounce is 120 cm.
Calculate the height of the fourth bounce.

24 A vitamin-C tablet contains 15 mg of vitamin C.
The total daily requirement is 60 mg.

(a) What fraction of the total daily requirement is one tablet?

Eating two oranges provides another $\frac{1}{5}$ of the total daily requirement.

(b) James takes one tablet and eats two oranges.

What fraction of the total daily requirement is still needed for James to reach 60 mg for the day?

25 Benjamin has £600 a month in his budget to cover food, rent, travel and leisure.
He spends $\frac{1}{4}$ on food, $\frac{1}{5}$ on rent, and $\frac{3}{8}$ on travel.
How much does he have in his budget for leisure?

26 In 2002, Shorebridge Chess Club's total income came from a council grant and members' fees.

    Council grant   £50
    Members' fees   240 at £5 each

(a) (i) Work out the total income of the club for the year 2002.

(ii) Find the council grant as a fraction of the club's total income for the year 2002.
Give your answer in its simplest form.

In 2001, the club's total income was £1000.
The club spent 60% of its total income on a hall.
It spent a further £250 on prizes.

(b) Work out the ratio
the amount spent on the hall : the amount spent on prizes.
Give your answer in its simplest form.   [E]

27 Martin cleaned his swimming pool.
He hired a cleaning machine to do this job.
The cost of hiring the cleaning machine was

      £35.50 for the first day,
    then £18.25 for each extra day.

Martin's total cost of hiring the machine was £163.25.

(a) For how many days did Martin hire the machine?

Martin had to buy some cleaning materials.
The cost of the cleaning materials was £64.00 plus VAT at $17\frac{1}{2}\%$.

(b) Work out the total cost of the cleaning materials.   [E]

Summary of key points

1 To write a percentage as a fraction, always use the denominator 100.

2 To write a percentage as a decimal, write the percentage as a fraction and convert the fraction to a decimal *or* divide the percentage by 100.

3 To change a decimal to a percentage, multiply the decimal by 100%.

4 To write a fraction as a percentage, change the fraction to a decimal and multiply the decimal by 100%.

5 To increase a quantity by a percentage, use a multiplier *or* find the percentage of the quantity and add it to the original quantity.

6 To decrease a quantity by a percentage, use a multiplier *or* find the percentage of the quantity and subtract it from the original quantity.

7 To write one quantity as a percentage of another:
- write one quantity as a fraction of the other;
- change the fraction to a decimal;
- multiply the decimal by 100%.

8 When a quantity changes (increases or decreases), find the percentage change using

$$\text{Percentage change} = \frac{\text{actual change}}{\text{original quantity}} \times 100\%$$

9 A **ratio** is a way of showing the relationship between two numbers.

10 To simplify a ratio, divide its numbers by a common factor.

11 Two quantities are in **proportion** if their ratio stays the same when the quantities get larger or smaller.

12 A **scale** is a ratio that shows the relationship between a measurement on a map and the real distance.

13 The ratio $a:b$ can be written as the fraction $\frac{a}{b}$.

14 A useful way of solving proportion problems is to find the value of 1 unit first. This is called the **unitary method**.

15 Ratios can be used to share or divide quantities.

4 Elements of algebra

4.1 Algebraic language

- An **equation** has an $=$ sign.
- A **formula** is an equation with two or more variables, for example $V = l \times w \times h$. It represents the relationship between quantities. The subject of a **formula** is the variable on its own on one side of the $=$ sign.
- An **identity** is an equation where both sides are identical when fully simplified, for example $3x^2 + 6x = 3x(x + 2)$.
- A **term** is a single item separated from other items by symbols such as $+$, $-$, $=$, $<$ or $>$.

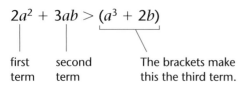

$$2a^2 + 3ab > (a^3 + 2b)$$

| first term | second term | The brackets make this the third term. |

- An **expression** is one or more terms together without a relation like $=$, $>$ or $<$.

> Simplifying by collecting like terms was covered in Chapter 4 of Foundation Unit 3.

Exercise 4A

1 Select the correct word from 'equation', 'formula', 'identity' and 'expression' to describe the following.
  (a) $2x + 1 = 7$
  (b) $3 - 3x = 9$
  (c) $15 + 7x$
  (d) $p = 2at$
  (e) $v = ut$
  (f) $\frac{1}{2}at$
  (g) $2x(x + 3) = 2x^2 + 6x$
  (h) $y(2y + 3) = 2y^2 + 3y$

2 Equation, formula, expression, identity.
  Select the word from the above list which describes each of the following.
  (a) $P = 2(a + b)$ (b) $x(2x + y) = 2x^2 + xy$
  (c) $\pi r^2 h$ (d) $2x + 5 = 13$
  (e) $D = \dfrac{M}{V}$ (f) $2\pi r$

4.2 Substituting numbers into expressions

- If you know the value of the letter or letters used in an algebraic expression, you can work out the value of the expression.
- Replacing letters by numbers is called **substituting**.

Example 1

$a = 5$ and $b = 3$
Work out the value of

(a) $2a - b$ (b) $4ab$ (c) $a^2 + 4$

(a) $2a - b = 2 \times 5 - 3$
$\qquad\quad = 10 - 3$
$\qquad\quad = 7$

(b) $4ab = 4 \times 5 \times 3$
$\qquad\quad = 60$

(c) $a^2 + 4 = 5^2 + 4$
$\qquad\qquad = 5 \times 5 + 4$
$\qquad\qquad = 25 + 4$
$\qquad\qquad = 29$

The numbers take the place of the letters they represent.

Exercise 4B

1 $p = 3$, $q = 2$, $r = 5$ and $s = 0$
Work out the value of the following expressions.

(a) $p + r$ (b) rs (c) $5p - 2r$
(d) pqr (e) $pr - pq$ (f) $6pq + 3qr$
(g) $4(p + 7)$ (h) $p(q + 4)$ (i) $p(r - q)$
(j) $r^2 + 1$ (k) $(q + 1)^2$ (l) $2p^3$
(m) $(p + r)^2$ (n) $(p - q)^3$

2 $p = \frac{3}{4}$, $q = \frac{1}{4}$, $r = 2$ and $s = 1$
Work out the value of the following expressions.

(a) $4q$ (b) $7qr$ (c) $4p - 6q$
(d) qrs (e) $qr - pq$ (f) $4qr - 5pq$
(g) $6(r - 2)$ (h) $r(r - 2)$ (i) p^2
(j) $3r^2 - 2$ (k) $(r - 4)^2$ (l) $6q^3$
(m) $(p + q)^3$

3 $p = 0.5, q = 2, r = 3$ and $s = 1.25$

Work out the value of the following expressions.

(a) pq (b) $6p + 4q$ (c) $7p + 8s$

(d) $pr + 4q$ (e) $qr + rs$ (f) $6pr - 7qs$

(g) $5(p + q)$ (h) $q(p + r)$ (i) $5p^2$

(j) $5q^2 + 7$ (k) r^3 (l) $p^2 + r^2$

(m) $p^3 - q^3$

4.3 Substituting negative numbers into expressions

- Sometimes you have to substitute negative numbers into algebraic expressions.

> For more on calculating with negative numbers see Section 1.2.

Example 2

$p = 2, q = -3$ and $r = -5$

Work out the value of

(a) $p + r$ (b) $q - r$ (c) pq (d) qr

(e) $p(q + r)$ (f) $r^2 + 6r$ (g) $(p + q)^2$ (h) $4r^3$

(a) $p + r = 2 + (-5)$
$\quad = 2 - 5$
$\quad = -3$

> Adding a negative number is the same as subtracting a positive number.

(b) $q - r = -3 - (-5)$
$\quad = -3 + 5$
$\quad = 2$

> Subtracting a negative number is the same as adding a positive number.

(c) $pq = 2 \times -3$
$\quad = -6$

> When you multiply two numbers which have different signs, the answer is negative. Remember: 2 means +2.

(d) $qr = -3 \times -5$
$\quad = 15$

> When you multiply two numbers which have the same sign, the answer is positive.

(e) $p(q + r) = 2 \times (-3 + (-5))$
$\quad\quad\quad = 2 \times (-3 - 5)$
$\quad\quad\quad = 2 \times -8$
$\quad\quad\quad = -16$

(f) $r^2 + 6r = (-5)^2 + 6 \times -5$
$\quad\quad\quad = (-5 \times -5) - 30$
$\quad\quad\quad = 25 - 30$
$\quad\quad\quad = -5$

(g) $(p + q)^2 = (2 + (-3))^2$
$\quad\quad\quad = (2 - 3)^2$
$\quad\quad\quad = (-1)^2$
$\quad\quad\quad = -1 \times -1$
$\quad\quad\quad = 1$

(h) $4r^3 = 4 \times (-5)^3$
$\quad\quad = 4 \times (-5 \times -5 \times -5)$
$\quad\quad = 4 \times -125$
$\quad\quad = -500$

Exercise 4C

In this exercise $a = -5$, $b = 6$, $c = -2$, $d = \frac{1}{2}$ and $e = 1$.

Work out the value of the following expressions.

1 $a + b$	**2** $a - b$	**3** $b - a$
4 $a - c$	**5** $b - c$	**6** $a + b + c$
7 $3a + 7$	**8** $4a + 3b$	**9** $2b + 5c$
10 $2a - 5c$	**11** $3b - 2a$	**12** ab
13 acd	**14** $3bc$	**15** $bd - 1$
16 $ab - bc$	**17** $2ab + 3ac$	**18** $3ac - 2bc$
19 $abcd$	**20** $3d(a + 1)$	**21** $5(c - 1)$
22 $a(b + c)$	**23** $b(c - a)$	**24** $c(a + b)$
25 a^2	**26** $3c^2d$	**27** $4a^2 - 3$
28 $5c^2 + 3c$	**29** $2a^2 - 3a$	**30** $(a + 1)^2$
31 $(c + 3)^2$	**32** $(a + b)^2$	**33** $(a + c)^2$
34 $(c - a)^2$	**35** $2b^3$	**36** $3a^3$
37 $6c^3$	**38** $2(b + c)^2$	**39** $a^2 - b^2$
40 $(a - c)^3$	**41** $(e - d)^2$	**42** $(c - 5d)^2$

4.4 Indices

- In the expression x^n, the number n is called the **index** or **power**.

> The plural of 'index' is 'indices'.

- These are the laws of indices:
  - To multiply powers of the same letter, add the indices.
    $$x^m \times x^n = x^{m+n}$$
  - To divide powers of the same letter, subtract the indices.
    $$x^m \div x^n = x^{m-n}$$
  - To raise a power of a letter to a further power, multiply the indices.
    $$(x^m)^n = x^{mn}$$

Example 3

Write in index form

(a) $x \times x \times x \times x$

(b) $7 \times x \times x \times x$

(a) $x \times x \times x \times x = x^4$

(b) $7 \times x \times x \times x = 7x^3$

> x^4 is read as 'x to the power four' or 'x to the fourth'.

> $7x^3$ is read as 'seven x cubed'.

Example 4

Simplify

(a) $x^8 \times x^3$ (b) $x^8 \div x^3$ (c) $(x^8)^3$

(a) $x^8 \times x^3 = x^{8+3} = x^{11}$ (b) $x^8 \div x^3 = x^{8-3} = x^5$

(c) $(x^8)^3 = x^{8 \times 3} = x^{24}$

• Any letter raised to the power 1 is equal to the letter itself.
  $x^1 = x$

Example 5

Simplify

(a) $x^3 \times x^5 \times x^4$ (b) $\dfrac{x^7 \times x^4}{x^6}$ (c) $\dfrac{x^4 \times x}{x^2}$

(a) $x^3 \times x^5 \times x^4 = x^{3+5+4} = x^{12}$

(b) $\dfrac{x^7 \times x^4}{x^6} = \dfrac{x^{7+4}}{x^6} = \dfrac{x^{11}}{x^6} = x^{11-6} = x^5$

(c) $\dfrac{x^4 \times x}{x^2} = \dfrac{x^4 \times x^1}{x^2} = \dfrac{x^{4+1}}{x^2} = \dfrac{x^5}{x^2} = x^{5-2} = x^3$

Example 6

Simplify

(a) $3x^2 \times 5x^4$ (b) $20x^6 \div 4x^2$

(a) $3x^2 \times 5x^4 = 3 \times x^2 \times 5 \times x^4$
$$= 3 \times 5 \times x^2 \times x^4$$
$$= 15 \times x^{2+4}$$
$$= 15x^6$$

(b) $20x^6 \div 4x^2 = \frac{20}{4}x^{6-2}$
$$= 5x^4$$

Exercise 4D

1 Write in index form
   (a) $x \times x \times x \times x \times x \times x \times x$
   (b) $3 \times x \times x \times x \times x \times x \times x \times x$

2 Simplify
    (a) $x^2 \times x^7$ **(b)** $x^4 \times x^5$ **(c)** $x^3 \times x^8$
    (d) $x^6 \times x^7$ **(e)** $x^7 \div x^4$ **(f)** $x^9 \div x^3$
    (g) $x^{12} \div x^7$ **(h)** $x^{11} \div x^9$ **(i)** $(x^5)^2$
    (j) $(x^9)^4$ **(k)** $(x^7)^5$ **(l)** $(x^4)^8$

3 Simplify
    (a) $x^6 \times x^5 \times x^7$ **(b)** $\dfrac{x^8 \times x^9}{x^4}$ **(c)** $\dfrac{x^6 \times x^7}{x^5 \times x^3}$

4 Simplify
    (a) $2x^3 \times 7x^5$ **(b)** $6x^4 \times 5x^6$ **(c)** $8x^7 \times 5x^2$
    (d) $2x^5 \times 5x^6 \times 3x^2$ **(e)** $18x^8 \div 3x^5$ **(f)** $36x^6 \div 12x^2$
    (g) $28x^9 \div 4x^3$ **(h)** $40x^{12} \div 8x^7$ **(i)** $(x^3)^2$
    (j) $(x^5)^3$ **(k)** $(x^6)^4$ **(l)** $(x^4)^5$

5 Simplify
    (a) $x^9 \times x$ **(b)** $x \times x^6$ **(c)** $x^9 \div x$
    (d) $7x^4 \times x$ **(e)** $5x \times 8x^5$ **(f)** $8x^7 \times 3x$
    (g) $5x^4 \div x$ **(h)** $12x^8 \div 4x$ **(i)** $30x^{10} \div 5x$
    (j) $x^9 \div x^8$ **(k)** $x^{20} \div x^{19}$ **(l)** $20x^6 \div 4x^5$
    (m) $28x^9 \div 4x^8$

Mixed exercise 4

1 Copy the table. Tick the box which represents the
   algebraic item in the first column.

Algebra	Expression	Formula	Equation	Identity
$P = 2ab$				
$2ab + 3c$				
$2(x^2 + 3x) = 2x^2 + 6x^3$				
$3(x + 1) = 9$				
πr^2				

2 $w = 4$, $x = 7$, $y = 0$ and $z = 0.25$
   Work out the value of
    (a) $w + x$ **(b)** $3x$ **(c)** $5xy$
    (d) $2wx$ **(e)** $3w + 2x$ **(f)** $2(w + 3)$
    (g) $4(x - 1)$ **(h)** $y(3x - w)$ **(i)** $2x^2$
    (j) $(x + 2)^2$ **(k)** w^3 **(l)** $(x - w)^3$
    (m) $w^2 z$ **(n)** z^2 **(o)** $4xz$

3 $v = 3$, $w = -2$, $x = -4$ and $y = \frac{1}{2}$

Work out the value of

(a) $v + w$	**(b)** $v - x$	**(c)** $w - x$
(d) vw	**(e)** wxy	**(f)** vwx
(g) $2v + 5w$	**(h)** $2w - x$	**(i)** $6(v - 5)$
(j) $3w^2$	**(k)** $w^3 + 5w$	**(l)** $2x^3$
(m) y^2	**(n)** x^2y^2	**(o)** $y(wx + 2)$

4 Simplify

(a) $x^6 \times x^3$	**(b)** $x^8 \div x^5$	**(c)** $(x^3)^5$
(d) $x^5 \div x^4$	**(e)** $x \times x^4$	**(f)** $(x^6)^2$
(g) $x^8 \div x^8$	**(h)** $x^7 \div x$	**(i)** $x^2 \times x^6 \times x^3$
(j) $x^8 \times x$	**(k)** $\dfrac{x^6 \times x^4}{x^7}$	**(l)** $\dfrac{x^3 \times x^7}{x^4 \times x^5}$

5 Simplify

(a) $4x^3 \times x^5$	**(b)** $3x^2 \times 5x^6$	**(c)** $7x \times 3x^4$
(d) $8x^9 \div 2x^5$	**(e)** $24x^6 \div 3x$	**(f)** $36x^9 \div 4x^8$
(g) $(x^5)^2$	**(h)** $(x^3)^3$	

6 **(a)** Simplify $a^3 \times a^4$

   (b) Simplify $3x^2y \times 5xy^3$ [E]

Summary of key points

1 An **equation** has an $=$ sign.

2 A **formula** is an equation with two or more variables, for example $V = l \times w \times h$. It represents the relationship between quantities. The **subject** of a formula is the variable on its own on one side of the $=$ sign.

3 An **identity** is an equation where both sides are identical when fully simplified, for example $3x^2 + 6x = 3x(x + 2)$.

4 A **term** is a single item separated from other items by symbols such as $+$, $-$, $=$, $<$ or $>$.

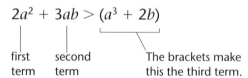

$2a^2 + 3ab > (a^3 + 2b)$

first term   second term   The brackets make this the third term.

5 An **expression** is one or more terms together without a relation like $=$, $>$ or $<$.

6 If you know the value of the letter or letters used in an algebraic expression, you can work out the value of the expression.

7 Replacing letters by numbers is called **substituting**.

8 Sometimes you have to substitute negative numbers into algebraic expressions.

9 In the expression x^n, the number n is called the **index** or **power**.

10 These are the laws of indices:
- To multiply powers of the same letter, add the indices.
$$x^m \times x^n = x^{m+n}$$
- To divide powers of the same letter, subtract the indices.
$$x^m \div x^n = x^{m-n}$$
- To raise a power of a letter to a further power, multiply the indices.
$$(x^m)^n = x^{mn}$$

11 Any letter raised to the power 1 is equal to the letter itself.
$$x^1 = x$$

5 Equations and inequalities

5.1 Equations

- In an **equation**, a symbol or letter represents an unknown number.

$4 \times \square + 3 = 11$ and $4x + 3 = 11$ are equations.

Example 1

Write these equations using letters.

(a) $\square + 7 = 13$ (b) $3 \times \square - 2 = 19$

(a) The equation is $x + 7 = 13$
(b) The equation is $3x - 2 = 19$

You can use any letter to stand for the number but we usually use x.

Example 2

I think of a number.
When I multiply my number by 6, the answer is 48.

(a) Express this problem as an equation.
(b) What number did I think of?

(a) Let x stand for the number I thought of.
The equation is $6x = 48$.
(b) $8 \times 6 = 48$
The number I thought of was 8.

$48 \div 6 = 8$

$x \times 6 = 48$
Write $x \times 6$ as $6x$.

Example 3

Here is a number machine.

$$\text{number} \longrightarrow \boxed{\text{add } 3} \longrightarrow \boxed{\begin{array}{c}\text{multiply} \\ \text{by } 2\end{array}} \longrightarrow 16$$

(a) Express this problem as an equation.
(b) What number was put in?

(a) Let x stand for the number put in.
The equation is $2(x + 3) = 16$.

$x \xrightarrow{\text{add } 3} (x + 3)$
$\xrightarrow{\times 2} 2(x + 3)$

(b) Work backwards through the number machine using inverse operations.

$$5 \longleftarrow \boxed{\begin{array}{c}\text{subtract} \\ 3\end{array}} \longleftarrow \boxed{\begin{array}{c}\text{divide} \\ \text{by 2}\end{array}} \longleftarrow 16$$

The number put in was 5.

> The inverse of an operation 'undoes' the operation. For example, 'add 2' is the inverse of 'subtract 2'.

Exercise 5A

In questions **1–10**, write each equation using a letter.

1 $\square - 7 = 9$ **2** $\square + 3 = 11$

3 $8 \times \square = 32$ **4** $9 + \square = 20$

5 $7 \times \square - 3 = 32$ **6** $\square \times 3 = 21$

7 $3 \times (\square + 1) = 24$ **8** $\square \times 4 + 5 = 13$

9 $(5 + \square) \times 2 = 16$ **10** $7 + 5 \times \square = 27$

In questions **11–15**

(a) express the problem as an equation

(b) find the number.

11 Amy thinks of a number and adds 7 to it. The answer is 11.

12 Ben thinks of a number and multiplies it by 5. The answer is 45.

13 Fatima thinks of a number. She adds 2 to it and multiplies the result by 4. The answer is 36.

14 Floyd thinks of a number. He multiplies it by 2 and subtracts 5 from the result. The answer is 12.

15 Dara thinks of a number. She multiplies it by 6 and adds 7 to the result. The answer is 31.

In questions **16–20**

(a) express the problem as an equation

(b) find the number put into the machine.

16 $\text{number} \longrightarrow \boxed{\begin{array}{c}\text{subtract} \\ 8\end{array}} \longrightarrow 7$

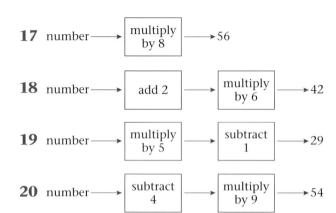

17 number $\longrightarrow$ | multiply by 8 | $\longrightarrow$ 56

18 number $\longrightarrow$ | add 2 | $\longrightarrow$ | multiply by 6 | $\longrightarrow$ 42

19 number $\longrightarrow$ | multiply by 5 | $\longrightarrow$ | subtract 1 | $\longrightarrow$ 29

20 number $\longrightarrow$ | subtract 4 | $\longrightarrow$ | multiply by 9 | $\longrightarrow$ 54

5.2 Solving equations by balancing

11 Algebra scales

- In an equation, a letter represents an unknown number.
- You can solve an equation to find the number that the letter represents. This number is called the **solution** of the equation.
- You can solve an equation by rearranging it so that the letter is on its own on one side of the equals sign.
- To rearrange an equation you can
  - add the same quantity to both sides
  - subtract the same quantity from both sides
  - multiply both sides by the same quantity
  - divide both sides by the same quantity.
- Whatever you do to one side of an equation you must also do to the other side. This is called the **balance method**.

Example 4

Solve the equation $a + 3 = 7$

$$a + 3 = 7$$
$$a + 3 - 3 = 7 - 3 \quad \text{Subtract 3 from both sides.}$$
$$a = 7 - 3$$
$$a = 4$$

-3 is the inverse of $+3$.

Example 5

Solve the equation $b - 5 = 3$

$$b - 5 = 3$$
$$b - 5 + 5 = 3 + 5 \quad \text{Add 5 to both sides.}$$
$$b = 3 + 5$$
$$b = 8$$

$+5$ is the inverse of -5.

Example 6

Solve the equation $5c = 15$ This means $5 \times c = 15$

$$\frac{5 \times c}{5} = \frac{15}{5}$$ Divide both sides by 5. $\div 5$ is the inverse of $\times 5$.

$$c = \frac{15}{5}$$

$$c = 3$$

Example 7

Solve the equation $\frac{d}{6} = 2$ This means $d \div 6 = 2$

$$\frac{d \times 6}{6} = 2 \times 6$$ Multiply both sides by 6. $\times 6$ is the inverse of $\div 6$.

$$d = 2 \times 6$$

$$d = 12$$

Exercise 5B

Solve these equations.

1 $p + 4 = 7$ **2** $a + 7 = 12$ **3** $h + 6 = 15$

4 $9 + c = 20$ **5** $n + 5 = 5$ **6** $3 + g = 8$

7 $t - 2 = 7$ **8** $n - 5 = 3$ **9** $x - 6 = 8$

10 $v - 7 = 4$ **11** $3d = 24$ **12** $8c = 40$

13 $6q = 42$ **14** $9f = 63$ **15** $7k = 0$

16 $\frac{y}{2} = 5$ **17** $\frac{r}{6} = 7$ **18** $\frac{g}{5} = 9$

19 $\frac{b}{8} = 6$ **20** $\frac{m}{7} = 0$

5.3 Equations with two operations

Example 8

Solve the equation $6x + 5 = 23$

$$6x + 5 = 23$$

$$6x = 23 - 5$$ Subtract 5 from both sides.

$$6x = 18$$

$$x = \frac{18}{6}$$ Divide both sides by 6.

$$x = 3$$

- The solution of an equation is not always a whole number. It can be a fraction or a decimal.

Example 9

Solve the equation $3y - 5 = 9$

$$3y - 5 = 9$$
$$3y = 9 + 5 \qquad \text{Add 5 to both sides.}$$
$$3y = 14$$
$$y = \frac{14}{3} \qquad \text{Divide both sides by 3.}$$
$$y = 4\frac{2}{3}$$

Exercise 5C

Solve these equations.

1 $2y + 3 = 11$ **2** $3a - 2 = 13$ **3** $4h + 1 = 13$

4 $5e - 7 = 8$ **5** $7d + 5 = 19$ **6** $8c - 1 = 7$

7 $3u + 8 = 8$ **8** $2v + 1 = 8$ **9** $3x + 4 = 1$

10 $4p + 3 = 10$ **11** $5q - 6 = 7$ **12** $8k + 1 = 20$

13 $10f - 8 = 7$ **14** $5n + 3 = 20$ **15** $6e - 10 = 5$

5.4 Equations with the unknown on both sides

- You can use the balance method to solve equations with the letter on both sides. Rearrange the equation so that on one side there is the letter with a positive number in front of it and on the other side there is a number.

Example 10

Solve the equation $6x - 5 = 2x + 7$

$$6x - 5 = 2x + 7$$
$$4x - 5 = 7 \quad\text{——— Take } 2x \text{ away from both sides}$$
$$\text{to collect all the } x \text{ terms on one side.}$$
$$4x = 12\quad\text{——— Add 5 to both sides.}$$
$$x = 3 \quad\text{——— Divide both sides by 4.}$$

If you took $6x$ away from both sides, you would not affect the balance of the equation, but you would get $-4x$, with a negative number in front of x.

Example 11

Solve the equation $8y + 7 = 3y + 11$

$$8y + 7 = 3y + 11$$
$$5y + 7 = 11 \qquad \text{Take } 3y \text{ away from both sides.}$$
$$5y = 4 \qquad \text{Take 7 away from both sides.}$$
$$y = \tfrac{4}{5} \qquad \text{Divide both sides by 5.}$$

Exercise 5D

Solve the equations in questions **1–20**.

1 $2a + 9 = a + 5$ **2** $3c - 1 = c + 9$

3 $5p - 7 = 2p + 11$ **4** $8b + 9 = 3b + 14$

5 $9q - 8 = 2q + 13$ **6** $x + 13 = 5x + 1$

7 $4d + 17 = 8d - 3$ **8** $7y = 2y + 15$

9 $3n + 14 = 5n$ **10** $5k + 1 = 2k + 1$

11 $4u + 3 = 2u + 8$ **12** $7r - 3 = 2r + 9$

13 $6v - 7 = 3v + 7$ **14** $9t + 5 = 4t + 9$

15 $7m - 2 = 3m + 8$ **16** $3g + 4 = 9g - 1$

17 $5b + 6 = 7b + 5$ **18** $2h + 7 = 8h - 1$

19 $3e = 7e - 18$ **20** $9f = 3f + 4$

21 (a) Solve $7x = 21$

    (b) Solve $5y + 1 = 3y + 13$ [E]

5.5 Equations with brackets

- Equations with brackets can always be solved by expanding the brackets first.

> You learned how to expand brackets in Chapter 4 of Foundation Unit 3.

Example 12

Solve the equation $3(q - 4) = 15$ using the balance method.

$$3(q - 4) = 15$$
$$3q - 12 = 15 \qquad \text{Expand the brackets.}$$
$$3q = 27 \qquad \text{Add 12 to both sides.}$$
$$q = 9 \qquad \text{Divide both sides by 3.}$$

> Alternative method for solving $3(q - 4) = 15$:
> Divide both sides by 3:
> $$q - 4 = 5$$
> Add 4 to both sides:
> $$q = 9$$

Example 13

Solve the equation $\frac{t-7}{4} = 2$ using the balance method.

$$\frac{t-7}{4} = 2$$

$$t - 7 = 8 \qquad \text{Multiply both sides by 4.}$$

$$t = 15 \qquad \text{Add 7 to both sides.}$$

In the expression $\frac{t-7}{4}$, the division line acts as a bracket.
$\frac{t-7}{4} = \frac{1}{4}(t-7)$

Exercise 5E

Solve the equations in questions **1–20** using the balance method.

1 $5(a - 5) = 70$

2 $6b = 30$

3 $\frac{c}{6} = 4$

4 $3(d - 5) = 15$

5 $5(e + 2) = 40$

6 $\frac{f+4}{5} = 4$

7 $4g + 5 = 29$

8 $\frac{h}{3} - 5 = 2$

9 $4(m - 4) = 12$

10 $\frac{n-3}{6} = 2$

11 $9p - 1 = 2$

12 $6(q + 5) = 30$

13 $\frac{t+10}{6} = 1$

14 $5v + 3 = 7$

15 $\frac{x}{3} + 7 = 5$

16 $3(y - 1) = 2$

17 $3c + 5 = 2$

18 $2(b - 3) = 3$

19 $\frac{3c+4}{3} = 2$

20 $3(2d - 5) = -27$

21 Solve the equation
$5(x - 3) = 2x - 22$ [E]

5.6 Equations with negative coefficients

- A **coefficient** is the number in front of an unknown.
- You can use the balance method to solve equations with negative coefficients.
- The solution of an equation can be a negative number.

In $4 - 3x$ the coefficient of x is -3.

Example 14

Solve the equation $7 - 3x = 19$

Method 1

$$7 - 3x = 19$$
$$7 = 3x + 19 \qquad (+ 3x)$$
$$3x = -12 \qquad (- 19)$$
$$x = -4 \qquad (\div 3)$$

Method 2

$$7 - 3x = 19$$
$$-3x = 12 \qquad (- 7)$$
$$x = \frac{12}{-3} \qquad (\div -3)$$
$$x = -4$$

Example 15

Solve the equation $4 + 3x = 9 - 2x$

$$4 + 3x = 9 - 2x$$
$$4 + 5x = 9 \qquad (+ 2x)$$
$$5x = 5 \qquad (- 4)$$
$$x = 1 \qquad (\div 5)$$

You could subtract $3x$ from both sides, giving
$$4 = 9 - 5x$$
but positive coefficients are easier to work with.

Example 16

Solve the equation $4 - 3x = 7 - 5x$

$$4 - 3x = 7 - 5x$$
$$4 + 2x = 7 \qquad (+ 5x)$$
$$2x = 3 \qquad (- 4)$$
$$x = 1\frac{1}{2} \qquad (\div 2)$$

Adding $5x$ to both sides gives positive coefficients.

Exercise 5F

Solve these equations.

1 $8 - x = 6$

2 $9 - 2x = 1$

3 $40 - 3x = 1$

4 $3x + 2 = 10 - x$

5 $4(x + 1) = 11 - 3x$

6 $9 - 2x = x$

7 $9 - 5x = 3x + 1$

8 $2 - x = 10 - 3x$

9 $1 - 6x = 9 - 7x$

10 $5 - 6x = 9 - 8x$

11 $3 - 4x = 8 - 9x$

12 $17 - 6x = 5 - 3x$

13 $3 - 4x = 15$ **14** $7 - 6x = 7$

15 $8 - 2x = 3$ **16** $5 + 2x = 8 - 3x$

17 $8 + 3x = 1 - 4x$ **18** $5(4 - x) = 5 + 4x$

19 $13 - 2x = 3 - 7x$ **20** $3 - 9x = 5 - 6x$

5.7 Using equations to solve problems

- You can use equations to solve problems.

Example 17

I think of a number. I multiply it by 3 and add 14 to the result. The answer is the same as when I multiply the number by 5 and subtract 4.
What number did I think of?

Write an equation. Let x stand for the number.

$$3x + 14 = 5x - 4$$
$$14 = 2x - 4 \quad (- 3x)$$
$$2x = 18 \quad (+ 4)$$
$$x = 9 \quad (\div 2)$$

The number is 9.

Example 18

In the diagram, ABC is a straight line.
Find the size of angle ABD.

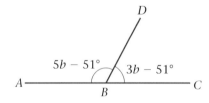

Write an equation in b. Use the fact that the sum of the angles on a straight line is 180°.

$$4b + 50 + 2b + 40 = 180$$
$$6b + 90 = 180$$
$$6b = 90 \quad (- 90)$$
$$b = 15 \quad (\div 6)$$

Angle $ABD = 4b + 50 = 4 \times 15 + 50 = 110$
So angle ABD is 110°.

Exercise 5G

1 I think of a number. I multiply it by 7 and subtract 9.
The result is 47.
Find the number.

2 The sizes of the angles of a triangle are $a + 30°$, $a + 40°$
and $a - 10°$.
Find the size of the largest angle of the triangle.

3 I think of a number. I multiply it by 3 and subtract the
result from 50. The answer is 14.
Find the number.

4 The diagram shows three angles at a point.
Find the size of each angle.

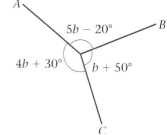

5 The lengths, in centimetres, of the sides of a triangle are
$3x - 4$, $x + 5$ and $15 - 2x$.
The perimeter of the triangle is 24 cm.
Find the length of each side.

6 I think of a number. I multiply it by 7 and subtract 6 from
the result. The answer is the same as when I multiply the
number by 4 and add 27 to the result.
Find the number.

7 The length of each side of a square is $2y - 5$ centimetres.
The perimeter of the square is 36 cm.
Find the value of y.

8 Gwen is 39 years older than her son.
She is also 4 times as old as he is.
Find Gwen's age.

9 The length of a rectangle is 3 cm greater than its width.
The perimeter of the rectangle is 54 cm.
Find its length.

10 The diagram shows a rectangle.

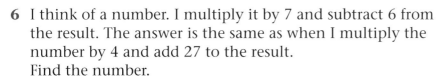

Find the values of x and y.

5.8 Quadratic equations

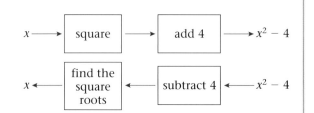

28 Solving quadratic equations

- A **quadratic** equation is one in which the highest power of x is x^2. For example, $x^2 + 4 = 29$, $3x^2 - 6 = 42$ and $25x^2 = 9$ are quadratic equations.

- You can solve some simple quadratic equations by using inverse operations.

- The inverse operation of 'square' is 'find the square roots'.

- A quadratic equation usually has two solutions.

> The square root of 36 can be 6 or -6 because $6 \times 6 = 36$ and $-6 \times -6 = 36$.

Example 19

Solve the quadratic equation $x^2 + 4 = 29$

Method 1
This is the number machine for $x \to x^2 + 4$ with the inverse number machine.

$x \longrightarrow$ square $\longrightarrow$ add 4 $\longrightarrow x^2 - 4$

$x \longleftarrow$ find the square roots $\longleftarrow$ subtract 4 $\longleftarrow x^2 - 4$

Send 29 through the inverse number machine.
The solutions are $x = 5$ and $x = -5$, which is usually written as $x = \pm 5$.

Method 2
$$x^2 + 4 = 29$$
$$x^2 = 25 \qquad (-4)$$
$$x = \pm 5 \qquad \text{(square roots)}$$

Example 20

Solve the quadratic equation $3x^2 - 6 = 42$

Method 1
This is the number machine for $x \to 3x^2 - 6$ with the inverse number machine.

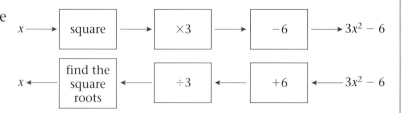

$x \longrightarrow$ square $\longrightarrow \times 3 \longrightarrow -6 \longrightarrow 3x^2 - 6$

$x \longleftarrow$ find the square roots $\longleftarrow \div 3 \longleftarrow +6 \longleftarrow 3x^2 - 6$

Send 42 through the inverse number machine.
The solutions are $x = \pm 4$.

Method 2
$$3x^2 - 6 = 42$$
$$3x^2 = 48 \qquad (+6)$$
$$x^2 = 16 \qquad (\div 3)$$
$$x = \pm 4 \qquad \text{(square roots)}$$

Example 21

Solve the quadratic equation $25x^2 = 9$

$$25x^2 = 9$$

$$x^2 = \frac{9}{25} \qquad (\div 25)$$

$$x = \pm\sqrt{\frac{9}{25}}$$

$$= \pm\frac{\sqrt{9}}{\sqrt{25}}$$

$$x = \pm\frac{3}{5}$$

Exercise 5H

Solve these quadratic equations.

1 $x^2 + 1 = 50$ **2** $x^2 - 7 = 57$ **3** $3x^2 = 75$

4 $8x^2 = 72$ **5** $\frac{x^2}{3} = 12$ **6** $4x^2 + 5 = 41$

7 $7x^2 + 3 = 31$ **8** $x^2 = \frac{9}{64}$ **9** $x^2 = \frac{25}{4}$

10 $4x^2 = 1$ **11** $49x^2 = 9$ **12** $25x^2 = 36$

13 $16x^2 = 1$ **14** $4x^2 = 81$ **15** $25x^2 = 100$

5.9 Solving equations by trial and improvement

- You can find approximate solutions to complicated equations by **trial and improvement**.

Example 22

Use trial and improvement to solve the equation $x^3 + x = 16$. Give your answer correct to 2 d.p.

$x^3 + x + 16$ is a **cubic equation**. The highest power of x is x cubed.

Method
Guess a value for x.
Calculate $x^3 + x$ using your guess.
Compare your answer with 16.
If your answer is too small, choose a bigger value for x.
If your answer is too big, choose a smaller value for x.

Keep repeating this process until you find a value for x correct to 2 d.p. which makes $x^3 + x$ as close as possible to 16.

x	$x^3 + x$	Bigger or smaller than 16?
2	10	too small
3	30	too big
2.5	18.125	too big
2.4	16.224	too big
2.3	14.467	too small
2.35	15.327 875	too small
2.36	15.504 256	too small
2.37	15.682 053	too small
2.38	15.861 272	too small
2.39	16.041 919	too big
2.385	15.951 416 63	too small

Try $x = 2.385$ to find out whether the solution is closer to 2.38 or 2.39.

The solution lies between 2.385 and 2.39.
So $x = 2.39$ correct to 2 d.p.

Exercise 5I

1 Use a trial and improvement method to solve $x^3 + x = 8$, giving your answer correct to 2 d.p.

2 Use a trial and improvement method to solve $x^2 + \dfrac{x}{5} = 17$, giving your answer correct to 2 d.p.

3 Use a trial and improvement method to solve $x^3 + 4x = 100$, giving your answer correct to 1 d.p.

4 Use trial and improvement to solve $\dfrac{x^3}{2} + x = 500$, giving your answer correct to 1 d.p.

5 Use trial and improvement to solve $x^2 + \dfrac{1}{x} = 10$, giving your answer correct to 2 d.p.

6 Use trial and improvement to solve $2x^3 + 2x = 50$, giving your answer correct to 2 d.p.

7 The equation $x^3 - 4x = 24$ has a solution between 3 and 4.
Use a trial and improvement method to find this solution.
Give your answer correct to 1 decimal place.
You must show all your working. [E]

5.10 Inequalities

⊙ **21** Showing inequalities on a number line

- $a > b$ means 'a is greater than b'.
- $x \leqslant y$ means 'x is less than or equal to y'.
- There are four signs to use: $> < \geqslant \leqslant$
  Notice that the larger value is at the wide end of the sign.

> means 'greater than'
< means 'less than'
$\geqslant$ means 'greater than or equal to'
$\leqslant$ means 'less than or equal to'

Example 23

Show $x > -1$ on a number line.

x can be any number greater than -1.

An empty circle shows that -1 is not included.

Example 24

Show $3 \geqslant x$ on a number line.

x can be 3 or any number less than 3.

A solid circle shows that 3 is included.

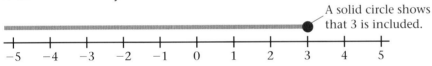

Example 25

Write down the inequality represented by the shading on this number line:

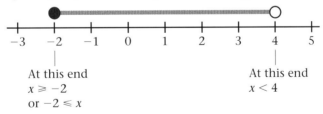

At this end
$x \geqslant -2$
or $-2 \leqslant x$

At this end
$x < 4$

These two inequalities combine as $-2 \leqslant x < 4$

Exercise 5J

1 Show each inequality on a number line.

(a) $x > 2$ (b) $x < -2$ (c) $x \leqslant 0$ (d) $x \geqslant -1$ (e) $x > -5$

(f) $x \leqslant 4$ (g) $3 < x$ (h) $-2 > x$ (i) $5 \leqslant x$ (j) $-3 \geqslant x$

Draw a new number line for each.

2 Replace * by the correct sign in each statement.

(a) 4 * 7   (b) −15 * −9

(c) 3 * −11   (d) −23 * −27

(e) (2 + 3) * (5 − 1)   (f) (−2 + 3) * (2 − 3)

(g) (15 − 4) * (3 − 14)   (h) (0 − 6) * (0 − 15)

3 Write down the inequalities represented by the shading.

(a)
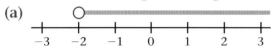

(b)
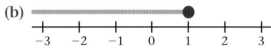

(c)
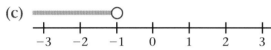

(d)
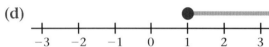

4 Draw separate number lines to show these inequalities.

(a) $-2 < x < 3$ (b) $-5 \leqslant x \leqslant -2$

(c) $1 < x \leqslant 4$ (d) $-3 \leqslant x < 2$

5 Write down the inequalities shown on these number lines.

(a)
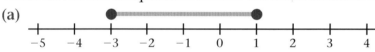

(b)

(c)

5.11 Solving inequalities

- To solve an inequality you can
  - add the same quantity to both sides
  - subtract the same quantity from both sides
  - multiply both sides by the same **positive** quantity
  - divide both sides by the same **positive** quantity.

  But you must *not*
  - multiply both sides by the same **negative** quantity
  - divide both sides by the same **negative** quantity.

> You solve inequalities in the same way as linear equations, except that you must not multiply or divide both sides by a **negative** number.

Example 26

(a) Solve the inequality $2x - 1 < 4$

(b) Show the solution on a number line.

(a) $2x - 1 < 4$

$\qquad 2x < 5$ $\qquad$ Add 1 to both sides.

$\qquad x < 2\frac{1}{2}$ $\qquad$ Divide both sides by 2.

(b)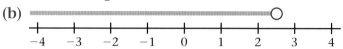

Example 27

(a) Solve the inequality $2x + 3 \leqslant 5x + 7$

(b) Write down the smallest integer which satisfies this inequality.

(a) $2x + 3 \leqslant 5x + 7$

$\qquad 3 \leqslant 3x + 7$ $\qquad$ Subtract $2x$ from both sides.

$\qquad -4 \leqslant 3x$ $\qquad$ Subtract 7 from both sides.

$\qquad x \geqslant -1\frac{1}{3}$ $\qquad$ Divide both sides by 3.

$-4 \leqslant 3x$ is the same as $3x \geqslant -4$.

(b) The smallest integer which satisfies this inequality is -1.

Example 28

Find all the integers which satisfy the inequality $-9 \leqslant 3x < 5$

$-9 \leqslant 3x < 5$

$-3 \leqslant x < \frac{5}{3}$ $\qquad$ Divide each term in the inequality by 3.

The integer solutions are $-3, -2, -1, 0, 1$.

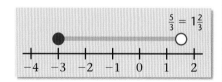

Exercise 5K

In questions **1–12** solve the inequality.

1 $x + 3 < 7$

2 $x - 1 \geqslant 5$

3 $2x \leqslant 12$

4 $\frac{x}{3} > 2$

5 $x - 4 < 5$

6 $5x > 20$

7 $x + 9 \geqslant 9$

8 $3x - 7 \leqslant 8$

9 $4x + 3 \geq 15$

10 $5x - 7 < 3$

11 $7x - 2 > 3x + 10$

12 $4x - 3 \leq 9x - 8$

In questions **13–18**, solve the inequality and show the solution on a number line.

13 $4x > 11$

14 $6x \leq 3$

15 $3x + 7 \geq 1$

16 $8x - 3 > 7$

17 $2x + 5 < 2$

18 $7x - 5 \leq 3x - 2$

In questions **19–27**, find all the **integers** which satisfy the inequality.

19 $4 \leq 2x \leq 8$

20 $-9 \leq 3x < 6$

21 $-15 < 5x \leq 5$

22 $0 \leq 6x < 24$

23 $-16 < 4x \leq 0$

24 $2 \leq 2x < 7$

25 $-7 < 5x \leq 15$

26 $-5 < 2x < 5$

27 $-10 < 3x < 0$

In questions **28–54**, solve the inequality.

28 $8x < 20$

29 $4x \geq 3$

30 $5x > -15$

31 $3x \geq -8$

32 $\frac{x}{4} > -2$

33 $21 < 6x$

34 $4x - 9 \geq 2$

35 $6x + 7 \leq 3$

36 $8x - 1 > 6$

37 $9 < 7x + 2$

38 $5x + 3 \geq 2x + 9$

39 $7x + 2 \leq 3x - 2$

40 $8x - 1 > 5x - 6$

41 $9x - 7 < 5x + 3$

42 $2x + 9 \geq 7x - 6$

43 $2(x - 3) \geq 8$

44 $5(x + 2) > 10$

45 $3(x + 1) < x + 9$

46 $7 - x \leq 1$

47 $8 - 3x > 2$

48 $2 - 5x < 6$

49 $7 - 2x \geq 3x + 2$

50 $4(x - 3) \leqslant 3 - x$

51 $10 - 3x > 2x - 1$

52 $6 - 5x \leqslant 2 - 3x$

53 $3 - 5x \geqslant 4 - 7x$

54 $11 - 2x < 2 - 5x$

55 Solve the inequality $7x + 5 > 4x - 9$
Write down the smallest integer which satisfies it.

56 Solve the inequality $3x + 4 \leqslant 1 - 2x$
Write down the largest integer which satisfies it.

Mixed exercise 5

1 Solve these equations.
   (a) $a + 7 = 12$ (b) $c - 4 = 6$
   (c) $3p = 21$ (d) $\dfrac{d}{4} = 3$
   (e) $5x + 4 = 19$ (f) $6b - 7 = 17$
   (g) $2r + 7 = r + 10$ (h) $3x - 2 = x + 8$
   (i) $5c + 4 = 2c + 19$ (j) $3b + 4 = b + 5$
   (k) $5d - 2 = 2d + 3$ (l) $7y - 9 = 2y - 5$
   (m) $3t + 8 = 6t + 1$ (n) $2w = 8w - 15$

2 Solve these equations.
   (a) $a + 7 = 3$ (b) $5b = -30$
   (c) $c - 2 = -3$ (d) $2e = -11$
   (e) $3h + 7 = 1$ (f) $4m + 5 = 2$
   (g) $6p + 19 = 2$ (h) $6q + 7 = 3$
   (i) $7u - 6 = 4u - 15$ (j) $5w + 8 = 3w - 5$
   (k) $3y - 5 = 7y + 5$

3 Solve these equations.
   (a) $3(a + 5) = a + 21$ (b) $5(b - 4) = 2b + 1$
   (c) $7c - 2 = 3(c + 6)$ (d) $6(d - 2) = 5(d - 1)$
   (e) $8(e - 1) = 5(e + 2)$ (f) $9(f - 2) = 2(f + 3)$
   (g) $4(2m + 1) = 3(5m - 1)$ (h) $2(3t + 4) = 5(2t - 1)$
   (i) $8 - a = 5$ (j) $13 - 3b = 1$
   (k) $5 - 4d = 3$ (l) $5 - 3g = 7$
   (m) $4 - 3p = 18$

4 The perimeter of a rectangle is $120 \, \text{cm}$.
The length of the rectangle is 4 times its
width. Find the length of the rectangle.

> Let the width of
> the rectangle be x
> centimetres.

5 (a) Solve $4x - 1 = 7$

(b) Solve $5(2y + 3) = 20$ [E]

6 (a) Solve $4x + 3 = 19$

(b) Solve $4y + 1 = 2y + 8$

(c) Simplify $2(t + 5) + 13$ [E]

7 Solve $4(x + 3) = 6$ [E]

8 In the diagram, all measurements are in centimetres.

ABC is an isosceles triangle.

$AB = 2x$

$AC = 2x$

$BC = 10$

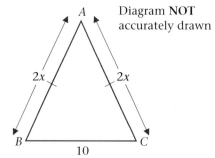

Diagram **NOT** accurately drawn

(a) Find an expression, in terms of *x*, for the **perimeter** of the triangle. Simplify your expression.

The perimeter of the triangle is 34 cm.

(b) Find the value of *x*. [E]

9 Solve these equations.

(a) $a^2 - 3 = 6$

(b) $5b^2 - 3 = 17$

(c) $9b^2 = 64$

(d) $11 = 36 - d^2$

10 Use the method of trial and improvement to find solutions to these equations.

(a) $x^3 + 3x - 20 = 0$ (to 2 d.p.)

(b) $x^3 - 20x - 3 = 0$ (to 2 d.p.)

(c) $x^3 - 4x^2 - 5 = 0$ (to 2 d.p.)

(d) $x^3 - 2x^2 = 25$ (to 2 d.p.)

(e) $x^3 + 5x = 26$ (to 1 d.p.)

(f) $x^3 - 2 = 2x$ (to 2 d.p.)

11 The equation $x^3 + 10x = 21$ has a solution between 1 and 2. Use a trial and improvement method to find this solution. Give your answer correct to 1 decimal place. You must show ALL your working. [E]

12 Tariq and Yousef have been asked to find the solution, correct to 1 decimal place, of the equation

$$x^3 + 2x = 56$$

(a) Work out the value of $x^3 + 2x$ when $x = 3.65$

Tariq says 3.6 is the solution.
Yousef says 3.7 is the solution.

(b) Use your answer to part **(a)** to decide whether Tariq or Yousef is correct.
You must give a reason. [E]

13 Show each inequality on a number line.

(a) $x > 1$ (b) $x \leqslant 3$ (c) $x \leqslant 0$
(d) $-2 \leqslant x < 1$ (e) $-1 < x \leqslant 3$ (f) $1 \leqslant x < 4$
(g) $-1 \leqslant x < 3$

14 Write down the inequalities represented on these number lines.

(a)
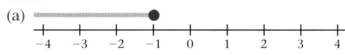

(b)
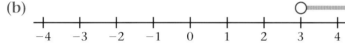

(c)
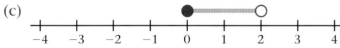

(d)
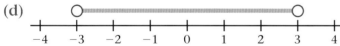

(e)
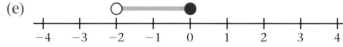

(f)
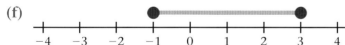

15 For each of these inequalities, list the integers which satisfy it.

(a) $-3 \leqslant x < 1$ (b) $0 < x \leqslant 3$
(c) $-2 \leqslant x \leqslant 4$ (d) $-4 < x < -1$

16 Solve each inequality.

(a) $x - 6 > 4$ (b) $6x \leqslant 30$
(c) $2x - 5 < 4$ (d) $5x + 11 \leqslant 1$
(e) $8x + 9 \geqslant 4x + 3$ (f) $7x - 1 < 4x - 1$
(g) $3x - 1 < 5x$ (h) $2(x - 3) < 7$
(i) $4 - x \leqslant x + 8$

17 Solve each inequality and show the solution on a number line.

(a) $2x < 5$ (b) $4x \geqslant -2$

(c) $3x - 4 > 1$ (d) $6x + 7 \leqslant 1$

(e) $9x - 5 < 4x + 5$ (f) $6x + 7 < 8x + 7$

18 (a) Solve the inequality $6x < 7 + 4x$

(b) Expand and simplify $(y + 3)(y + 4)$ [E]

19 (a) Solve $5 - 3x = 2(x + 1)$

(b) $-3 < y \leqslant 3$ y is an integer.
Write down all the possible values of y.   [E]

20 (a) Solve $7x = 21$

(b) Solve $5y + 1 = 3y + 13$ [E]

Summary of key points

1 In an **equation**, a symbol or letter represents an unknown number.

2 You can solve an equation to find the number that the letter represents. This number is called the **solution** of the equation.

3 You can solve an equation by rearranging it so that the letter is on its own on one side of the equals sign.

4 To rearrange an equation you can
  ○ add the same quantity to both sides
  ○ subtract the same quantity from both sides
  ○ multiply both sides by the same quantity
  ○ divide both sides by the same quantity.

5 Whatever you do to one side of an equation you must also do to the other side. This is called the **balance method**.

6 The solution of an equation is not always a whole number. It can be a fraction or a decimal.

7 You can use the balance method to solve equations with the letter on both sides. Rearrange the equation so that on one side there is the letter with a positive number in front of it and on the other side there is a number.

8 Equations with brackets can always be solved by expanding the brackets first.

9 A **coefficient** is the number in front of an unknown.

10 You can use the balance method to solve equations with negative coefficients.

11 The solution of an equation can be a negative number.

12 You can use equations to solve problems.

13 A **quadratic** equation is one in which the highest power of x is x^2. For example, $x^2 + 4 = 29$, $3x^2 - 6 = 42$ and $25x^2 = 9$ are quadratic equations.

14 You can solve some simple quadratic equations by using inverse operations.

15 The inverse operation of 'square' is 'find the square roots'.

16 A quadratic equation usually has two solutions.

17 You can find approximate solutions to complicated equations by **trial and improvement**.

18 $a > b$ means 'a is greater than b'.

19 $x \leqslant y$ means 'x is less than or equal to y'.

20 There are four signs to use: $> < \geqslant \leqslant$
Notice that the larger value is at the wide end of the sign.

> $>$ means 'greater than'
> $<$ means 'less than'
> $\geqslant$ means 'greater than or equal to'
> $\leqslant$ means 'less than or equal to'

21 To solve an inequality you can
  ○ add the same quantity to both sides
  ○ subtract the same quantity from both sides
  ○ multiply both sides by the same **positive** quantity
  ○ divide both sides by the same **positive** quantity.
  But you must *not*
  ○ multiply both sides by the same **negative** quantity
  ○ divide both sides by the same **negative** quantity.

> You solve inequalities in the same way as linear equations, except that you must not multiply or divide both sides by a **negative** number.

6 Graphs

6.1 General straight line graphs

- Every **straight line graph** has an equation of the form
    $$y = mx + c$$
    where m and c are numbers.
    For example,
    $$y = 3x + 2, \; y = -2x + 7 \text{ and } y = \tfrac{1}{2}x - 1$$
    are equations of straight line graphs.

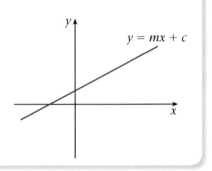

Example 1

Draw the graph of $y = 2x + 1$, taking values of x between -3 and 2.

Table of values: | Find 3 points on the graph.

x	-3	0	2
y	-5	1	5

When $x = -3$
$y = 2 \times -3 + 1$
$\quad = -6 + 1$
$\quad = -5$

This gives coordinates $(0, 1)$

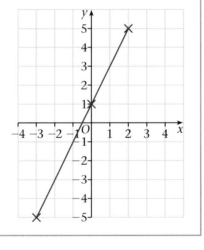

Plotting linear graphs was covered in Chapter 6 of Foundation Unit 3.

Exercise 6A

1 Draw the graph of $y = 3x + 2$ between $x = -2$ and $x = 3$.

2 Draw the graph of $y = -2x - 1$ between $x = -2$ and $x = 2$.

3 Draw the graph of $y = \tfrac{1}{2}x + 3$ between $x = -4$ and $x = 4$.

6.2 Gradients and intercepts

- In the equation

    $y = mx + c$

    the value of c is where the straight line graph crosses the vertical (y) axis.

    The graph crosses the y-axis at the point with coordinates $(0, c)$. c is called the y-**intercept**.

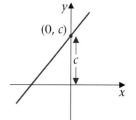

- In the equation

    $y = mx + c$

    the value of m represents the **gradient**. It is the increase in the y-value caused by an increase of 1 in the x-value.

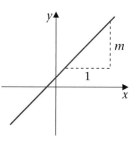

- To find the gradient of a straight line, draw a right-angled triangle.

    $$\text{Gradient} = \frac{\text{rise}}{\text{tread}}$$

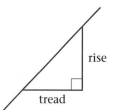

Example 2

Find the gradient and y-intercept of the line shown.

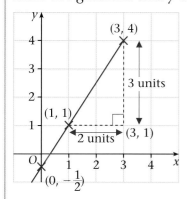

y-intercept is $(0, -\frac{1}{2})$.

$c = -\frac{1}{2}$

Gradient, $m = \dfrac{\text{rise}}{\text{tread}} = \dfrac{3}{2}$

The equation of the line is

$y = \frac{3}{2}x - \frac{1}{2}$

- Lines with the same gradient are **parallel**.

Example 3

Write down the equation of a line parallel to $y = 3x - 7$.

All lines parallel to $y = 3x - 7$ have the form
$$y = 3x + c$$
Choose any value for c, for example 1.
$$y = 3x + 1 \text{ is parallel to } y = 3x - 7.$$

- If a point lies on a line, its coordinates satisfy the equation of the line.

Example 4

Does the point with coordinates (4, 10) lie on the line with equation $y = 3x - 2$?

Substitute $x = 4$ into the expression $3x - 2$
$$3 \times 4 - 2 = 12 - 2 = 10$$
So the point with coordinates (4, 10) lies on the line with equation $y = 3x - 2$.

Exercise 6B

1 Write down the gradient and y-intercept of the lines with these equations.
   (a) $y = 2x - 3$ (b) $y = -x + 5$
   (c) $y = 3x - 6$ (d) $y = \frac{1}{2}x + 2$

2 In each part, write down the pairs of equations which represent parallel lines.
   (a) (i) $y = 3x - 2$ (b) (i) $y = \frac{3}{2}x - \frac{7}{2}$
       (ii) $y = -3x + 4$ (ii) $y = \frac{3}{2}x + 5$
       (iii) $y = 3x + 2$ (iii) $y = -\frac{2}{3}x + 1$
       (iv) $y = -3x - 2$ (iv) $y = \frac{3}{2}x - 17$
   (c) (i) $y = \frac{1}{2}x + 1$
       (ii) $y = \frac{x}{2} + 3$
       (iii) $y = -\frac{1}{2}x + 7$
       (iv) $y = -2x$

3 Which of the following points lie on the line with equation $y = 3x + 2$?

(i) (2, 0)   (ii) (0, 2)   (iii) (1, 5)

(iv) (5, 1)   (v) (−1, −5)   (vi) (−1, −1)

4 Which of the following points lie on the line with equation $y = -x + 6$?

(i) (6, 0)   (ii) (0, 6)   (iii) (1, 5)

(iv) (5, 1)   (v) (−2, 4)   (vi) (−2, 8)

5

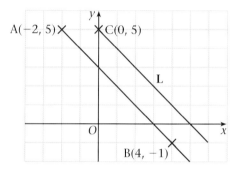

The diagram shows three points A(−2, 5), B(4, −1) and C(0, 5).

The line **L** is parallel to AB and passes through C.

Find the equation of the line **L**.   [E]

6.3 Simultaneous equations – graphical solutions

- Two equations in two unknowns with a common solution are called **simultaneous** equations, for example $y = 2x - 1$ and $y = -x + 8$.
- You can solve simultaneous equations graphically.
  - Draw the two straight lines represented by the two simultaneous equations.
  - Their point of intersection represents the common solution.

Example 5

Solve the simultaneous equations

$$y = 2x - 1$$
$$y = -x + 8$$

Make a table of values for each equation.

$y = 2x - 1$

x	0	1	2
y	−1	1	3

$y = -x + 8$

x	0	1	2
y	8	7	6

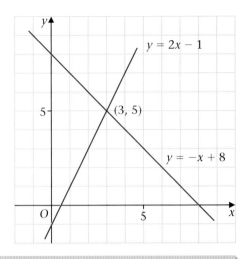

Draw the two straight lines.
The coordinates of the point of intersection
of the lines give the solution:

$x = 3$
$y = 5$

Check: Substitute $x = 3$ into both the expressions.
$2 \times 3 - 1 = 5$ ✓
$8 - 3 = 5$ ✓

Example 6

Use the diagram to solve the
simultaneous equations
$y = x - 1$
$y = -\frac{1}{2}x + 5$

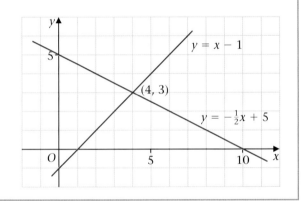

The coordinates of the point of
intersection give the solution:
$x = 4$
$y = 3$

Exercise 6C

1 Use the diagram to solve the
simultaneous equations
$y = x + 3$
$y = 3x - 1$

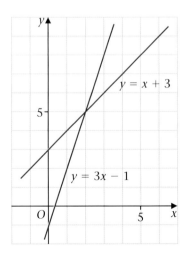

2 Use the diagram below to solve the simultaneous equations

$$y = 2x - 3$$
$$y = -x + 9$$

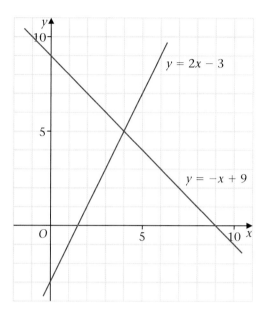

3 Use the diagram below to solve the simultaneous equations

$$y = -\tfrac{1}{2}x + 2$$
$$y = \tfrac{2}{3}x - 5$$

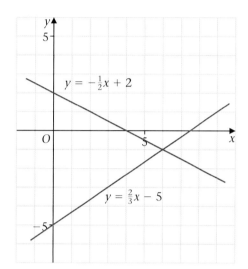

4 Use the diagram on the right to solve the pairs of simultaneous equations

(a) $y = -0.5x + 3.5$
   $y = \tfrac{1}{3}x - \tfrac{2}{3}$

(b) $y = 2x + 6$
   $y = -0.5x + 3.5$

(c) $y = 2x + 6$
   $y = \tfrac{1}{3}x - \tfrac{2}{3}$

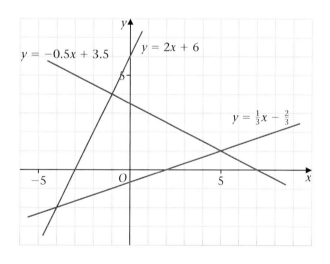

5 On separate diagrams, draw appropriate straight lines to solve these pairs of simultaneous equations.

(a) $y = x + 4$
   $y = 3x$

(b) $y = x + 2$
   $y = 2x - 1$

(c) $y = 2x - 1$
   $y = 3x + 1$

(d) $y = x + 3$
   $y = 7 - x$

(e) $y = x - 4$
   $2x + y = 5$

(f) $x + y = 3$
   $y = 1 - 2x$

In parts (d), (e) and (f) rearrange the equations into the form
$$y = mx + c$$

6.4 Equations of lines of best fit

- You can draw a **line of best fit** for any data whose graph is almost a straight line.
- You can find the equation of a line of best fit by using the gradient and *y*-intercept.
- In real-life examples, *m* and *c* are rarely whole numbers.

> You often need to draw a line of best fit for a scatter graph.

Example 7

In an experiment, the length of a spring is measured when different loads are hung from it. The table shows the results.

Load in kg	1	2	3	4	5
Length in cm	25.8	27.8	30.5	31.4	34.6

(a) Plot the points.   (b) Draw the line of best fit.
(c) Find the equation of the line of best fit.

(a) (b)

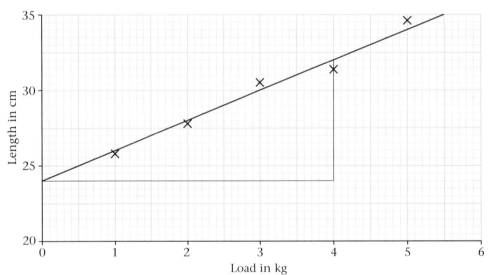

(c) The *y*-intercept is where the line of best fit crosses the length axis, at 24 cm.

To find the gradient, draw a right-angled triangle.

$$\text{Gradient} = \frac{\text{rise}}{\text{tread}} = \frac{8}{4} = 2$$

The equation is

Length = 2 × load + 24
or $L = 2w + 24$ where *w* is the load in kilograms

> This is when there is no load. It is the natural length of the spring.

Exercise 6D

For each question, (a) plot the points from the table (b) draw
the line of best fit (c) find the equation of the line of best fit.

1

Age (years)	4	5	6	7	8
Depreciation (%)	62	70	75	80	83

2

Age (years)	11	12	13	14	15
Weight (kg)	40	45	53	62	70

3

Distance travelled (km)	120	150	200	270	350
Litres used	20	24	35	42	60

4

IQ	90	95	102	105	108
Total Key Stage score	8	9	13	14	15

5

Journey distance (miles)	55	83	120	134	165
Fare (£)	21	30	40	45	52

6.5 Using straight line graphs for real-life problems

16 Distance-time graphs

- Straight line graphs arise from a variety of real-life problems. Examples are conversion graphs and distance–time graphs.
- A **conversion graph** is used to convert a measurement into different units.

Example 8

This graph can be used to
convert between miles
and kilometres.

(a) Convert 34 miles
to kilometres.

(b) Convert 115 km
to miles.

(a) 34 miles = 55 km

(b) 115 km = 72 miles

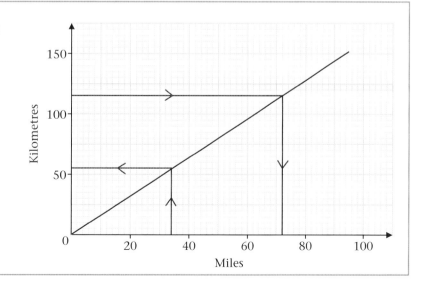

- On a **distance–time graph**
  - a straight line represents constant speed
  - a horizontal line represents a stop, or zero speed.

Example 9

Here is the distance–time graph for Peter's cycle ride.

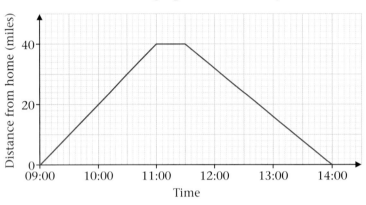

(a) Find Peter's distance from home at 10:15.

(b) Describe the three stages of Peter's journey.

(c) Work out Peter's average speed between
    (i) 09:00 and 11:00   (ii) 11:30 and 14:00.

(d) Work out Peter's average speed for the whole journey.

(a)

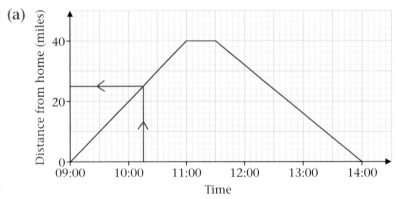

At 10:15, Peter is 25 miles from home.

(b) Between 09:00 and 11:00, Peter cycles 40 miles. His speed is constant because this part of the graph is a straight line.
Between 11:00 and 11:30 (the horizontal part of the graph), Peter is in the same place. He has stopped for a rest, perhaps.
Between 11:30 and 14:00, Peter cycles 40 miles back home at a constant speed.

(c) Average speed = $\dfrac{\text{total distance travelled}}{\text{total time taken}}$

> Calculating speeds was covered in Chapter 9 of Foundation Unit 3.

    (i) Between 9:00 and 11:00

        Average speed = $\dfrac{40}{2}$ = 20 mph

> You do *not* work out $\dfrac{40}{2.30}$
> 2 hours 30 minutes = 2.5 hours

    (ii) Between 11:30 and 14:00

        Average speed = $\dfrac{40}{2.5}$ = 16 mph •

(d) Average speed = $\dfrac{80}{5}$ = 16 mph

> Total distance = 40 + 40 miles
> Total time is 9:00 to 14:00

Exercise 6E

1 This graph can be used to convert between pounds and Swiss francs (SF).

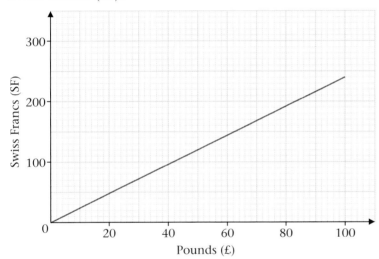

  (a) Convert to Swiss francs.

    (i) £50   **(ii)** £12   **(iii)** £38   **(iv)** £87

  (b) Convert to pounds.

    (i) SF100   **(ii)** SF130   **(iii)** SF210   **(iv)** SF185

2 (a) 1 kilogram (kg) = 2.2 pounds (lb).

    Copy and complete the table.

Kilograms (kg)	0	10	20	30	40	50
Pounds (lb)	0			66		

  (b) Using a scale of 1 cm to 5 kg on the horizontal axis and a scale of 1 cm to 10 lb on the vertical axis, plot the points given by the pairs of values in your table. Join the points with a straight line.

  (c) Use your graph to convert

    (i) 33 kg to pounds   **(ii)** 42 lb to kilograms.

3 Paul drove from Birmingham to Liverpool and back.
Here is the distance–time graph for his journey.

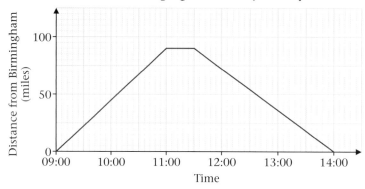

(a) Find his distance from Birmingham at 10:00.

(b) At what time did he reach Liverpool?

(c) For how long did he stay in Liverpool?

(d) Work out his average speed for
   (i)   the journey from Birmingham to Liverpool
   (ii) the journey from Liverpool to Birmingham
   (iii) the whole journey, including his stay in Liverpool.

4 Aishya set off from home at 1 pm. She cycled 36 km in
2 hours and then rested for an hour. She cycled a further
12 km in half an hour and finally cycled the 48 km home,
arriving at 7 pm.

> Assume that she cycled at a constant speed during each stage of her journey.

(a) Draw a distance–time graph for her journey.

(b) Work out her average speed for the whole journey,
including the rest time.

5 Here is a distance–time graph for Tristan's bus journey to
work.

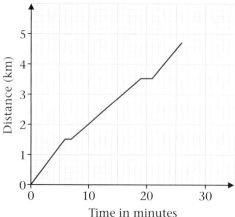

(a) How long does the bus wait at the first stop?

(b) In which stage of the journey is the bus travelling fastest?

(c) Work out the average speed for the whole journey.

6.6 Graphs that describe real-life situations

- Graphs can be used to describe a wide variety of real-life situations.
  You may have to interpret or sketch graphs of this type.

Example 10

The diagram represents a bottle.

Water is poured into the bottle at a steady rate.

Sketch a graph of the height of the water in the bottle against time.

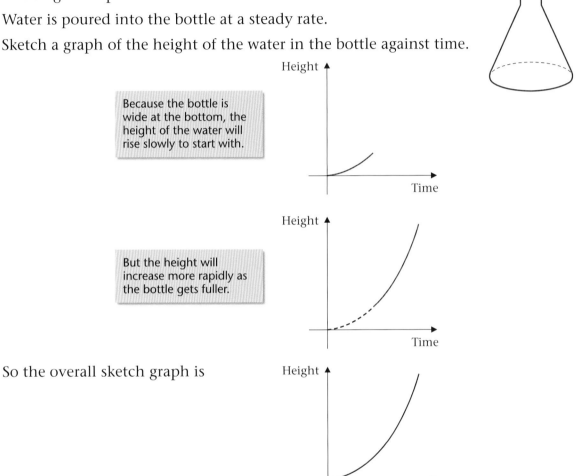

Because the bottle is wide at the bottom, the height of the water will rise slowly to start with.

But the height will increase more rapidly as the bottle gets fuller.

So the overall sketch graph is

Example 11

Here is a speed–time graph for a car. Describe what happened.

The car was travelling at a steady speed and then stopped suddenly.

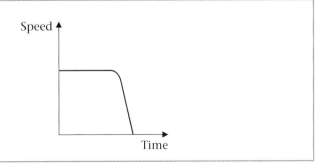

Exercise 6F

1 Water is poured into each of these containers at a steady rate.
   For each container, sketch a graph of the water level against time.

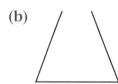

   (a)   (b)   (c)

2 Here are speed–time graphs for two cars. For each one, describe what happened.

   (a) 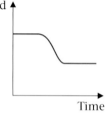   (b)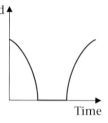

3 Sketch a graph to show the relationship between the total cost of the petrol and the number of litres bought.

4 Sketch a graph to show how the value of a new car changes over a number of years.

5 The diagram shows the cross-section of a swimming pool. The pool is filled with water at a steady rate. Sketch a graph to show how the depth of water in the pool varies with time.

6 The graph shows how Ben's weekly wage depends on the number of hours' overtime he works.
   Describe the relationship.

7 Sketch a graph to show how the cost of a mobile phone call depends on the length of the call.

8 Lester ran a 100 metres sprint in 10 seconds.
   The graph of his speed against time is shown.
   Comment as fully as possible on his speed during the sprint.

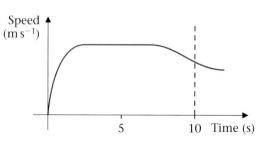

9 Helen threw a rounders ball.

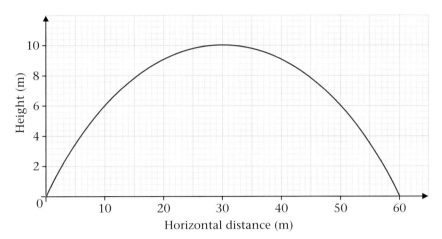

The graph above shows the height of the ball above the ground against the horizontal distance travelled by the ball.

(a) How far did the ball travel horizontally?

(b) Find the maximum height of the ball above the ground.

(c) Find the height of the ball above the ground when it had travelled 12 metres horizontally.

10 Tom travels by car to his meetings.
Tom's company works out the amount it will pay him for the distance he travels.
It uses the graph below.

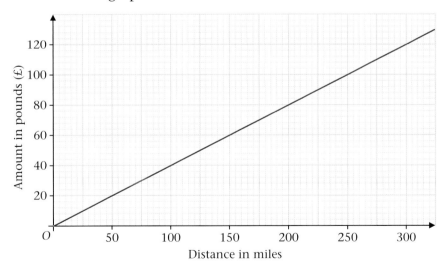

Use the graph to write down

(a) the amount Tom's company pays him when he travels 200 miles

(b) the distance Tom travels when his company pays him £50. **[E]**

6.7 Graphs of quadratic functions

- A **quadratic function** is one in which the highest power of x is x^2. For example, $x^2 + 5$, $3x^2 - 4x + 7$ and $4x^2 + 5x$ are quadratic functions.
- The graph of a quadratic function is called a **parabola**.

Example 12

(a) Draw the graph of $y = x^2 + 3$ for values of x from -3 to 3.

(b) Write down the minimum value of y and the value of x for which it occurs.

(a) Draw up a table of values.

x	-3	-2	-1	0	1	2	3
y	12	7	4	3	4	7	12

Plot the points and join them with a smooth curve.

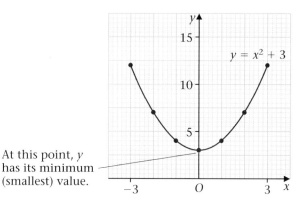

At this point, y has its minimum (smallest) value.

(b) The minimum value of y is 3, which occurs when $x = 0$.

Example 13

(a) Draw the graph of $y = 2 + 4x - x^2$, taking values of x from -1 to 5.

(b) Draw the graph's line of symmetry and write down its equation.

(c) Write down the maximum value of y and the value of x for which it occurs.

When $x = 3$
$y = 2 + 4 \times 3 - 3^2$
$= 2 + 12 - 9$
$= 5$

(a)

x	-1	0	1	2	3	4	5
y	-3	2	5	6	5	2	-3

At this point, y has its maximum (greatest) value.

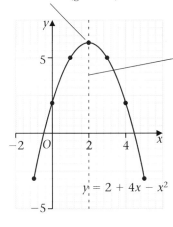

Line of symmetry

$y = 2 + 4x - x^2$

(b) The line of symmetry has equation $x = 2$.

(c) The maximum value of y is 6, which occurs when $x = 2$.

- Graphs of functions of the form $y = ax^2 + bx + c$ have a ∪-shape where a is positive and a ∩-shape where a is negative. The parabola cuts the y-axis at $(0, c)$.

Exercise 6G

1 Draw the graph of each of the following for values of x from -4 to 4.

(a) $y = x^2 + 4$

(b) $y = x^2 - 5$

(c) $y = 3x^2$

(d) $y = \frac{1}{2}x^2$

(e) $y = -x^2$

(f) $y = x^2 + 2x$

(g) $y = 3x^2 - 8$

(h) $y = (x + 2)^2$

For $y = (x + 2)^2$:
when $x = -3$,
$y = (-3 + 2)^2$
$= (-1)^2$
$= 1$

2 (a) Copy and complete the table of values for
$y = x^2 + 4x + 2$.

x	-4	-3	-2	-1	0	1	2
y		-1					14

(b) Draw the graph of $y = x^2 + 4x + 2$.

(c) Draw the graph's line of symmetry and write down its equation.

3 (a) Draw the graph of $y = x^2 - 2x - 1$ for values of x from -2 to 4.

(b) Write down the minimum value of y and the value of x for which it occurs.

4 (a) Draw the graph of $y = x^2 - 4x + 4$ for values of x from -1 to 5.

(b) Draw the graph's line of symmetry and write down its equation.

(c) Write down the minimum value of y and the value of x for which it occurs.

5 (a) Copy and complete the table of values for
$y = 2x^2 + 4x - 5$.

x	-4	-3	-2	-1	0	1	2
y		1			-5		

(b) Draw the graph of $y = 2x^2 + 4x - 5$.

(c) Draw the graph's line of symmetry and write down its equation.

(d) Write down the minimum value of y and the value of x for which it occurs.

6 (a) Draw the graph of $y = 2x^2 - 6x + 7$ for values of x from -1 to 4.

(b) Draw the graph's line of symmetry and write down its equation.

7 (a) Draw the graph of $y = 3 + 4x - x^2$ for values of x from -1 to 5.

(b) Draw the graph's line of symmetry and write down its equation.

(c) Write down the maximum value of y and the value of x for which it occurs.

6.8 Solving a quadratic equation from its graph

- You can estimate solutions to a quadratic equation from its graph.
- Quadratic equations can have 0, 1 or 2 solutions.

Example 14

Find the solutions of $6x^2 - x - 3 = 0$.

Make a table of values and draw the graph.

x	-2	-1	0	1	2
$6x^2$	24	6	0	6	24
$-x$	2	1	0	-1	-2
-3	-3	-3	-3	-3	-3
y	23	4	-3	2	19

The graph is of $y = 6x^2 - x - 3$.

The line $y = 0$ is the x-axis.
So the intercepts with the x-axis are the solutions of the
quadratic equation.

The solutions are $x = -0.6$ and 0.8

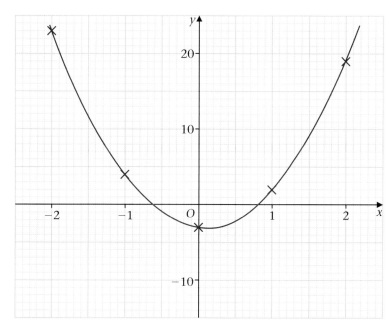

Note: to solve the equation $6x^2 - x - 3 = 5$ you would need to find the intercepts with $y = 5$.

The solutions are $x = -1.1$ and 1.25

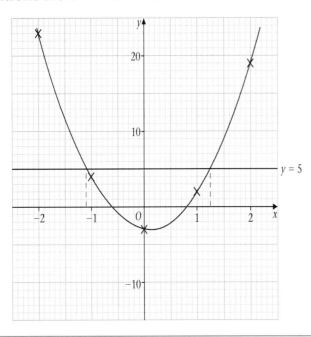

Exercise 6H

1 Draw the graph of $y = x^2 - 2x - 2$. Make a table using values of x from -2 to 4.
   (a) Use your graph to solve the following quadratic equations.
      (i) $x^2 - 2x - 2 = 0$ (ii) $x^2 - 2x - 2 = 3$
      (iii) $x^2 - 2x - 2 = -3$
   (b) What are the coordinates of the minimum point?
   (c) Give a value of y for which $y = x^2 - 2x - 2$ has no solution.

In each of questions **2–7** draw the graph using the given values of x.
Use your graph to solve the equation for the given values of y
and give the coordinates of the maximum or minimum value.

2 $y = x^2 - 5x + 3$ for $x = 0$ to $x = 6$. Solve for $y = -1, 4$ and 8.

3 $y = x^2 - 3x + 1$ for $x = 0$ to $x = 4$. Solve for $y = -1, 0$ and 3.

4 $y = x^2 - x - 3$ for $x = -2$ to $x = 4$. Solve for $y = -1, 0$ and 5.

5 $y = 2x^2 - 7x + 2$ for $x = -1$ to $x = 4$. Solve for $y = -1, 0$ and 6.

6 $y = 6x - 6 - x^2$ for $x = 0$ to $x = 4$. Solve for $y = 1, 0$ and -5.

7 $y = 3 - x^2 + x$ for $x = -2$ to $x = 4$. Solve for $y = 1$, 0 and -5.

8 (a) Copy and complete the table of values for $y = 2x^2$.

x	-3	-2	-1	0	1	2	3
y	18				2	8	

(b) On a copy of the grid, draw the graph of $y = 2x^2$.

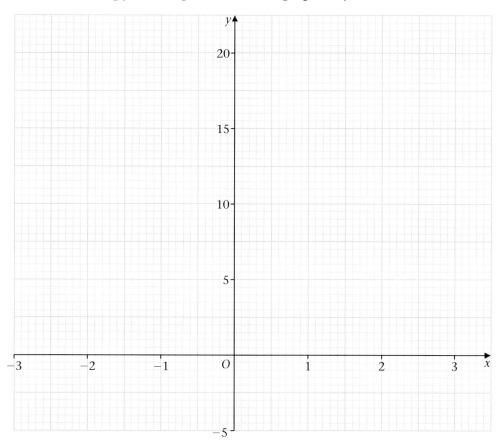

(c) Use your graph to find
  (i) the value of y when $x = 2.5$
  (ii) the values of x when $y = 12$.   [E]

Mixed exercise 6

1 The graphs of the straight lines with equations
$3y + 2x = 12$ and $y = x - 1$ have been drawn on the grid.

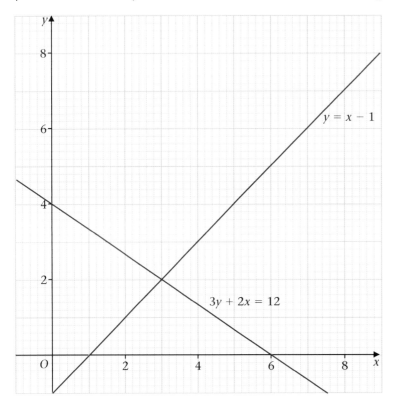

Use the graphs to solve the simultaneous equations
$$3y + 2x = 12$$
$$y = x - 1$$ [E]

2 On separate diagrams, draw appropriate straight lines to
solve these pairs of simultaneous equations.
  (a) $y = x - 3$ (b) $y = -2x + 8$ (c) $x + y = 3$
      $x + y = 5$ $y = x - 1$ $x - 2y = 6$

3 The table shows the estimated value of a factory robot
at the end of each month as a percentage of its original
value.

Time (months)	1	2	3	4	5	6	7	8	9	10	11	12
Value (%)	92	88	80	78	75	71	69	65	61	59	54	51

  (a) Plot this data as a graph.
  (b) Draw the line of best fit.
  (c) Write the equation of the line of best fit.

4 **(a)** £1 = 1.6 euros.
Make a conversion graph for amounts up to £50.
Plot (0, 0) and at least two more points on your line.
Use a scale of 1 cm to £5 on the horizontal axis and a
scale of 1 cm to 10 euros on the vertical axis.

(b) Use your graph to convert
(i) £44 to euros
(ii) 37 euros to pounds.

5 This rule can be used to work out the time, in minutes,
needed to cook a turkey:

Multiply the weight in pounds by 15 and then add 15.

(a) Use the rule to copy and complete the table.

Weight (lb)	Cooking time (minutes)
5	
10	
15	240
20	

(b) Draw a graph to show this information.

Do not join the straight
line to the origin.

(c) Use your graph to find
(i) the cooking time for a 17 lb turkey
(ii) the weight of a turkey if its cooking time is 3 hours.

6 **(a)** The graph below shows how the depth of water in a
bath changes while Kate has a bath. Describe what
happens from when she starts to fill the bath.

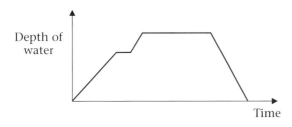

(b) The graph below shows how the temperature of the
water changes while Kate is in the bath.
Describe what happens.

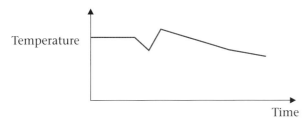

7 These two mugs are filled with tea at a steady rate. Draw a sketch graph for each to show the level of tea against time.

(a)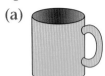

(b)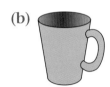

8 (a) Copy and complete the table of values for $y = x^2 + 2x - 2$.

x	-3	-2	-1	0	1	2	3
y		-2					13

   (b) Draw the graph of $y = x^2 + 2x - 2$.

   (c) Draw the graph's line of symmetry and write down its equation.

   (d) Use your graph to estimate the solutions to $x^2 + 2x - 2 = 0$.

9 (a) Draw the graph of $y = x^2 - 6x + 11$ for values of x from -1 to 5.

   (b) Write down the minimum value of y and the value of x for which it occurs.

10 (a) Draw the graph of $y = 4x^2 - 20x + 15$ for values of x from 0 to 5.

   (b) Draw the graph's line of symmetry and write down its equation.

   (c) Use your graph to estimate the solutions to $4x^2 - 20x + 15 = 0$.

11 A man left home at 12 noon to go for a cycle ride.
The travel graph represents part of the man's journey.

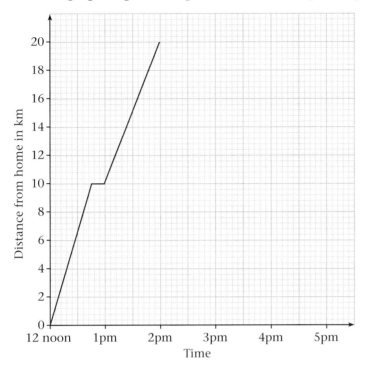

At 12:45 pm the man stopped for a rest.

(a) For how many minutes did he rest?

(b) Find his distance from home at 1:30 pm.

The man stopped for another rest at 2 pm.
He rested for one hour.
Then he cycled home at a steady speed.
It took him 2 hours.

(c) Copy and complete the travel graph.   [E]

12 (a) Copy and complete the table of values for
$y = x^2 - 3x + 1$.

x	-2	-1	0	1	2	3	4
y	11			-1			5

(b) Draw the graph of $y = x^2 - 3x + 1$.

(c) Use your graph to estimate the values of x for which
$y = 3$.   [E]

Summary of key points

1 Every **straight line graph** has an equation of the form

$$y = mx + c$$

where m and c are numbers.

For example,

$$y = 3x + 2, y = -2x + 7 \text{ and } y = \tfrac{1}{2}x - 1$$

are equations of straight line graphs.

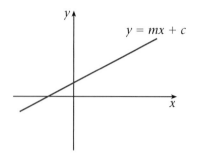

2 In the equation

$$y = mx + c$$

the value of c is where the straight line graph crosses the vertical (y) axis.

The graph crosses the y-axis at the point with coordinates $(0, c)$. c is called the y-**intercept**.

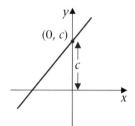

3 In the equation

$$y = mx + c$$

the value of m represents the **gradient**. It is the increase in the y-value caused by an increase of 1 in the x-value.

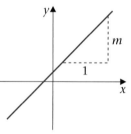

4 To find the gradient of a straight line, draw a right-angled triangle.

$$\text{Gradient} = \frac{\text{rise}}{\text{tread}}$$

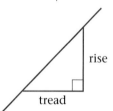

5 Lines with the same gradient are **parallel**.

6 If a point lies on a line, its coordinates satisfy the equation of the line.

7 Two equations in two unknowns with a common solution are called **simultaneous** equations, for example $y = 2x - 1$ and $y = -x + 8$.

8 You can solve simultaneous equations graphically.
   - Draw the two straight lines represented by the two simultaneous equations.
   - Their point of intersection represents the common solution.

9 You can draw a **line of best fit** for any data whose graph is almost a straight line.

10 You can find the equation of a line of best fit by using the gradient and y-intercept.

11 In real-life examples, m and c are rarely integers.

12 Straight line graphs arise from a variety of real-life problems. Examples are conversion graphs and distance–time graphs.

13 A **conversion graph** is used to convert a measurement into different units.

14 On a **distance–time graph**
   ○ a straight line represents constant speed
   ○ a horizontal line represents a stop, or zero speed.

15 Graphs can be used to describe a wide variety of real-life situations. You may have to interpret or sketch graphs of this type.

16 A **quadratic function** is one in which the highest power of x is x^2. For example, $x^2 + 5$, $3x^2 - 4x + 7$ and $4x^2 + 5x$ are quadratic functions.

17 The graph of a quadratic function is called a **parabola**.

18 Graphs of functions of the form $y = ax^2 + bx + c$ have a ∪-shape where a is positive and a ∩-shape where a is negative. The parabola cuts the y-axis at $(0, c)$.

19 You can estimate solutions to a quadratic equation from its graph.

20 Quadratic equations can have 0, 1 or 2 solutions.

7 Formulae

7.1 Using word formulae

- A **word formula** uses words to represent a relationship between quantities.

Example 1

This word formula can be used to work out the perimeter of an equilateral triangle.

Perimeter = 3 × length of side

Work out the perimeter of an equilateral triangle with sides of length 9 cm.

Perimeter = 3 × 9 = 27 cm

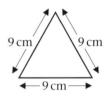

Example 2

Suki is paid £6.50 per hour.
(a) Write a word formula for her weekly pay.
(b) Work out her pay for a week when she works 24 hours.

(a) Pay = hourly rate × hours worked
(b) Pay = £6.50 × 24
       = £156

Exercise 7A

1 This word formula can be used to work out the perimeter of a regular pentagon.

   Perimeter = 5 × length of side

Work out the perimeter of a regular pentagon with sides of length 7 cm.

2 Gwen uses this word formula to work out her wages.

   Wages = rate per hour × number of hours worked

Gwen's rate per hour is £5 and she worked for 37 hours. Work out her wages.

3 This word formula can be used to work out the perimeter of a rectangle.

Perimeter = 2 × length + 2 × width

Work out the perimeter of a rectangle with a length of 8 cm and a width of 3 cm.

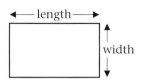

4 Owen uses this word formula to work out his phone bill.

Total bill = cost per minute × number of minutes + monthly charge

The cost per minute is 6p. Owen made 70 minutes of calls. The monthly charge is £15. Work out his total bill.

Remember the order of operations: multiplication before addition.

Work in £
6p = £0.06

5 This word formula can be used to work out the area of a triangle.

Area = $\frac{1}{2}$ × base × vertical height

A triangle has base 8 cm and vertical height 10 cm. Work out the area of the triangle.

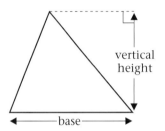

6 Kirsty buys 12 stamps at 42p each.
  (a) Write a word formula for the total cost of the stamps.
  (b) Work out the cost of the stamps.

Area of a triangle was covered in Chapter 10 of Foundation Unit 3.

7 **(a)** Write a word formula to work out the number of packets of crisps in a machine after a number have been sold.
  (b) Use your formula to work out the number of packets in a machine that holds 56 packets, when 27 have been sold.

8 Georgina uses this word formula to work out her take-home pay:

Take-home pay =
rate per hour × number of hours worked − deductions

Georgina's rate per hour is £7. She worked for 40 hours and her deductions were £96. Work out her take-home pay.

Remember the order of operations: multiplication before subtraction.

9 For each part write a word formula, then use it to calculate the answers.
  (a) Alix shared a bag of sweets equally between herself and her three brothers. There were 84 sweets in the bag. How many did each person have?
  (b) At a buffet lunch there were 36 slices of pizza. Every person at the lunch had 3 slices. How many people were at the lunch?

10 This word formula can be used to work out the average speed for a journey.

$$\text{Average speed} = \frac{\text{total distance travelled}}{\text{total time taken}}$$

Raj travels 215 miles in 5 hours.
Work out his average speed.

> When distance is in miles and time is in hours, the average speed is in miles per hour (mph).

11 This word formula can be used to work out the angle sum, in degrees, of a polygon.

$$\text{Angle sum} = (\text{number of sides} - 2) \times 180$$

Work out the angle sum of a polygon with 7 sides.

> Brackets first.

> For more on angles in polygons see Chapter 9.

12 This word formula can be used to work out the size, in degrees, of each exterior angle of a regular polygon.

$$\text{Exterior angle} = \frac{360}{\text{number of sides}}$$

Work out the size of each exterior angle of a regular polygon with 8 sides.

13 This word formula can be used to work out the area inside a circle.

$$\text{Area} = \pi \times \text{radius} \times \text{radius}$$

Work out the area of a circle with a radius of 4 cm.
Give your answer to the nearest whole number.

> If you haven't got a calculator with a π key, use $\pi = 3.14$

> For more on area of a circle see Chapter 10.

7.2 Rearranging word formulae

- In a word formula, you can find the value of any term, if you know the values of all the other terms.
- You can rearrange a word formula using the balance method. Whatever you do to one side you must also do to the other.

Example 3

This word formula can be used to work out the area of a rectangle.

$$\text{Area} = \text{length} \times \text{width}$$

The area of a rectangle is 63 cm². Its length is 9 cm.
Work out the width of the rectangle.

$$63 = 9 \times \text{width}$$

$$\text{So width} = \frac{63}{9} = 7 \text{ cm} \qquad \text{Divide both sides by 9.}$$

> For more on the balance method see Chapter 5.

Exercise 7B

1 This word formula can be used to work out the perimeter of a regular octagon.

   Perimeter = 8 × length of side

   The perimeter of a regular octagon is 56 cm.
   Work out the length of each side.

2 Jan uses this word formula to work out her wages.

   Wages = rate per hour × number of hours worked

   Jan's wages are £198 and her rate per hour is £6.
   Work out the number of hours she worked.

3 This word formula can be used to work out the perimeter of a rectangle.

   Perimeter = 2 × length + 2 × width

   The perimeter of a rectangle is 34 cm and its length is 10 cm.
   Work out the width of the rectangle.

4 Ben uses this word formula to work out his total phone bill.

   Total bill = cost per minute × number of minutes + monthly charge

   Ben's bill is £15. The cost per minute is 10p and he made 51 minutes of calls.
   Work out the monthly charge.

5 This word formula can be used to work out the average speed for a journey.

   $$\text{Average speed} = \frac{\text{total distance travelled}}{\text{total time taken}}$$

   Dec's average speed for a journey was 53 miles per hour.
   The total time taken for the journey was 3 hours.
   Work out the total distance he travelled.

6 Liz uses this word formula to work out her take-home pay.

   Take-home pay =
   rate per hour × number of hours worked − deductions

   Liz's take-home pay is £64. Her rate per hour is £5 and her deductions are £26.
   Work out the number of hours she worked.

7 This word formula can be used to work out the volume of a cuboid.

Volume = length × width × height

The volume of a cuboid is $90 \, \text{cm}^3$. Its length is $6 \, \text{cm}$ and its width is $5 \, \text{cm}$. Work out the height of the cuboid.

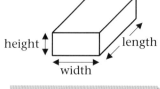

Volume of a cuboid was covered in Chapter 10 of Foundation Unit 3.

8 This word formula can be used to work out the distance travelled by an object moving at a constant speed.

Distance = speed × time

Hayley walked 10 miles at a constant speed of 4 miles per hour. Work out the time she took.

9 This word formula can be used to work out the roasting time, in minutes, for a joint of lamb.

Roasting time = 20 × weight in lb + 20

The roasting time for a joint of lamb is 2 hours. Work out the weight of the joint.

10 This word formula can be used to work out the area of a triangle.

Area = $\frac{1}{2}$ × base × vertical height

A triangle has an area of $20 \, \text{cm}^2$ and a base $10 \, \text{cm}$ long. Work out the vertical height of the triangle.

7.3 Using algebraic formulae

- An **algebraic formula** uses letters to show a relationship between quantities, for example $A = lw$.

- The letter which appears on its own on one side of the = sign and does not appear on the other side is called the **subject** of the formula.

- You can substitute number values for the letters in a formula to work out a quantity.

A is the subject of the formula $A = lw$.

Example 4

The formula for the perimeter of this isosceles triangle is $P = 2a + b$.
Work out the value of P when $a = 8$ and $b = 5$.

$P = 2 \times 8 + 5 = 16 + 5 = 21$

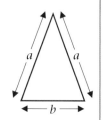

$2a$ is short for $2 \times a$.

Example 5

Nathan's pay is worked out using this formula.

Pay = hours worked × rate of pay + bonus

Write this as an algebraic formula.

$P = h \times r + b$

$P = hr + b$

P = pay
h = hours worked
r = rate of pay
b = bonus

Exercise 7C

1 Write a formula for the perimeter P of this regular hexagon, with side l.
   Work out the value of P when
   (a) $l = 3$ (b) $l = 7$ (c) $l = 29$ (d) $l = 8.6$

2 The formula for the area of a parallelogram is $A = bh$.
   Work out the value of A when
   (a) $b = 7$ and $h = 3$ (b) $b = 9$ and $h = 7$
   (c) $b = 6$ and $h = 3.7$ (d) $b = 8.4$ and $h = 4.5$

3 The formula for the circumference of a circle is $C = \pi d$. Work out, to the nearest whole number, the value of C when
   (a) $d = 2$ (b) $d = 5$
   (c) $d = 3.7$ (d) $d = 9.3$

> For more on the circumference of a circle see Chapter 10.

4 Euler's formula for the number of edges of a solid is $E = F + V - 2$, where E is the number of edges, F is the number of faces and V is the number of vertices.
   Work out the value of E when
   (a) $F = 6$ and $V = 8$ (b) $F = 16$ and $V = 9$

5 $y = 2x + 3$ is the equation of a straight line.
   Work out the value of y when
   (a) $x = 4$ (b) $x = 6$ (c) $x = 10$ (d) $x = 7.5$

6 Write a formula for the perimeter of this isosceles triangle.
   Work out the perimeter when
   (a) $a = 6$ and $b = 4$ (b) $a = 12$ and $b = 7$
   (c) $a = 5.3$ and $b = 3.4$ (d) $a = 4.7$ and $b = 8.5$

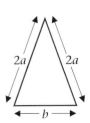

7 The formula $F = 1.8C + 32$ can be used to convert a temperature from degrees Celsius to degrees Fahrenheit. Work out the value of F when
   (a) $C = 10$ (b) $C = 100$ (c) $C = -30$ (d) $C = 0$

8 The formula for the volume of a cuboid is $V = lwh$. Work out the value of V when
   (a) $l = 5$, $w = 4$ and $h = 2$ (b) $l = 8$, $w = 5$ and $h = 3.5$
   (c) $l = 10$, $w = 6$ and $h = 4$ (d) $l = 9.3$, $w = 4.2$ and $h = 5.1$

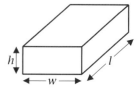

9 The formula $v = u + at$ can be used to work out velocity. Work out the value of v when

Velocity means speed in a particular direction.

   (a) $u = 8$, $a = 4$ and $t = 3$ (b) $u = 0$, $a = 10$ and $t = 2$
   (c) $u = 7$, $a = 2.6$ and $t = 5$ (d) $u = 12$, $a = 10$ and $t = 4.7$

10 The formula $T = 15(W + 1)$ can be used to work out the time needed to cook a turkey. Work out the value of T when
   (a) $W = 5$ (b) $W = 8$ (c) $W = 12$ (d) $W = 18$

11 (a) Write an algebraic formula for the price of a number of pens that cost 70p each.
   (b) Use your formula to work out the cost of
       (i)   4 pens   (ii) 6 pens   (iii) 12 pens.

12 The formula for the volume of this cuboid is $V = l^2h$. Work out the value of V when
   (a) $l = 2$ and $h = 5$ (b) $l = 7$ and $h = 9.8$
   (c) $l = 2.5$ and $h = 4.3$

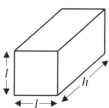

7.4 Rearranging algebraic formulae

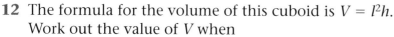

- To find the value of a term which is not the subject of a formula, put the values you are given into the formula and solve the resulting equation.

Example 6

$P = 2a + b$
Work out the value of a when $P = 25$ and $b = 7$.

$25 = 2a + 7$	Solve this equation.
$2a = 18$	Subtract 7 from both sides.
$a = 9$	Divide both sides by 2.

Check:
   $2 \times 9 + 7 = 18 + 7$
   $= 25$

Exercise 7D

1 $P = 6l$
   Work out the value of l when
   (a) $P = 24$ (b) $P = 54$ (c) $P = 138$ (d) $P = 35.4$

2 $A = bh$
   (a) Work out the value of h when
       (i) $A = 45$ and $b = 5$ (ii) $A = 54$ and $b = 3$
   (b) Work out the value of b when
       (i) $A = 35$ and $h = 7$ (ii) $A = 120$ and $h = 8$

3 $E = F + V - 2$
   (a) Work out the value of F when
       (i) $E = 9$ and $V = 5$ (ii) $E = 21$ and $V = 9$
   (b) Work out the value of V when
       (i) $E = 15$ and $F = 10$ (ii) $E = 30$ and $F = 12$

4 $y = 2x + 3$
   Work out the value of x when
   (a) $y = 15$ (b) $y = 27$ (c) $y = -10$ (d) $y = -3$

5 $P = 2a + b$
   (a) Work out the value of b when
       (i) $P = 15$ and $a = 6$ (ii) $P = 23$ and $a = 4.5$
   (b) Work out the value of a when
       (i) $P = 11$ and $b = 5$ (ii) $P = 19$ and $b = 8$

6 $y = 4x - 5$
   Work out the value of x when
   (a) $y = 3$ (b) $y = -31$ (c) $y = 75$ (d) $y = -6$

7 $V = hwl$
   Work out the value of h when
   (a) $V = 24$, $l = 3$ and $w = 2$
   (b) $V = 60$, $l = 6$ and $w = 2$
   (c) $V = 80$, $l = 4$ and $w = 5$

8 $v = u + at$
   (a) Work out the value of u when
       (i) $v = 19$, $a = 7$ and $t = 2$
       (ii) $v = 25$, $a = 6$ and $t = 3$
   (b) Work out the value of a when $v = 17$, $u = 5$ and $t = 2$
   (c) Work out the value of t when $v = 31$, $u = 3$ and $a = 7$

9 $y = \dfrac{x}{5}$

Work out the value of x when

(a) $y = 4$ (b) $y = 17$ (c) $y = 7.4$ (d) $y = 0$

10 $t = \dfrac{d}{s}$

Work out the value of d when

(a) $t = 3$ and $s = 5$ (b) $t = 9$ and $s = -8$

(c) $t = 7.5$ and $s = 6$ (d) $t = 5.6$ and $s = -10.4$

7.5 Changing the subject of a formula

- You can rearrange a formula to make a different letter the subject.

Example 7

Make t the subject of the formula $v = u + at$.

$$v = u + at$$
$$v - u = at \qquad \text{Subtract } u \text{ from both sides.}$$
$$t = \frac{v - u}{a} \qquad \text{Divide both sides by } a.$$

Example 8

Make l the subject of the formula $P = 2(l + b)$.

$$P = 2(l + b)$$
$$P = 2l + 2b \qquad \text{Multiply out the brackets.}$$
$$2l = P - 2b \qquad \text{Subtract } 2b \text{ from both sides.}$$
$$l = \frac{P - 2b}{2} \qquad \text{Divide both sides by 2.}$$

Alternatively, you can divide both sides by 2:
$$\frac{P}{2} = l + b$$
and then subtract b from both sides:
$$l = \frac{P}{2} - b$$

Example 9

Make h the subject of the formula $V = \frac{1}{3}Ah$.

$$V = \tfrac{1}{3}Ah$$
$$3V = Ah \qquad \text{Multiply both sides by 3.}$$
$$h = \frac{3V}{A} \qquad \text{Divide both sides by } A.$$

$h = \dfrac{V}{\frac{1}{3}A}$ is also correct but it is best not to have a fraction within another fraction.

Exercise 7E

In questions **1–27**, rearrange the formula to make the letter in square brackets the subject.

1 $P = 5d$ $\qquad$ [d] $\qquad\qquad$ **2** $P = IV$ $\qquad$ [I]

3 $A = lw$ $\qquad$ [w] $\qquad\qquad$ **4** $C = \pi d$ $\qquad$ [d]

5 $V = lwh$ $\qquad$ [h] $\qquad\qquad$ **6** $A = \pi rl$ $\qquad$ [r]

7 $y = 4x - 3$ $\qquad$ [x] $\qquad\qquad$ **8** $t = 3n + 5$ $\qquad$ [n]

9 $P = 2x + y$ $\qquad$ [y] $\qquad\qquad$ **10** $y = mx + c$ $\qquad$ [m]

11 $v = u - gt$ $\qquad$ [u] $\qquad\qquad$ **12** $v = u - gt$ $\qquad$ [t]

13 $A = \frac{1}{2}bh$ $\qquad$ [b] $\qquad\qquad$ **14** $I = \dfrac{PRT}{100}$ $\qquad$ [T]

15 $T = \dfrac{D}{V}$ $\qquad$ [V] $\qquad\qquad$ **16** $\dfrac{PV}{T} = k$ $\qquad$ [V]

17 $\dfrac{PV}{T} = k$ $\qquad$ [T] $\qquad\qquad$ **18** $I = m(v - u)$ $\qquad$ [v]

19 $A = \frac{1}{2}(a + b)h$ $\qquad$ [b] $\qquad\qquad$ **20** $y = \frac{1}{3}x - 2$ $\qquad$ [x]

21 $y = 2(x - 1)$ $\qquad$ [x] $\qquad\qquad$ **22** $x = 3(y + 2)$ $\qquad$ [y]

23 $H = 17 - \dfrac{A}{2}$ $\qquad$ [A] $\qquad\qquad$ **24** $3x - 2y = 6$ $\qquad$ [x]

25 $3x - 2y = 6$ $\qquad$ [y]

26 $P = 6(q - 7) - 5(q - 6)$ $\qquad$ [q]

27 $4y^2 - 2x = 6(x - 8y)$ $\qquad$ [x]

Mixed exercise 7

1 This word formula can be used to work out the total cost, in pounds, of running a car.

$$\text{Total cost} = \text{fixed costs} + \frac{\text{number of miles travelled}}{6}$$

(a) Flora's fixed costs were £500 and she travelled 9000 miles. Work out her total cost.

(b) Harry's total cost was £2700 and he travelled 12 000 miles. Work out his fixed costs.

(c) Ali's total cost was £1600 and his fixed costs were £400. Work out the number of miles he travelled.

2 The formula $v = u - gt$ can be used to work out velocity.
   (a) Work out the value of v when $u = 45$, $g = 10$ and $t = 3$.
   (b) Work out the value of u when $v = 8$, $g = 10$ and $t = 2$.

3 (a) Write a formula for the area of a square of side l.
   (b) Work out the area when $l = 9$.

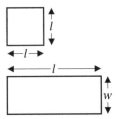

4 (a) Write a formula for the perimeter of a rectangle.
   (b) Work out the perimeter when
      (i) $l = 9$ and $b = 4$ (ii) $l = 6.7$ and $b = 3.4$

5 The formula $d = \dfrac{a + b}{3}$ can be used to work out the
   distance apart two bushes should be planted.
   (a) Work out the value of d when $a = 50$ and $b = 43$.
   (b) Work out the value of b when $d = 29$ and $a = 59$.

6 $F = 1.8C + 32$ is a formula which links temperatures
   in degrees Fahrenheit (F) with temperatures in degrees
   Celsius (C).
   (a) Use the formula to convert
      (i) $20\,°C$ (ii) $45\,°C$ (iii) $70\,°C$ into $°F$.
   (b) Use the formula to convert
      (i) $212\,°F$ (ii) $122\,°F$ (iii) $77\,°F$ into $°C$.

7 The cost, C, in £, of buying t trees and b bushes together
   with delivery is given by the formula
   $$C = 10t + 6b + 15$$
   Greg has £315 to spend and needs 35 bushes.
   How many trees can be afford?

8 The width of a rectangle is x centimetres.
   The length of the rectangle is $(x + 4)$ centimetres.

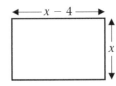

   (a) Find an expression, in terms of x, for the perimeter of
      the rectangle.
      Give your expression in its simplest form.

   The perimeter of the rectangle is 54 centimetres.
   (b) Work out the length of the rectangle.   [E]

9 The diagram shows a trapezium.
All the lengths are in centimetres.
The perimeter of the trapezium is P cm.

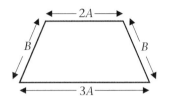

Diagram **NOT**
accurately drawn

Find a formula, in terms of x and y, for P.
Give your answer in its simplest form.   [E]

10 $s = ut + \frac{1}{2}at^2$ is a formula for working out the distance, s,
moved by an object.
Work out s when
(a) $u = 4.2$, $a = 10$ and $t = 3$
(b) $u = 5$, $a = -10$ and $t = 5.7$
(c) $u = -3$, $a = -32$ and $t = 6$

11 $A = \frac{1}{2}bh$ is the formula for working out the area of a
triangle. Work out the area of a triangle when
(a) $b = 30$ cm and $h = 20$ cm
(b) $b = 15$ cm and $h = 26$ cm
(c) $b = 7.3$ cm and $h = 2.9$ cm
(d) $b = 2.3$ cm and $h = 1.3$ cm

12 $V = \frac{1}{3}\pi r^2 h$ is the formula for finding the volume of a cone.
Work out the volume of a cone with
(a) $r = 5$ cm and $h = 10$ cm
(b) $r = 7$ cm and $h = 15$ cm
(c) $r = 4.6$ cm and $h = 9.2$ cm

13 $v = u + at$ is a formula for finding the speed of an object.
Find v when
(a) $u = 6$, $a = 10$ and $t = 5$
(b) $u = 8$, $a = -10$ and $t = 6$
(c) $u = 20$, $a = -32$ and $t = 4\frac{1}{2}$

14 $p = 2$ Work out the value of $5p^2$ [E]

15 $S = 2p + 3q$ $p = -4$ $q = 5$
(a) Work out the value of S

$T = 2m + 20$ $T = 30$
(b) Work out the value of m [E]

16 $v = u + 10t$

Work out the value of v when

(a) $u = 10$ and $t = 7$

(b) $u = -2.5$ and $t = 3.2$ [E]

17 (a) Work out the value of $2a + ay$ when $a = 5$ and $y = -3$

(b) Work out the value of $5t^2 - 7$ when $t = 4$ [E]

18 Make b the subject of the formula $P = 2a + 2b$ [E]

In questions **18–23**, rearrange the formula to make the letter in square brackets the subject.

19 $P = 2x + y$ [x]   **20** $s = \dfrac{a + b + c}{2}$ [a]

21 $T = \dfrac{D}{V}$ [D]   **22** $A = \frac{1}{2}(a + b)h$ [h]

23 $y = \dfrac{5 - x}{2}$ [x]

Summary of key points

1 A **word formula** uses words to represent a relationship between quantities.

2 In a word formula, you can find the value of any term, if you know the values of all the other terms.

3 You can rearrange a word formula using the balance method. Whatever you do to one side you must also do to the other.

4 An **algebraic formula** uses letters to show a relationship between quantities, for example $A = lw$.

5 The letter which appears on its own on one side of the $=$ sign and does not appear on the other side is called the **subject** of the formula.

6 You can substitute number values for the letters in a formula to work out a quantity.

7 To find the value of a term which is not the subject of a formula, put the values you are given into the formula and solve the resulting equation.

8 You can rearrange a formula to make a different letter the subject.

8 Symmetry and transformations

8.1 Reflective symmetry in 2-D shapes

18 Introduction to symmetry
18 Completing symmetrical patterns

- A **line of symmetry** is sometimes called a **mirror line**.
- A 2-D shape has a line of symmetry if there is a line that divides the shape into two halves and one half is the mirror image of the other half.

butterfly

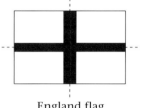

England flag

Example 1

Half of a symmetrical shape is shown.
The dotted line is the mirror line.
Copy and complete the shape.

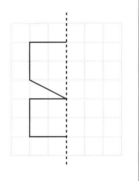

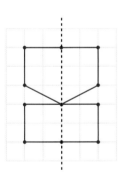

Mark each corner (vertex) with a dot.

Each dot has an image the same distance from the mirror line but on the other side.

Example 2

Draw in all the lines of symmetry for each shape.

(a)

(b)

(a)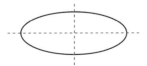

(b)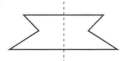

Exercise 8A

1 Half of some symmetrical shapes are shown. The dotted line is the mirror line. Copy and complete each shape.

(a)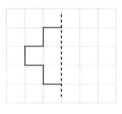

(b)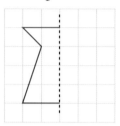

(c)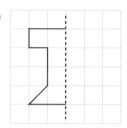

2 Copy each shape and draw in all the lines of symmetry.

(a)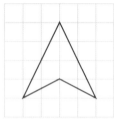

(b)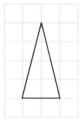

(c)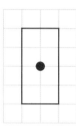

(d)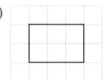

(e)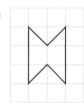

(f)

3 Write down these numbers. Draw in any lines of symmetry.

8, 3, 4, 10, 5

4 Copy each design and draw in the lines of symmetry:

(a)

(b)

(c)

(d)

(e)

(f)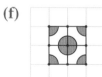

8.2 **Rotational symmetry**

- A 2-D shape with **rotational symmetry** looks the same as it did in its starting position two or more times during a full turn.
- The **order** of rotational symmetry is the number of times the shape looks the same in a full turn.

18 Rotational symmetry
18 Rotational symmetry activity

A cross looks the same 4 times during a full turn. The order of rotational symmetry of the cross is 4.

Example 3

Write down the order of rotational symmetry of each shape.

(a)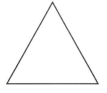

(b)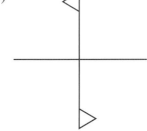

(c)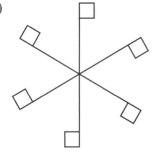

(d)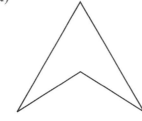

You can make a tracing to check rotational symmetry.

(a)
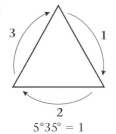

$5°35° = 1$

(b)
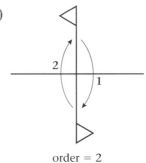

order = 2

(c)
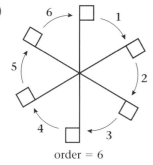

order = 6

(d)
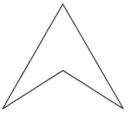

No rotational symmetry. The shape does not look the same again until it completes a whole turn.

- Regular polygons have the same number of lines of symmetry as they have sides.

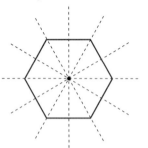

Hexagon (6 sides)
6 lines of symmetry
Rotational symmetry of order 6

A **regular polygon** has
- all sides equal length
- all interior angles equal.

- The order of rotational symmetry of a regular polygon is the same as the number of sides.

Exercise 8B

You may find tracing paper helpful in this exercise.

1 Write down the order of rotational symmetry of each shape.

(a)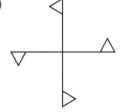

(b)

(c)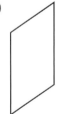

(d)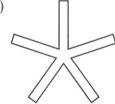

(e)

(f)

2 Write down the order of rotational symmetry for each regular polygon.

(a)

(b)

(c)

(d)
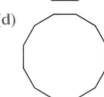

8.3 Reflection

- In a mathematical **reflection**, the image is the same distance from the mirror line as the object, but on the other side.
- To describe a reflection fully you need to specify the mirror line.
- After a reflection, the image is the same size as the object, and corresponding angles on the object and image are equal.

For example, the y-axis ($x = 0$) or the line $y = 3$.

Example 4

Reflect the shape in the mirror line.

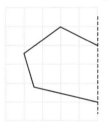
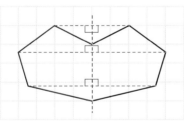

Lines on the image are the same distance on the other side measured at right angles to the mirror line.

- Mirror lines are two-way. The mirror line may go through the object.

Example 5

Reflect the shape in the mirror line.

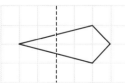
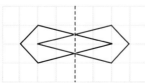

Exercise 8C

1 Copy each shape.

Draw the image of the object after reflection in the mirror line (dotted).

(a)

(b)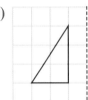

(c)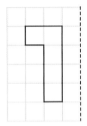

(d)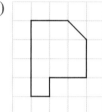

(e)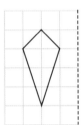

(f)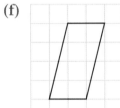

(g)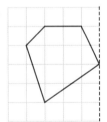

(h)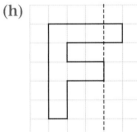

(i)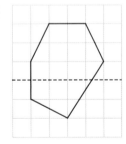

(j)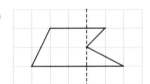

2 Copy the diagram. Reflect the shaded shape P in
  (a) the *y*-axis   **(b)** the *x*-axis   **(c)** the line $x = -2$ **(d)** the line $y = 3$

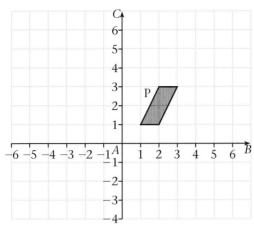

3 Copy the diagram. Reflect the shaded shape Q in
  (a) the *x*-axis   **(b)** the line $y = x$ **(c)** the line $y = -x$

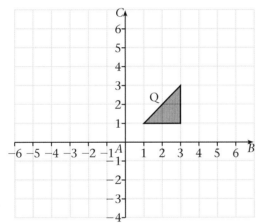

4 All the transformations shown are reflections of shape P.
  Write down the line that shape P is reflected in to get
  (a) shape Q   **(b)** shape R   **(c)** shape S   **(d)** shape T

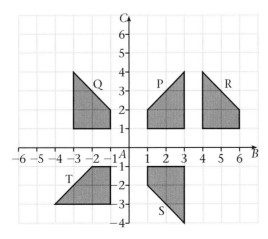

8.4 Rotation

- Images of a shape that are formed by turning are called **rotations** of the shape.
- The point about which the turning occurs is called the **centre of rotation**.
- To describe a rotation fully, you need to specify
  - ○ the angle of rotation
  - ○ the direction (clockwise or anticlockwise)
  - ○ the centre of rotation.
- After a rotation, the image is the same size as the object, and corresponding angles on the object and image are equal.

Example 6

Draw the image of the shape
after it has been rotated through
(a) $\frac{1}{4}$ turn clockwise about A
(b) $\frac{1}{2}$ turn about A.

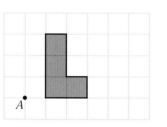

(a)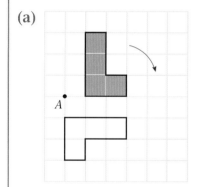

(b)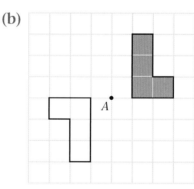

Use tracing paper to help.

$\frac{1}{2}$ turn anticlockwise is the same as $\frac{1}{2}$ turn clockwise.

Example 7

Describe fully the transformation
that maps triangle A onto triangle B.

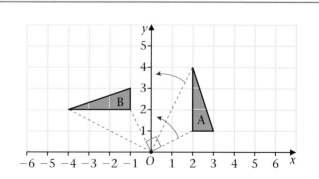

Anticlockwise rotation by 90°
(or by $\frac{1}{4}$ turn)
Centre (0, 0)

Example 8

Rotate the shaded shape below about the centre (0, 0) through

(a) $\frac{1}{4}$ turn anticlockwise (label the image A)

(b) $\frac{1}{2}$ turn anticlockwise (label the image B)

(c) $\frac{3}{4}$ turn anticlockwise (label the image C).

(a) (b) (c)

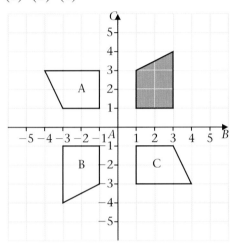

Exercise 8D

1 Copy these shapes.
  Draw the image after an anticlockwise rotation of 90°
  about each of the centres marked.

(a)

(b)

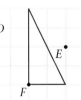

(c)

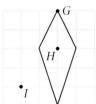

(d)

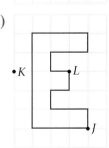

2 Describe fully the transformation that maps triangle A onto

(a) triangle B   (b) triangle C   (c) triangle D

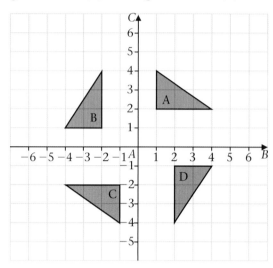

3 Copy each diagram and rotate each shape about the point (1, 0) through
  (i) 90° clockwise
  (ii) 270° clockwise.

(a)

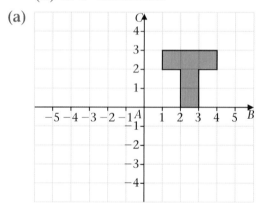

(b)

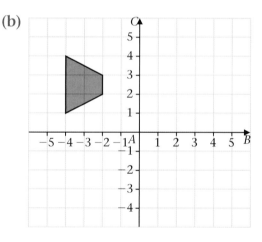

8.5 Translation

- A **translation** moves every point on a shape the same distance in the same direction.
- To describe a translation fully you need to give the distance moved and the direction of the movement.
- After a translation, the image is the same size as the object, and corresponding angles on the object and image are equal.

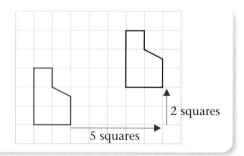

2 squares

5 squares

Example 9

Translate this shape 3 squares right
and 4 squares up.

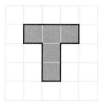

Each vertex (corner) moves
3 squares right and 4 squares up.

4 squares

3 squares

- On a coordinate grid a translation can be described by the
  number of units moved in the x-direction and the number of
  units moved in the y-direction, *or* by a column vector.

Example 10

The triangle ABC is shown on the grid.

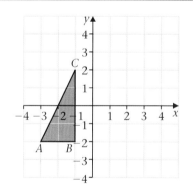

ABC is translated to $A'B'C'$ by the translation that
moves A to A' $(0, -3)$.
(a) Plot A' and draw the image $A'B'C'$.
(b) Describe the translation that moves ABC to $A'B'C'$.

(a)

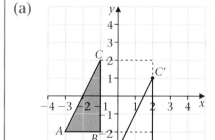

Check that $A'B'C'$ is correct by
tracing ABC and sliding it to $A'B'C'$.

(b) Translation by 3 squares in the x-direction and -1 unit in the y-direction,
   or by $\begin{pmatrix} 3 \\ -1 \end{pmatrix}$.

Example 11

(a) Translate the shape *ABCD* so that the point *A* moves to the point *P*.

P is the image of A.

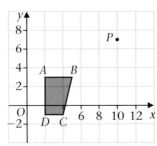

(b) Describe the translation.

(a)

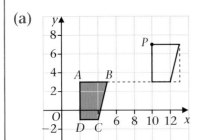

(b) Translation by 8 units in the *x*-direction and 4 units in the *y*-direction, or by $\begin{pmatrix} 8 \\ 4 \end{pmatrix}$.

Exercise 8E

1 Draw each shape on squared paper and translate it as shown.

(a)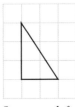

3 squares left

(b)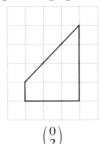

$\begin{pmatrix} 0 \\ 2 \end{pmatrix}$

(c)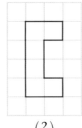

$\begin{pmatrix} 2 \\ 3 \end{pmatrix}$

(d)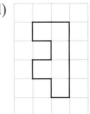

4 squares right
2 squares down

(e)

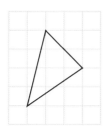

$\begin{pmatrix} -2 \\ -2 \end{pmatrix}$

(f)

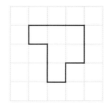

$\begin{pmatrix} -4 \\ 3 \end{pmatrix}$

(g)

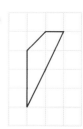

4 squares left
2 squares down

2 For each of parts **(a)** to **(d)**, copy the diagram and answer
(i) and **(ii)**.
ABCD is translated to *A'B'C'D'* by the translation that
moves *A* to *A'*(1, −2).

   (i) Plot *A'* and draw the image *A'B'C'D'*.

   (ii) Describe the translation that moves *ABCD*
      to *A'B'C'D'*.

(a)

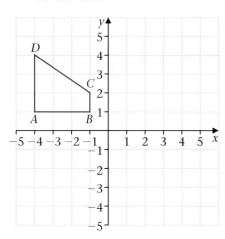

(b)

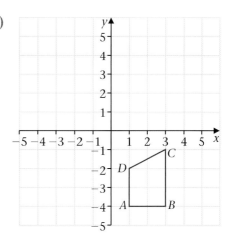

(c)

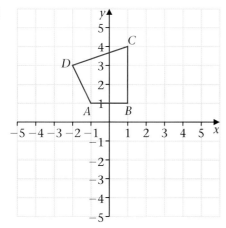

(d)

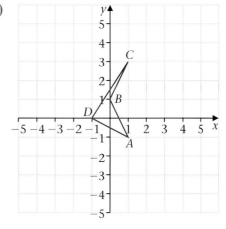

3 Describe the translation for each object–image pair.

(a)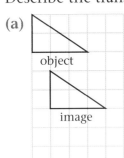

(b)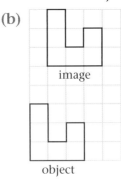

(c)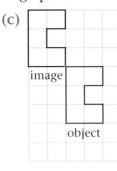

(d)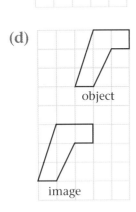

(e)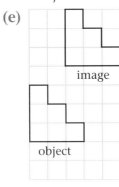

(f)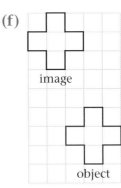

8.6 Enlargement

- In an **enlargement**, all angles stay the same and lengths are changed in the same proportion.
- The **scale factor** is a multiplier for lengths.
- The **centre of enlargement** determines the final position of the image.
- In an enlargement, image lines are parallel to their corresponding lines on the object.
- Scale factors greater than 1 make shapes larger.
- Scale factors between 0 and 1 make shapes smaller.
- To describe an enlargement fully, you need to specify
  - the centre of enlargement
  - the scale factor.
- After an enlargement, the image is larger or smaller than the object. Corresponding angles on the object and image are equal.

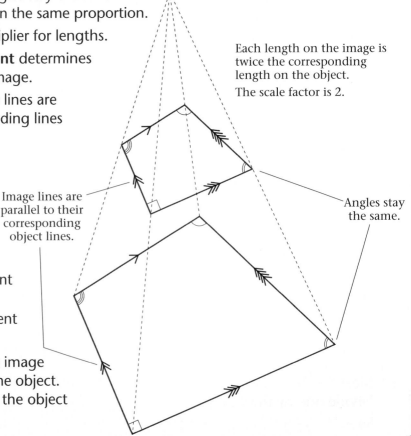

centre of enlargement

Each length on the image is twice the corresponding length on the object.

The scale factor is 2.

Image lines are parallel to their corresponding object lines.

Angles stay the same.

Example 12

On the grid, enlarge shape *ABC* by scale factor 3, centre the origin.

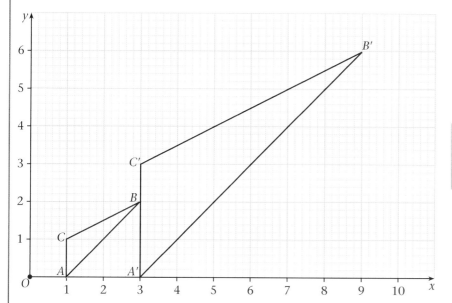

Note:
angle A = angle A'
angle B = angle B'
angle C = angle C'

Line *OA* is 1 across, so line *OA'* is 3 across.
OB is 3 across and 2 up, so *OB'* is 9 across and 6 up.
OC is 1 across and 1 up, so *OC'* is 3 across and 3 up.

Multiply each distance from the centre by 3.

Example 13

Work out
(a) the scale factor
(b) the centre of enlargement for these two similar triangles.

When one shape is an enlargement of another, they are called **similar**.

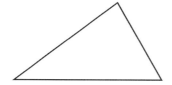

(a) Join the corresponding vertices (corners) of the triangles with straight lines.
Where the lines cross is the centre of enlargement.

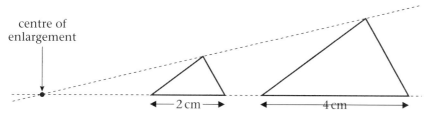

centre of
enlargement

(b) Measure the lengths of two corresponding sides of the triangles.
Divide one by the other. This gives the scale factor.
Small to large is $\frac{4}{2} = 2$ Large to small is $\frac{2}{4} = \frac{1}{2}$

Example 14

Enlarge triangle ABC by scale factor $\frac{1}{2}$ using B as the centre of enlargement

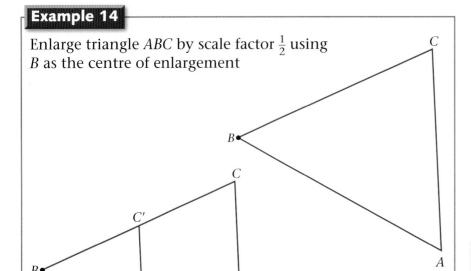

B is fixed as the centre of enlargement and does not move.

The scale factor is $\frac{1}{2}$, so all the other points move to $\frac{1}{2}$ the distance from B.
$BC' = \frac{1}{2}BC \quad BA' = \frac{1}{2}BA$

Exercise 8F

1 A scale factor and two centres of enlargement are given for each shape. Copy each diagram and draw the two enlargements.

Use squared paper.

(a)

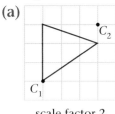

scale factor 2

(b)

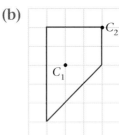

scale factor 3

(c)

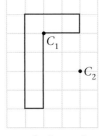

scale factor 2

(d)

scale factor $\frac{1}{2}$

2 Measure the lengths of the sides of the shapes in
   questions **1** (c) and **1** (d).
   Find the perimeter of each shape.
   Measure the lengths of your enlarged shapes and find the
   perimeter of each enlarged shape.
   What do you notice?

3 By counting squares, find the areas of the shapes in
   questions **1** (c) and **1** (d).
   Find the areas of your enlarged shapes.
   What do you notice?

4 Work out the centre and scale factor of the enlargement
   for each pair of similar triangles.

   (a)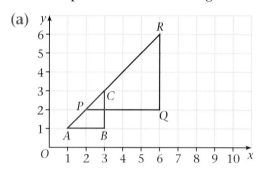

   (b)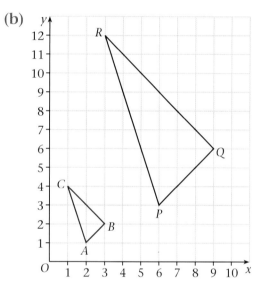

   (c)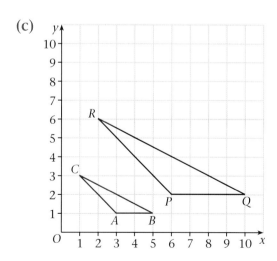

5 Write down the pairs of corresponding angles for each set of similar triangles in
   question **4**.

6 For each part of question **4** write down the scale factor of enlargement for the perimeter from *ABC* to *PQR*.

7 Copy shape *PQR* on to graph paper.
Enlarge the shape by scale factor $2\frac{1}{2}$, centre the origin.

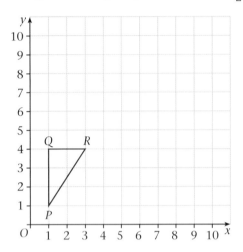

8 A unit cube is enlarged by scale factor 2.

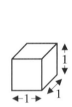 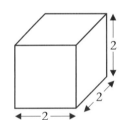

On the image, how many times bigger is
(a) an edge
(b) the area of a face
(c) the volume?

9 Draw three squares with different side lengths.
Is each square a similar shape to the others?

10 Draw three rectangles with different side lengths.
Is each rectangle a similar shape to the others?

8.7 Combined transformations

27 Transformations on a coordinate grid

- Sometimes you will have to carry out two transformations one after the other. This is called a **combination** of transformations.

Example 15

(a) Reflect triangle T in the y-axis. Label the image R.
(b) Reflect R in the x-axis. Label the image S.
(c) What single transformation takes T to S?
(d) What single transformation takes S to T?

(a) (b)

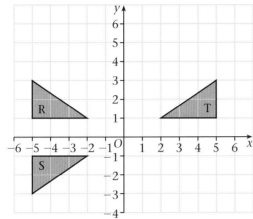

(c) From T to S: 180° rotation, centre (0, 0).
(d) From S to T: 180° rotation, centre (0, 0).

Reflection in the y-axis
and then in the x-axis is
the same as a rotation
through 180°.

Exercise 8G

Copy this diagram for each question in this exercise.

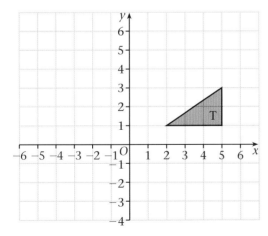

1 (a) Translate triangle T by $\begin{pmatrix} -4 \\ 2 \end{pmatrix}$ followed by a translation
of $\begin{pmatrix} 2 \\ -3 \end{pmatrix}$.

(b) What single translation is the same as this
combination of translations?

2 (a) Reflect triangle T in the *x*-axis. Label the image R.
   (b) Reflect R in the *y*-axis. Label the image S.
   (c) What single transformation takes T to S?
   (d) What single transformation takes S to T?

3 (a) Rotate triangle T by 90° anticlockwise centre (0, 0).
        Label the image R.
   (b) Rotate R by 180° centre (0, 0). Label this image S.
   (c) What single transformation takes T to S?
   (d) What single transformation takes S to T?

4 (a) Reflect triangle T in the line *y* = 3. Label the image R.
   (b) Reflect R in the line *x* = 1. Label this image S.
   (c) What single transformation takes T to S?
   (d) What single transformation takes S to T?

5 (a) Rotate triangle T by 90° anticlockwise centre (1, 1).
        Label the image R.
   (b) Rotate R by 90° anticlockwise centre (0, 1). Label this image S.
   (c) What single transformation takes T to S?
   (d) What single transformation takes S to T?

8.8 Symmetry in 3-D shapes

13 Planes of symmetry

• A **plane of symmetry** divides a 3-D
  shape into two equal halves which
  are mirror images of each other.

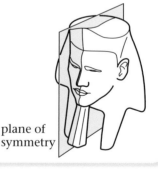

plane of
symmetry

This Japanese mask is not
symmetrical.
Can you see why?

Example 16

Draw in all the planes of
symmetry for this 3-D shape.

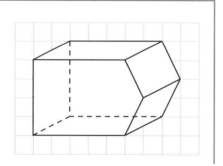

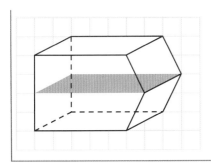
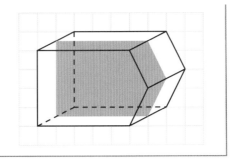

Exercise 8H

You may need tracing paper for this exercise.

1 Copy or trace each shape.
Draw in any planes of symmetry.

(a)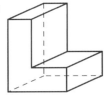

(b)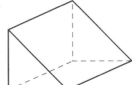

(c)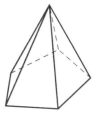

(d)

2 The drawings on the right each show half a 3-D solid.
Copy and complete each solid so that the shaded face forms a plane of symmetry.

(a)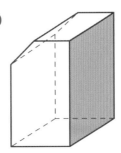

(b)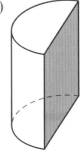

3 Copy or trace each shape.
Draw in the number of planes of symmetry indicated for each shape.

(a)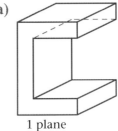

1 plane

(b)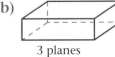

3 planes

Mixed exercise 8

You may need tracing paper for this exercise.

1 Copy each shape.
   Draw in any lines of symmetry.

(a)

(b)

(c)

(d)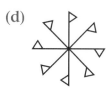

2 Write down the order of rotational symmetry for each shape in question **1**.

3 Draw two copies of each 3-D shape.
   Draw a different plane of symmetry on each copy.

(a)

(b)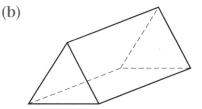

4 Draw a separate diagram for each shape A to D.
   Reflect each shape in the lines $x = 0$ and $y = 0$.
   Label the images P and Q respectively.

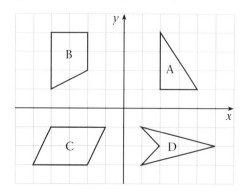

5 Repeat question **4** but reflect the shapes in the lines $y = x$ and $y = -x$.

6 Draw four separate coordinate grids with *x*- and *y*-axes from −6 to +6.
On each of the four grids copy one of shapes A, B, C and D.
Draw the image of each shape after

(a) a quarter turn of 90° anticlockwise about (0, 0)

(b) a half turn about (0, 0)

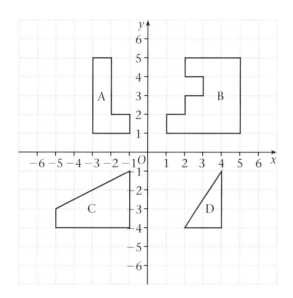

7 Shape P has been rotated three times.
Describe fully the rotation which takes P to
(a) position A   (b) position B   (c) position C.

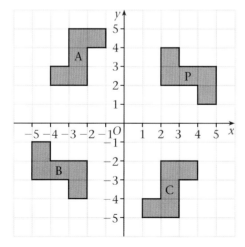

8 Transform shape P by the translation vector

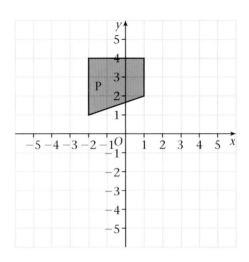

(a) $\begin{pmatrix} -1 \\ -3 \end{pmatrix}$

Label the image A.

(b) $\begin{pmatrix} 3 \\ -4 \end{pmatrix}$

Label the image B.

(c) $\begin{pmatrix} 4 \\ 2 \end{pmatrix}$

Label the image C.

(d) $\begin{pmatrix} -1 \\ 0 \end{pmatrix}$

Label the image D.

9 Write the translation vector which maps T onto
(a) shape A (b) shape B (c) shape C (d) shape D.

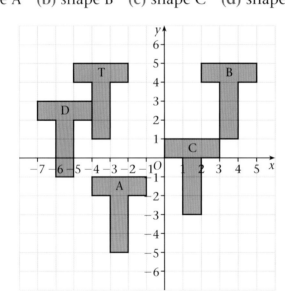

10 Copy the diagram.
Enlarge the shape by a scale factor of 2 using each centre of enlargement shown.

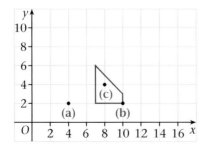

11 Copy and enlarge the shape by a scale factor of $\frac{1}{3}$, using each centre of enlargement shown.

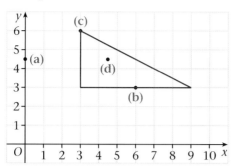

12 In each part give

    (i) the scale factor of the enlargement that maps A onto B

    (ii) the scale factor of the enlargement that maps B onto A

    (iii) the centre of enlargement.

(a) 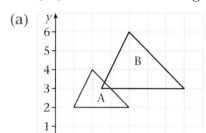   **(b)**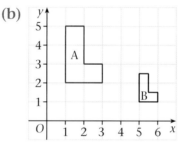

13

Shape A is rotated by 90° anticlockwise, centre (0, 1), to shape B.

Shape B is rotated by 90° anticlockwise, centre (0, 1), to shape C.

Shape C is rotated by 90° anticlockwise, centre (0, 1), to shape D.

(a) Copy the diagram and mark the position of shape D.

(b) Describe the single transformation that takes shape C to shape A.   [E]

Summary of key points

1 A **line of symmetry** is sometimes called a **mirror line**.

2 A 2-D shape has a line of symmetry if there is a line that divides the shape into two halves and one half is the mirror image of the other half.

3 A 2-D shape with **rotational symmetry** looks the same as it did in its starting position two or more times during a full turn.

4 The **order** of rotational symmetry is the number of times the shape looks the same in a full turn.

5 Regular polygons have the same number of lines of symmetry as they have sides.

A **regular polygon** has
• all sides equal length
• all interior angles equal.

6 The order of rotational symmetry of a regular polygon is the same as the number of sides.

7 In a mathematical **reflection**, the image is the same distance from the mirror line as the object, but on the other side.

8 To describe a reflection fully, you need to specify the mirror line.

9 After a reflection, the image is the same size as the object, and corresponding angles on the object and image are equal.

10 Mirror lines are two-way. The mirror line may go through the object.

11 Images of a shape that are formed by turning are called **rotations** of the shape.

12 The point about which the turning occurs is called the **centre of rotation**.

13 To describe a rotation fully, you need to specify
   ○ the angle of rotation
   ○ the direction (clockwise or anticlockwise)
   ○ the centre of rotation.

14 After a rotation, the image is the same size as the object, and corresponding angles on the object and image are equal.

15 A **translation** moves every point on a shape the same distance in the same direction.

16 To describe a translation fully, you need to give the distance moved and the direction of the movement.

17 After a translation, the image is the same size as the object, and corresponding angles on the object and image are equal.

18 On a coordinate grid, a translation can be described by the number of units moved in the x-direction and the number of units moved in the y-direction *or* by a column vector.

19 In an **enlargement**, all angles stay the same and lengths are changed in the same proportion.

20 The **scale factor** is a multiplier for lengths.

21 The **centre of enlargement** determines the final position of the image.

22 In an enlargement, image lines are parallel to their corresponding lines on the object.

23 Scale factors greater than 1 make shapes larger.

24 Scale factors between 0 and 1 make shapes smaller.

25 To describe an enlargement fully, you need to specify
   ○ the centre of enlargement
   ○ the scale factor.

26 After an enlargement, the image is larger or smaller than the object.
   Corresponding angles on the object and image are equal.

27 Sometimes you will have to carry out two transformations one after the other. This is called a **combination** of transformations.

28 A **plane of symmetry** divides a 3-D shape into two equal halves which are mirror images of each other.

9

Angles, bearings, drawings and constructions

9.1 Measuring, drawing and estimating angles ⊙ 7 Geometry set

- You can use a protractor to measure and draw angles.

Example 1

Measure the angle shown in the diagram.

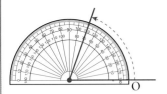

> You are turning anticlockwise from O. Use the inside scale on the protractor.

The angle is 70°.

Exercise 9A

1 Measure these angles.

(a)
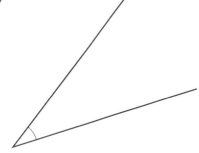

(b)
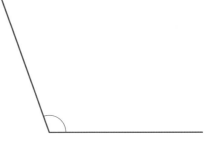

(c)
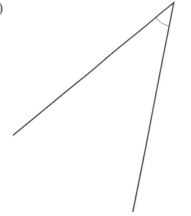

(d)
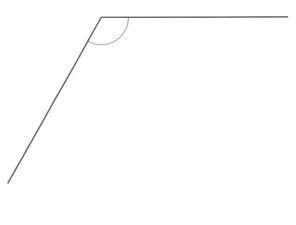

(e)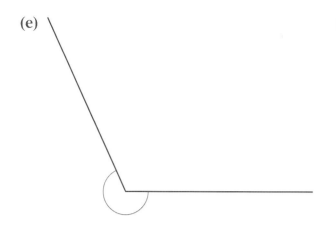

(f)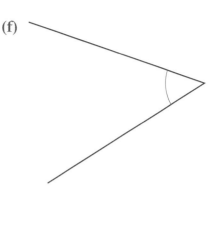

2 Use a ruler and protractor to draw these angles.
Draw a separate diagram for each.

(a) 25°   (b) 80°   (c) 115°
(d) 215°   (e) 320°   (f) 155°

3 Estimate the size of these angles.
Check your answers by measuring.

(a) 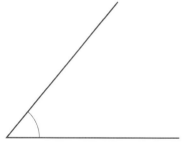   (b)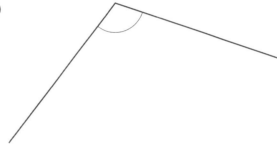

(c)    (d)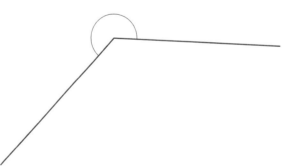

(e)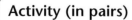

Activity (in pairs)

- Draw an angle. Each person estimates the size and writes down their estimate.
- Measure the angle. The person who is closer wins.
- A full game is a set of 9.

9.2 Accurate drawings

- You can construct triangles using a ruler and protractor.

> Make a sketch first to see the general shape. This helps to make sure your triangle fits on the paper.

Example 2

Construct a triangle with angle $A = 40°$, angle $B = 50°$ and $AB = 6$ cm.

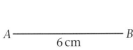

Draw side AB 6 cm long.

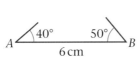

Draw the angles at each end using the protractor.

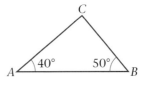

Complete the triangle.

Exercise 9B

1 Measure these lines to the nearest mm.

(a) _____

(b) _____

(c) _____

(d) _____

(e) _____

2 Draw lines with length

(a) 32 mm   (b) 57 mm   (c) 44 mm

(d) 61 mm   (e) 87 mm

3 Use a ruler and protractor to construct these triangles as accurately as possible. Measure and write down the length of the other side(s) and angle(s).

(a)

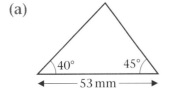

(b)

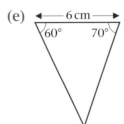

(c)

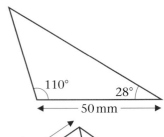

(d)

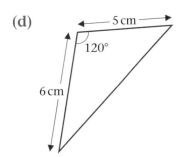

(e)

(f)

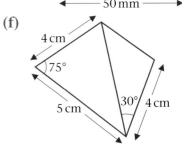

9.3 Bearings

- A **three-figure bearing** gives a direction in degrees.
  It is an angle measured clockwise from North.

Example 3

Find the bearing of A from B.

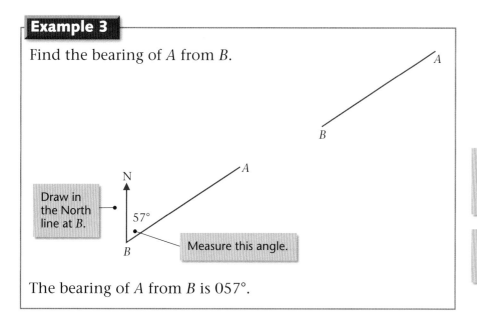

'From B' means: stand at B and face North. What angle do you need to turn clockwise to face A?

For a bearing like this, add a zero in front to give it three figures.

Draw in the North line at B.

Measure this angle.

The bearing of A from B is $057°$.

Exercise 9C

1 Measure and write down the bearing of
   (a) A from B
   (b) B from A.

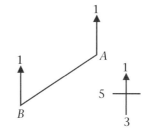

2 Measure and write down the bearing of
   (a) B from C
   (b) C from A
   (c) A from B
   (d) B from A.

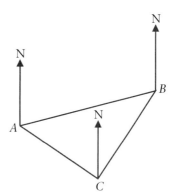

3 Using the map of East Anglia, find the bearing of

(a) Great Yarmouth from Norwich

(b) Colchester from London

(c) Cambridge from Luton

(d) Cambridge from Kings Lynn

(e) Spalding from Kings Lynn

(f) Boston from Norwich

(g) Ipswich from Bury St Edmunds

(h) Southend from Boston.

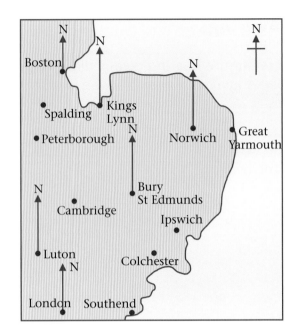

4

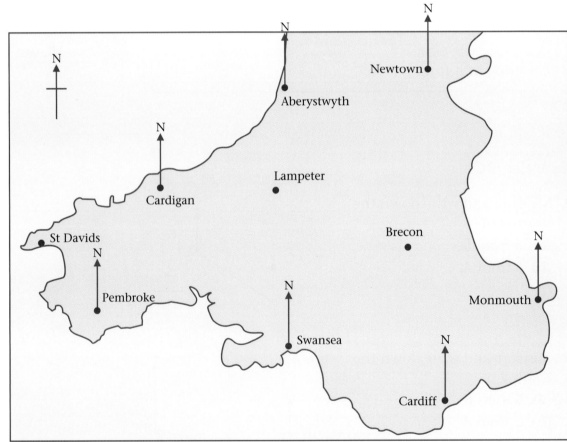

Using the map of South Wales, find the bearing of

(a) Brecon from Swansea
(b) Lampeter from Pembroke
(c) Cardigan from Aberystwyth
(d) St Davids from Cardigan
(e) Swansea from Cardiff
(f) Cardigan from Monmouth
(g) Lampeter from Newtown
(h) Swansea from Aberystwyth.

5 Measure and write down
the bearing of

(a) *B* from *C*

(b) *A* from *C*

(c) *C* from *B*

(d) *B* from *A*.

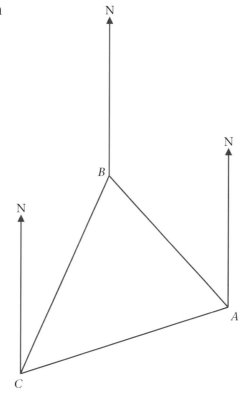

9.4 Maps and scale drawings

- A **scale** shows the relationship between a length on a
  drawing and the actual length in real life.

- A scale can be represented as a ratio (e.g. 1 : 25 000) or using
  an equals sign (e.g. 1 cm = 5 km).

Example 4

The scale of a map is 1 : 25 000.

(a) What is the actual distance between two points which
are 5.6 cm apart on the map?

(b) Two places are 9 km apart.
How far apart will they be on the map?

(a) Actual distance apart = 5.6 × 25 000 cm
= 5.6 × 250 m
= 1400 m
= 1.4 km

(b) 9 km = 9000 m = 900 000 cm
Distance on the map = 900 000 ÷ 25 000
= 36 cm

> This means that every
> 1 cm on the map
> represents 25 000 cm on
> the ground.

> 25 000 cm = 250 m

> First change to
> centimetres.

Exercise 9D

1 The scale of this map is 1 cm = 2 km.

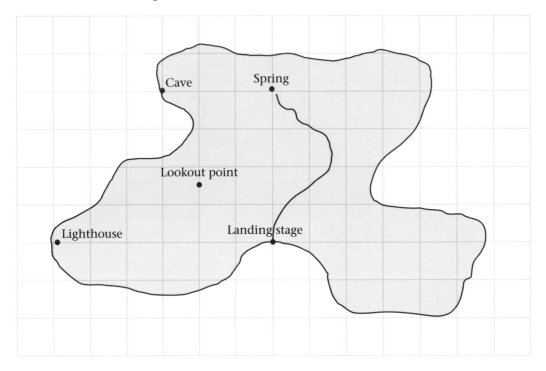

Find the actual distance between
(a) the landing stage and the lighthouse
(b) the landing stage and the spring
(c) the landing stage and the cave
(d) the landing stage and the lookout point
(e) the lighthouse and the lookout point.

2 Copy and complete the distance chart.
Give the distances in km.

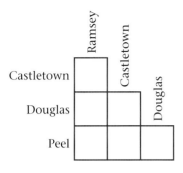

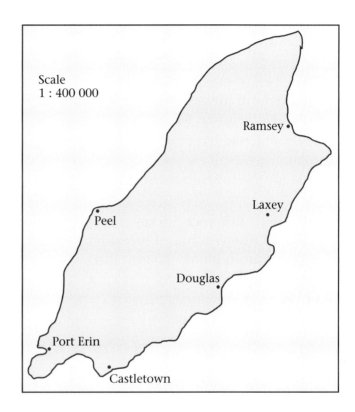

3 (a) Construct an accurate drawing for this sketch.
Use a scale of 1 cm = 5 km.

> Use a ruler and protractor.

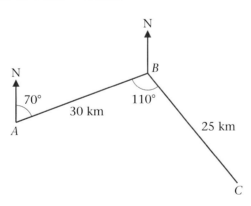

(b) How far is *A* from *C* in real life?

4 Make a sketch and construct an accurate drawing of the
following journey. Use a scale of 1 cm = 40 km.

170 km on a bearing of 120° followed by 220 km on a
bearing of 050°.

5 Make a sketch and construct an accurate drawing of the following journey. Use a scale of 1 cm = 12 km.

   66 km on a bearing of 250° followed by 78 km on a bearing of 320°.

6 A surveyor's plan has a scale of 1 : 2500.
   (a) A plot of land measures 1 cm by 13 mm on the plan. Work out the actual size.
   (b) A road which is 10 m wide and 125 m long is to be marked on this map. Work out the measurements on the map.

7 The scale of an Ordnance Survey map is 1 : 50 000. On the map, Brownsea Island measures 4 cm by 2.5 cm. Also, Bournemouth pier is 4.5 mm long. Work out the real sizes.

9.5 Constructing triangles and polygons

(○) **7** Constructing a triangle

- You can use a ruler and compasses to construct a triangle when all three sides are given.

Example 5

Construct an accurate triangle with sides 3 cm, 5 cm and 6 cm.

| Draw one of the sides (usually the longest is best). | Set the compasses at 3 cm, and with the centre at one end of the line, draw an arc. | Set the compasses at 5 cm and draw an arc from the other end of the line. | Complete the triangle. |

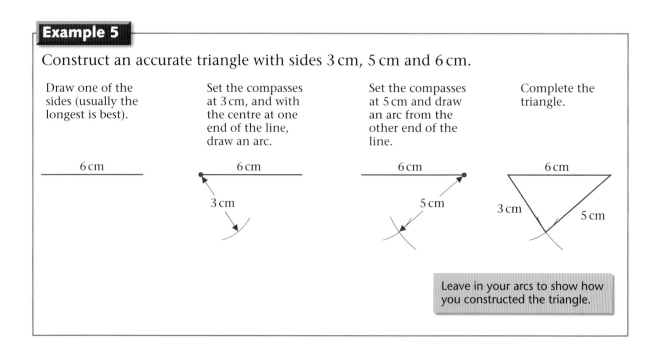

Leave in your arcs to show how you constructed the triangle.

- You can construct regular polygons in a circle.

For an octagon (8 sides) the centre angles are $\dfrac{360}{8} = 45°$

For an pentagon (5 sides) the centre angles are $\dfrac{360}{5} = 72°$

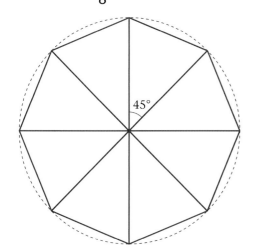

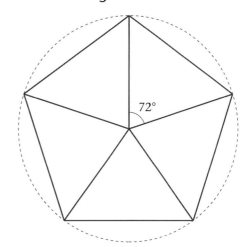

For more on regular polygons, see Section 9.12.

Exercise 9E

1 Construct accurate drawings of these triangles.

(a)

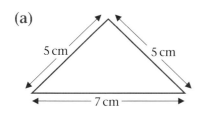

(b)

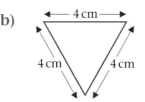

(c)

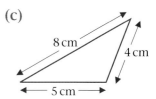

2 Construct accurate drawings of these triangles.

(a) Triangle ABC with $AB = 5$ cm, $BC = 6$ cm and $CA = 7$ cm

(b) Triangle PQR with $PQ = 4$ cm, $QR = 6$ cm and $RP = 8$ cm

(c) A triangle with sides 4 cm, 7 cm and 8 cm

(d) A triangle with sides $5\frac{1}{2}$ cm, 6 cm and $6\frac{1}{2}$ cm

3 Construct a regular hexagon inside a circle of radius 5 cm.

4 Construct accurately an equilateral triangle with side 4 cm.

9.6 More constructions

⊙ **7** Common constructions

- Two lines are **perpendicular** if they are at right angles to each other.

- The **perpendicular bisector** of line AB meets AB at right angles and cuts it into two halves.

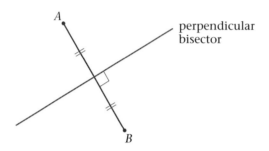

perpendicular bisector

- You can use a ruler and compasses to construct a perpendicular to a given line.

Example 6

Using a straight edge and compasses, construct accurately the perpendicular bisector of the line segment AB, which is 6 cm in length.
Label the midpoint of the line segment AB with a letter M.

A ruler is a 'straight edge'.

A —————— 6 cm —————— B A •—————————————— B

Draw a line segment 6 cm long and label its ends A and B.

Set your compasses to any radius greater than 3 cm (6 cm − 2). With the point at A, draw arcs above and below the line segment, roughly where you expect the bisector to be.

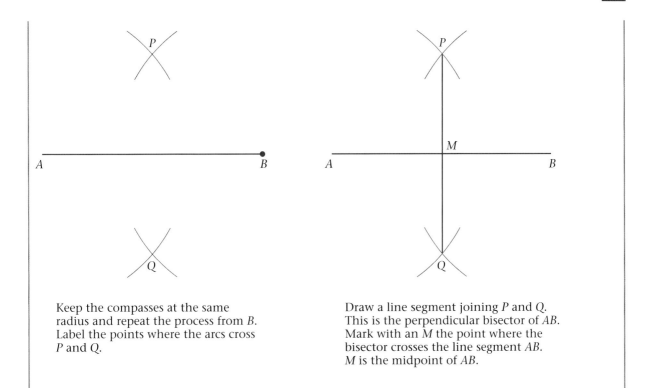

Keep the compasses at the same radius and repeat the process from B. Label the points where the arcs cross P and Q.

Draw a line segment joining P and Q. This is the perpendicular bisector of AB. Mark with an M the point where the bisector crosses the line segment AB. M is the midpoint of AB.

Example 7

Using a straight edge and compasses, construct accurately the line from P that is perpendicular to the line segment AB, which is 4 cm in length.

• P

A ——— 4 cm ——— B

• P

• P

Set your compasses to any radius greater than the distance from P to AB. With the point at P, draw two arcs on the line AB.

Move the point of your compasses to where one arc crosses AB, and draw a new arc roughly where you expect the perpendicular to be.

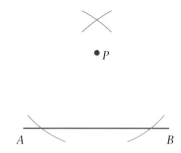

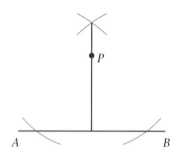

Keep the compasses at the same radius and repeat the process from the other arc on the line segment *AB*.

Draw a line from *P* to the point where the arcs cross. This is the line that is perpendicular to the line segment *AB*.

Example 8

Using a straight edge and compasses, construct accurately the line from *P* (any point on the line segment *AB*) that is perpendicular to the line segment *AB* (length 6 cm).

Draw a line segment *AB* 6 cm in length. Mark a point *P* on the line.

Set your compasses to any radius less than *AP* and *PB*. With the point at *P*, draw two arcs to cut the line segment *AB*.

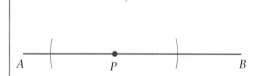

Make the radius on the compasses longer. Move the compasses to where one arc crosses *AB*, and draw a new arc roughly where you expect the perpendicular to be.

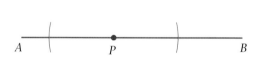

Keep the compasses at the same radius and repeat the process from the other arc on the line segment *AB*.

Draw a line from *P* to the point where the new arcs cross. This is the line from *P* that is perpendicular to the line segment *AB*.

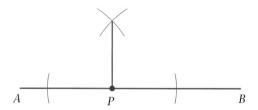

- An **angle bisector** is a line that divides an angle into two halves.
- You can use a ruler and compasses to construct an angle bisector.

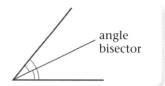

angle bisector

Example 9

Construct the angle bisector of angle A.

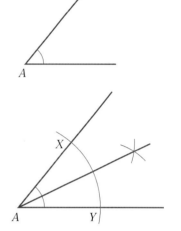

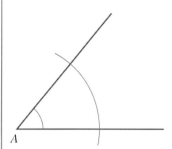

Put the compass point at A. Draw an arc that crosses both lines.

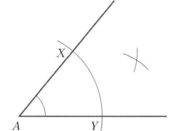

Put the compass point at X, then Y. Draw two arcs that cross.

Draw a line to bisect the angle.

Exercise 9F

In this exercise, use a straight edge and compasses only.

1 Construct accurately the perpendicular bisectors of the following line segments.
   (a) AB, length 4 cm
   (b) PQ, length 7 cm
   (c) RS, length 11 cm

2 Draw a line segment AB that is 8 cm long. Label a point about 5 cm above the line segment with a letter P. Construct accurately the line from P that is perpendicular to the line segment AB.

3 Construct accurately on the line segment AB, 9 cm in length, the perpendiculars from the points P, Q and R, which are 3 cm, 4 cm and 6 cm respectively from point A. Draw a separate construction for each part.

4 Construct these angles accurately.

   (a) 90°   **(b)** 60°   **(c)** 30°

   (d) 45°   **(e)** 135°

9.7 Loci

⊙ **7** Loci demonstrator

Loci is the plural of locus.

- A **locus** is a set of points that obey a given rule. For example, in dressage, part of the test is to follow the path shown by the dotted line. All points obey the rule:

    Each point is equidistant from B and E.
    This path is called the *locus* of the points.

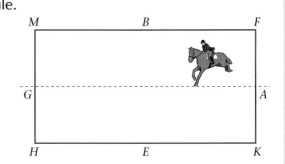

- The locus of the points equidistant from two points A and B is the perpendicular bisector of the line segment AB.

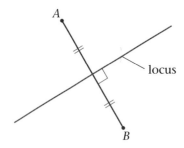

- The locus of the points a constant distance from a fixed point is a circle.

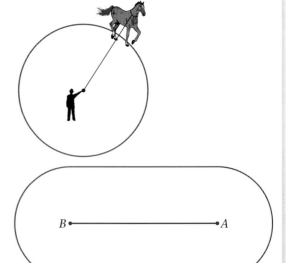

- The locus of the points a constant distance from a line segment AB is a pair of lines parallel to AB joined with semicircles whose centres are at A and B.

Example 10

Orion the horse is attached by a 10 metre rope to a bar that is 50 metres long.
Make an accurate drawing and shade the region that Orion can graze. Use a scale of 1 cm to 20 m.

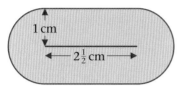

Exercise 9G

1 Construct the loci of the following points.

(a) 4 cm from a point A

(b) equidistant from the points B and C, where BC is 4 cm

(c) equidistant from two line segments AB and BC, where angle ABC is 45°

(d) 3 cm from the line segment PQ, length 5 cm

2 Make a full-size copy of this diagram.

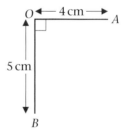

(a) Draw accurately on the diagram the locus of points which are the same distance from the line OA and the line OB.

(b) Some points are the same distance from the line OA and the line OB and are also 4 cm from the point B. Mark these points with crosses.

3 In triangle ABC, $AB = 5$ cm, angle $B = 38°$ and angle $A = 61°$.

(a) Make an accurate drawing of triangle ABC.

(b) Draw accurately the locus of all points that are the same distance from A and B.

(c) Draw the locus of all points that are 5 cm from C.

(d) Mark the points P and Q which are on both loci.

4 Construct an equilateral triangle with side 6 cm.
Draw the locus of all points outside the triangle that are 2 cm from the sides.

5 *ABC* is an equilateral triangle with side 6 cm.
  (a) Construct the triangle accurately.
  (b) Shade all the points inside this triangle which are
     (i)   nearer to *A* than to *B*
 and (ii) less than 4 cm from *C*.

6 *PQR* is a right-angled triangle.
  (a) Construct the triangle accurately.
  (b) Shade all the points that are
     (i)   nearer to *QR* than to *PR*
 and (ii) nearer to *QR* than to *PQ*.

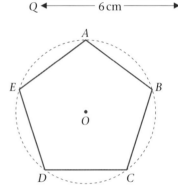

7 *ABCDE* are points on a circle, centre *O*, radius 6 cm.
  ABCDE is a regular pentagon.
  (a) Construct this diagram accurately.
  (b) Shade all points inside the pentagon that are
     (i)   less than 4 cm from *O*
 and (ii) more than 4 cm from *CD*.

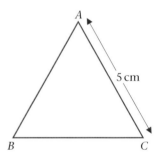

8 *ABC* is an equilateral triangle with side 5 cm.
  (a) Construct the triangle accurately.
  (b) Shade all points that are
     (i)   more than 3 cm from *B*
 and (ii) nearer to *BC* than to *BA*
 and (iii) inside triangle *ABC*.

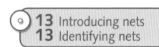

9.8 Nets

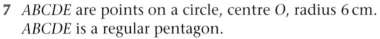

13 Introducing nets
13 Identifying nets

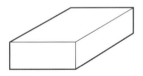
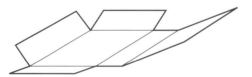
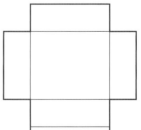

The box (cuboid) in the pictures has been opened out to
make a 2-D shape. This 2-D shape is called the **net** of the box.

• A **net** is a 2-D shape that folds up to make a 3-D shape.

Example 11

Construct the accurate net of this square-based pyramid on centimetre squared paper.

Leave the construction arcs in.

Use compasses and a ruler.

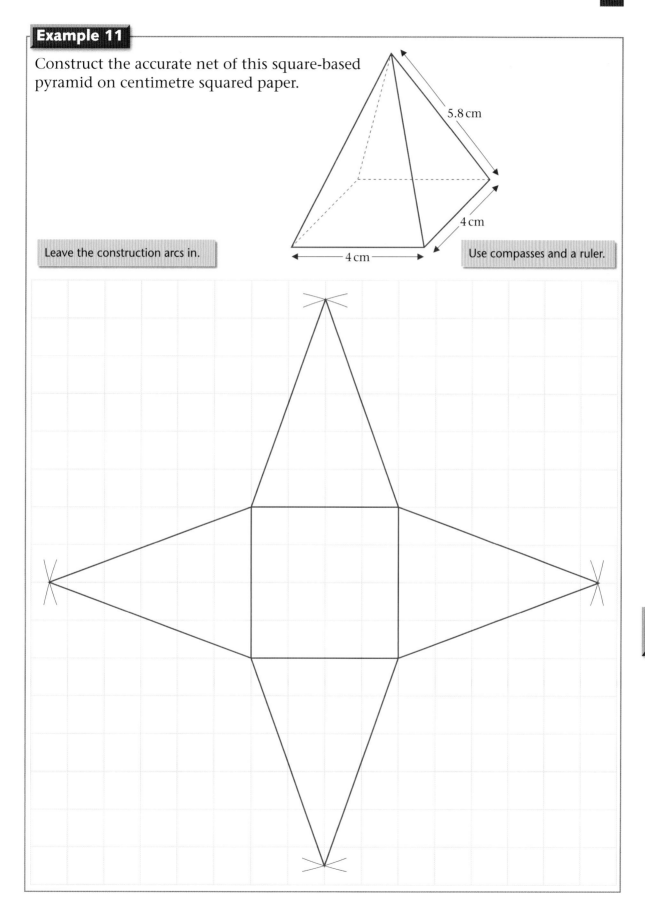

Example 12

This net will form a 3-D solid.

Draw a sketch of the solid.

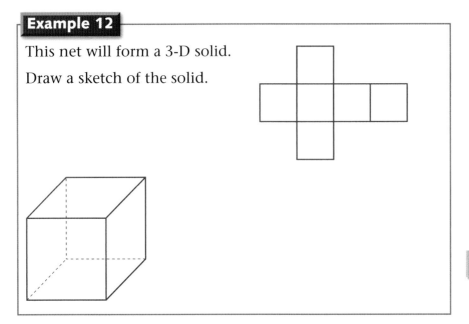

The solid is a cube.

Exercise 9H

You will need a ruler and a pair of compasses for some of the questions in this exercise.

1 Draw accurate nets of these shapes on centimetre squared paper.

(a)

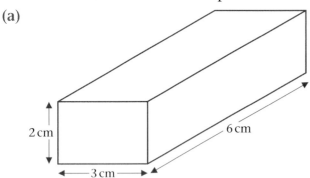

2 cm   3 cm   6 cm

(b)

9 cm   6 cm   6 cm

2 Construct an accurate net for this cuboid.

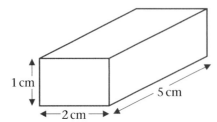

1 cm   2 cm   5 cm

3 Sketch a net for this prism.

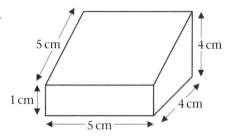

Label all the lengths on your sketch.

4 Draw an accurate net to construct a regular tetrahedron.

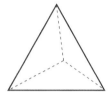

In a regular tetrahedron all faces are equilateral triangles.

5 What shape will this net make? Draw a sketch of the shape.

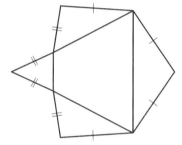

6 Could this be the net of a solid?
Give reasons for your answer.

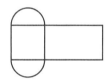

7 Which of these 2-D shapes are nets of a square-based pyramid?

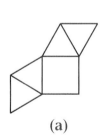

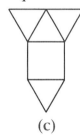

(a) (b) (c)

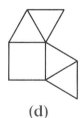

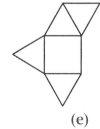

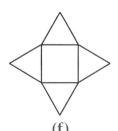

(d) (e) (f)

8 Copy and complete this 2-D shape to make it into a net of a cuboid.

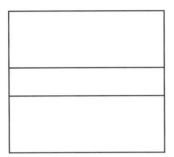

9 Draw an accurate net of this shape.

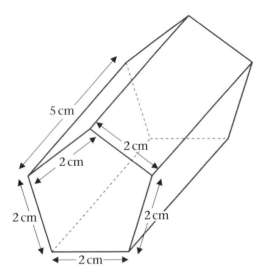

Make a sketch first.

10 These nets will each form a 3-D solid.
Draw a sketch of each solid.

(a)   (b)

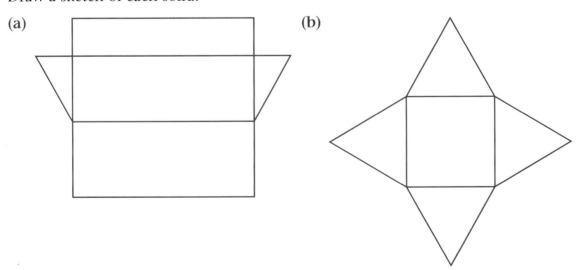

11 Sketch as many nets as possible that form the same cube.

9.9 Plan and elevation

13 Introducing plans and elevations
13 Identifying plans and elevations

- The **plan** of a solid is the view when seen from above.
- The **front elevation** is the view seen from the front.
- The **side elevation** is the view seen from the side.

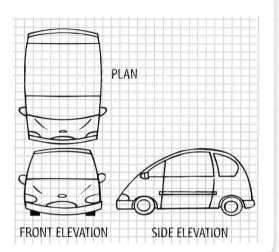

PLAN

FRONT ELEVATION   SIDE ELEVATION

Example 13

Draw the plan and elevations of this shape.

side

front

plan
(seen from above)

front elevation

side elevation

Example 14

Use this plan and these elevations to sketch the solid.

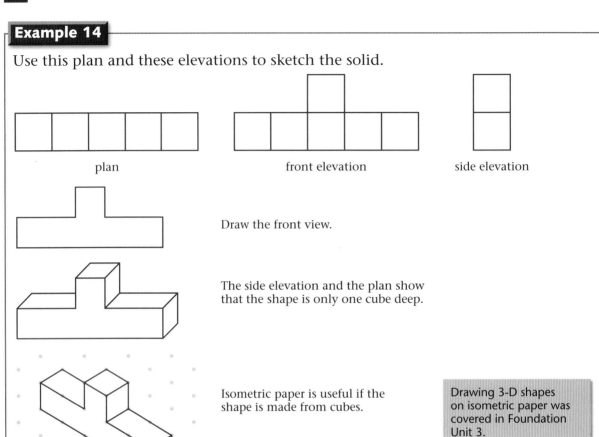

plan

front elevation

side elevation

Draw the front view.

The side elevation and the plan show that the shape is only one cube deep.

Isometric paper is useful if the shape is made from cubes.

Drawing 3-D shapes on isometric paper was covered in Foundation Unit 3.

Exercise 9I

1 Draw the plans and elevations of these shapes.

(a)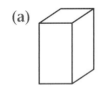

(b)

(c)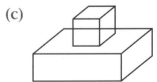

(d)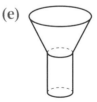

(e)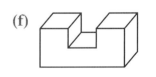

(f)

(g)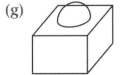

(h)

2 Draw the solid for each set of plan and elevations.

Plan	Front elevation	Right side elevation

(a)

> It may help to make the solid from cubes first.

(b)

(c)

(d)

(e)

(f)

(g)

9.10 **Congruent shapes**

> **7** Congruence
> **7** Identifying congruent shapes

- Shapes that are exactly the same size and shape are **congruent**.

> You can use tracing paper to check for congruence.

- Congruent shapes may be translations, rotations or reflections of each other.

Example 15

Which of these shapes are congruent?

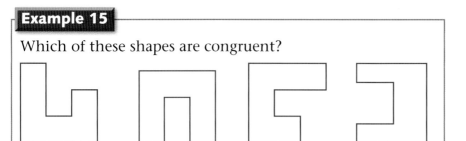

Shapes **A** and **C** are congruent.
They have the same length sides and the same size angles.

C is a rotation of *A*.

Example 16

Write down the letters of two pairs of congruent shapes.

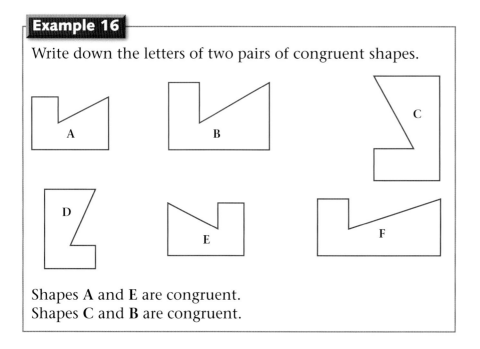

Shapes **A** and **E** are congruent.
Shapes **C** and **B** are congruent.

Exercise 9J

You may wish to use tracing paper.
In questions **1–5**, write down the letters of the shapes that are congruent.

1

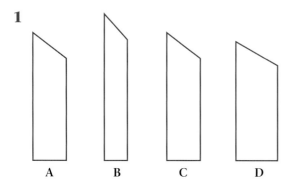

2

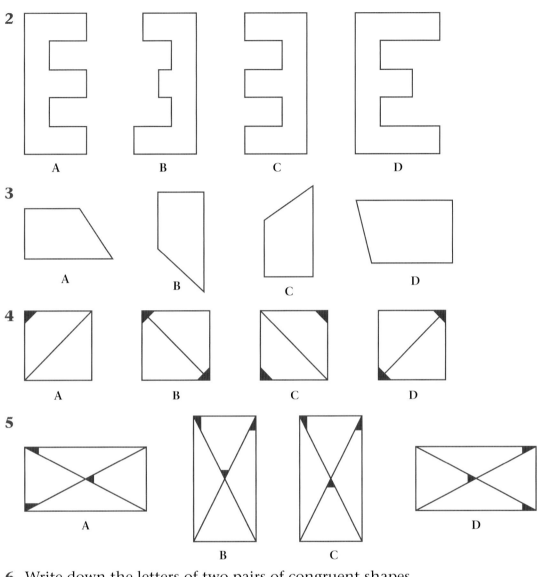

6 Write down the letters of two pairs of congruent shapes.

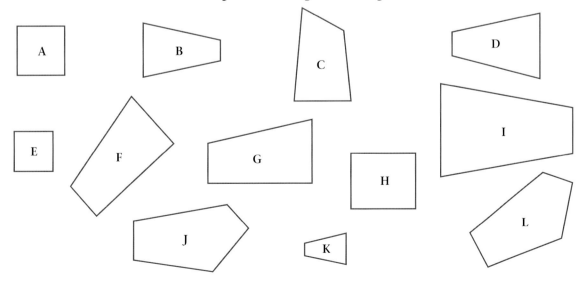

9.11 Angle properties of triangles

- Equilateral triangle
  - three sides equal
  - three angles equal, each 60°

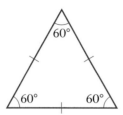

- Isosceles triangle
  - two sides equal
  - two angles equal

- Right-angled triangle
  - one angle 90°

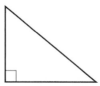

Example 17

BAC is an isosceles triangle
with $AB = AC$.
Angle $B = 20°$
$ACYX$ is a square.
Work out angle BCY.

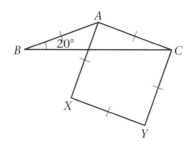

Angle $BCA = 20°$ (base angles of isosceles triangle)
Angle $ACY = 90°$ (corner of a square)
Angle BCY $=$ angle $ACY -$ angle BCA
          $= 90° - 20°$
so angle $BCY = 70°$

Exercise 9K

1 *ABCD* is a square.
AEB is an equilateral triangle.
Work out the size of angle *DAE*.

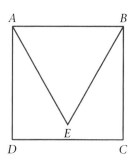

2

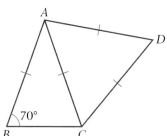

AB = *AC* = *AD* = *CD*
Angle *ABC* = 70°
Find angle *BCD* and angle *BAD*.

3

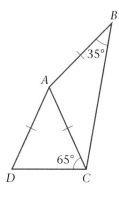

AB = *AC* = *AD*
Angle *ACD* = 65°
Angle *ABC* = 35°
Find angle *BCD* and angle *BAD*.

4

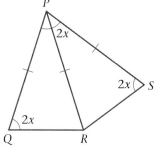

PQ = *PR* = *PS*
Angle *P* = angle *Q* = angle *S* = 2*x*
Find the value of *x*.

9.12 Polygons

- A **polygon** is a 2-D shape with straight sides.

The sides need not be the same length.

- A polygon is **regular** if its sides are all the same length and its angles are all the same size.

   Regular pentagon   Regular hexagon   Regular octagon

- The angles inside a polygon are called **interior angles**.
- The angles made by extending the sides outside a polygon are called **exterior angles**.

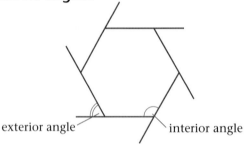

exterior angle   interior angle

Example 18

Show that the interior angles of any quadrilateral add up to 360°.

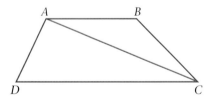

Draw any quadrilateral.

Draw a line to divide it into two triangles.

Quadrilateral *ABCD* is made from triangles *ABC* and *ACD*. The angle sum of each triangle is 180°.

So the sum of the angles in *ABCD* is

    angles in *ABC* + angles in *ACD* = 180° + 180° = 360°

- You can find the sum of the interior angles of any polygon by dividing it into triangles.

- For a polygon,
  Interior angle + exterior angle = 180°
- The exterior angles of a polygon always add up to 360°.
- The sum of the interior angles of a polygon with n sides is $(n \times 180°) - 360°$. This is usually written $(n - 2) \times 180°$.

Example 19

Work out
(a) the exterior angle of a regular octagon
(b) the interior angle of a regular octagon.

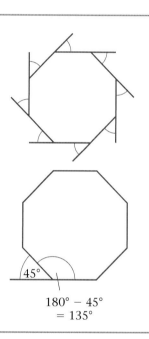

(a) A regular octagon has 8 equal sides and 8 equal exterior angles.
   The sum of the exterior angles = 360°
      So each exterior angle = 360° ÷ 8
                             = 45°

(b) Interior angle + exterior angle = 180°
      So each interior angle = 180° − 45°
                             = 135°

45°

180° − 45°
= 135°

Example 20

Work out the missing angle for this polygon.

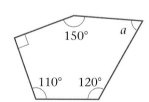

The sum of the interior angles is $(n - 2) \times 180°$
      $= (5 - 2) \times 180°$
      $= 3 \times 180°$
      $= 540°$

The angles given = 120° + 110° + 90° + 150°
                 = 470°

So missing angle a = 540° − 470°
                    = 70°

- For a **regular** polygon,

$$\text{Exterior angle} = \frac{360°}{\text{number of sides}}$$

Example 21

The exterior angle of a regular polygon is 60°.
Work out the number of sides.

$$\text{Exterior angle} = 60° = \frac{360°}{6}$$

So there are 6 sides.

Exercise 9L

1 Work out
  (a) the exterior angle of a regular 9-sided polygon
  (b) the interior angle of a regular 9-sided polygon.

2 Work out
  (a) the exterior angle of a regular hexagon
  (b) the interior angle of a regular hexagon.

3 The exterior angle of a regular polygon is 30°.
  Work out the number of sides.

4 The interior angle of a regular polygon is 162°.
  (a) Work out the exterior angle.
  (b) Work out how many sides it has.

5 Work out the missing angle in each polygon.
  (a)
  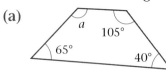

  (b)
  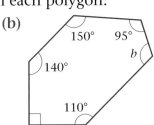

  (c)
  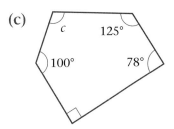

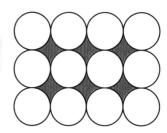

9.13 Tesselations

• A pattern of shapes which fit together without leaving any gaps or overlapping is called a **tesselation**.

Example 6

Tessellate this shape:

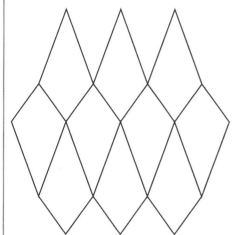

Here is one possible way. The tesselation must have at least six shapes.

Example 7

Show how a regular hexagon can tessellate.

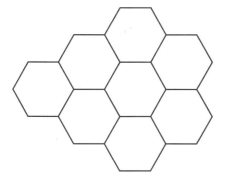

Exercise 9M

You may find squared or dotted paper useful in this exericse.

1 Show how these shapes tessellate:

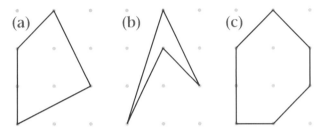

2 Show how a square and an octagon can tessellate.

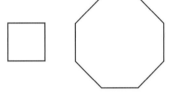

3 Design a pattern of at least 2 shapes that tessellate.

Mixed exercise 9

1 Construct each shape accurately using a protractor, compasses and ruler.

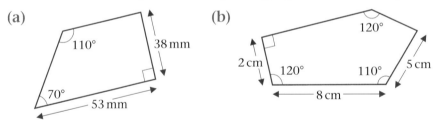

Write down the lengths of the unmarked sides.

2 Explain why this cannot be the net of a solid.

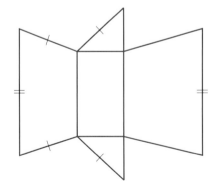

3 Which of these could possibly be the net of the dice shown?

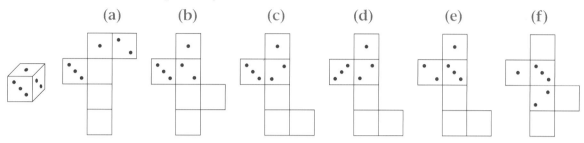

(a)   (b)   (c)   (d)   (e)   (f)

4 The exterior angle of a regular polygon is 9°.
   (a) How many sides has the polygon?
   (b) What is the sum of its interior angles?

5 Work out the size of the marked angles in each polygon.
   Give your reasons.

(a)

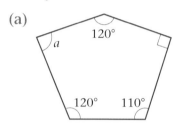

(b)

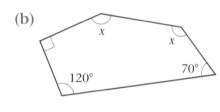

6 Work out the bearing of
   (a) *B* from *A*
   (b) *A* from *B*
   (c) *C* from *B*
   (d) *B* from *C*.

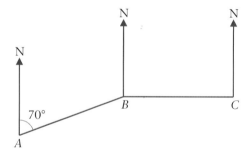

7 Skillington lies on a bearing
   of 230° from Cliftonbury,
   at a distance of 10 km.
   Henlow lies on a bearing
   of 120°, 4 km from
   Cliftonbury.

   (a) Draw a scale drawing
      to show these positions,
      using a scale of 1 cm to 1 km.
   (b) Meppershall water tower is equidistant from
      Cliftonbury and Skillington, and 7 km from Henlow.
      It is South of all 3 towns.
      Mark this position on your drawing.

8 *ABCD* is a rectangle with *AB* = 5 cm and *BC* = 3 cm.
  (a) Construct the rectangle.
  (b) Shade the set of points inside the rectangle which are
            (i) more than 3 cm from *A*
    and (ii) less than 3 cm from *BC*.

9 *ABCD* is a square with side 5 cm.
  (a) Construct the square.
  (b) Shade the set of points which are
            (i) nearer to *CD* than to *AB*
    and (ii) less than 4 cm from *A*.

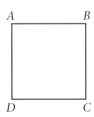

10 A goat is tied to a ring fixed
  to the midpoint of a wall,
  by a rope 20 m long.
  The wall is 50 m long.
  (a) Make an accurate scale
      drawing, using a scale
      of 1 cm to represent 5 m.
  (b) Shade the region where the goat can graze.

11 Sketch the solids shown by these plans and elevations.

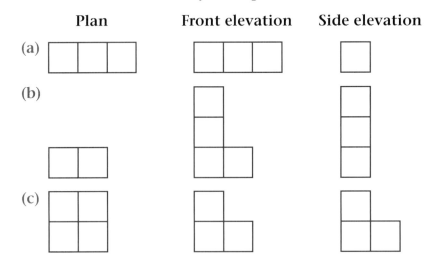

12 The diagram shows a sketch of a triangle *PQR*.
  PQ = 5.2 cm
  QR = 7.3 cm
  Angle *Q* = 115°
  (a) Make an accurate scale drawing of triangle *PQR*.
  (b) Measure *PQ* and angle *R*.

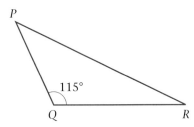

13 Use ruler and compasses to construct an angle of 150°.
Show all your construction lines.

14 Allton, Beeville and Cocester are three towns.
Allton is 15 km from Beeville on a bearing of 065°.
Cocester is 10 km from Allton on a bearing of 135°.
Using a scale of 1 cm = 2 km construct an accurate map
for the three towns.
(a) Find the distance between Beeville and Cocester.
(b) Find the bearing of Beeville from Cocester.

15 Draw the plan and elevations of each shape shown.

(a) 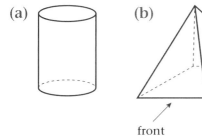 (b) 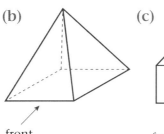 (c) 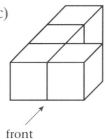 (d)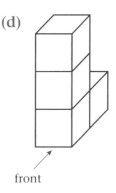

16 (a) Construct a regular octagon with 5 cm sides.
(b) Join each vertex to all the other vertices.
(c) Shade the congruent shapes in matching colours.

17 The diagram shows the exterior angles of a quadrilateral.

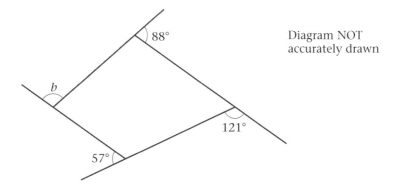

Diagram NOT
accurately drawn

Work out the value of b. [E]

18

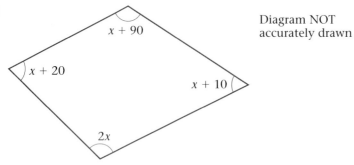

Diagram NOT accurately drawn

The sizes of the angles, in degrees, of the quadrilateral are

$x + 10$

$2x$

$x + 20$

$x + 90$

(a) Use this information to write down an equation in terms of x.

(b) Use your answer to part (a) to work out the size of the smallest angle of the quadrilateral.　　　[E]

19 *ABCD* is a rectangle.

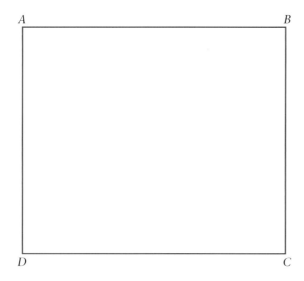

Copy the rectangle and shade the set of points inside the rectangle which are **both**

　　more than 4 centimetres from the point *A*

and more than 1 centimetre from the line *DC*.　　　[E]

20 Jill rolls a ball from point *C*.
At any point on its path, the ball is the same distance from point *A* and point *B*.

A

×*B*

×
C

(a) Trace the diagram. Draw accurately on your tracing the path that the ball will take.

(b) Shade the region that contains all the points that are no more than 3 cm from point *B*. [E]

21 Show how each of these shapes tessellates.

(a) 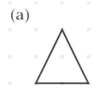 (b) 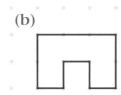 (c)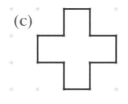

Summary of key points

1 You can use a protractor to measure and draw angles.

2 You can construct triangles using a ruler and protractor.

3 A **three-figure bearing** gives a direction in degrees. It is an angle measured clockwise from North.

4 A **scale** shows the relationship between a length on a drawing and the actual length in real life.

5 A scale can be represented as a ratio (e.g. 1 : 25 000) or using an equals sign (e.g. 1 cm = 5 km).

6 You can use a ruler and compasses to construct a triangle when all three sides are given.

7 You can construct regular polygons in a circle.

8 Two lines are **perpendicular** if they are at right angles to each other.

9 The **perpendicular bisector** of line AB meets AB at right angles and cuts it into two halves.

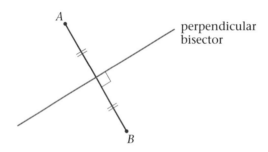

10 You can use a ruler and compasses to construct a perpendicular to a given line.

11 An **angle bisector** is a line that divides an angle into two halves.

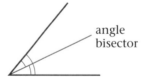

12 You can use a ruler and compasses to construct an angle bisector.

13 A **locus** is a set of points that obey a given rule.

14 The locus of the points equidistant from two points A and B is the perpendicular bisector of the line segment AB.

15 The locus of the points a constant distance from a fixed point is a circle.

16 The locus of the points a constant distance from a line segment AB is a pair of lines parallel to AB joined with semicircles whose centres are at A and B.

17 A **net** is a 2-D shape that folds up to make a 3-D shape.

18 The **plan** of a solid is the view when seen from above.

19 The **front elevation** is the view seen from the front.

20 The **side elevation** is the view seen from the side.

21 Shapes that are exactly the same size and shape are **congruent**.

22 Congruent shapes may be translations, rotations or reflections of each other.

23 Equilateral triangle
  ○ three sides equal
  ○ three angles equal, each 60°

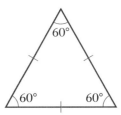

24 Isosceles triangle
  ○ two sides equal
  ○ two angles equal

25 Right-angled triangle
  ○ one angle 90°

26 A **polygon** is a 2-D shape with straight sides.

27 A polygon is **regular** if its sides are all the same length and its angles are all the same size.

28 The angles inside a polygon are called **interior angles**.

29 The angles made by extending the sides outside a polygon are called **exterior angles**.

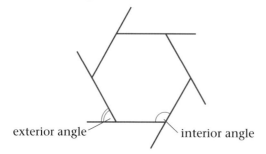

exterior angle — interior angle

30 You can find the sum of the interior angles of any polygon by dividing it into triangles.

31 For a polygon,

Interior angle + exterior angle = 180°

32 The exterior angles of a polygon always add up to 360°.

33 The sum of the interior angles of a polygon with n sides is $(n \times 180°) - 360°$.
This is usually written $(n - 2) \times 180°$.

34 For a **regular** polygon,

$$\text{Exterior angle} = \frac{360°}{\text{number of sides}}$$

10 Mensuration and Pythagoras' theorem

10.1 Converting units of area and volume

You need to know how to convert units of area and volume.
If you are working out an area or volume it is best to change
to the units you want before doing the calculation.

- **Area**
  - $1\,m^2 = 100 \times 100\,cm^2 = 10\,000\,cm^2$

  - $1\,cm^2 = 10 \times 10\,mm^2 = 100\,mm^2$

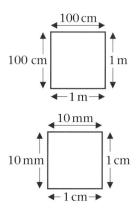

- **Volume**
  - $1\,m^3 = 100 \times 100 \times 100\,cm^3 = 1\,000\,000\,cm^3$

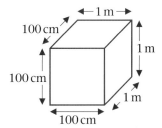

  - $1\,cm^3 = 10 \times 10 \times 10\,mm^3 = 1000\,mm^3$

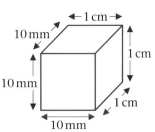

Example 1

The area of a stamp is $12\,cm^2$.
Write down its area in mm^2.

$$1\,cm^2 = 100\,mm^2$$
So $12\,cm^2 = 12 \times 100\,mm^2 = 1200\,mm^2$

Example 2

The volume of liquid in a small bottle is $35\,400\,\text{mm}^3$.
Write down this volume in cm^3.

$$1\,\text{cm}^3 = 1000\,\text{mm}^3$$
So $35\,400\,\text{mm}^3 = 35\,400 \div 1000\,\text{cm}^3 = 35.4\,\text{cm}^3$

Exercise 10A

1 Work out the number of
   (a) cm^2 in $5\,\text{m}^2$
   (b) cm^2 in $28\,\text{m}^2$
   (c) cm^2 in $1.2\,\text{m}^2$
   (d) cm^2 in $105\,\text{m}^2$
   (e) m^2 in $26\,000\,\text{cm}^2$
   (f) m^2 in $3400\,\text{cm}^2$
   (g) mm^2 in $8\,\text{cm}^2$
   (h) mm^2 in $22\,\text{cm}^2$
   (i) cm^2 in $2400\,\text{mm}^2$
   (j) cm^2 in $36\,200\,\text{mm}^2$

2 Work out the number of
   (a) cm^3 in $2.3\,\text{m}^3$
   (b) cm^3 in $0.04\,\text{m}^3$
   (c) cm^3 in $0.304\,\text{m}^3$
   (d) m^3 in $7\,000\,000\,\text{cm}^3$
   (e) m^3 in $530\,000\,\text{cm}^3$
   (f) m^3 in $26\,500\,\text{cm}^3$
   (g) mm^3 in $4\,\text{cm}^3$
   (h) mm^3 in $13.05\,\text{cm}^3$
   (i) cm^3 in $8400\,\text{mm}^3$
   (j) cm^3 in $430\,\text{mm}^3$

3 (a) Work out the total
       surface area in
       (i) m^2
       (ii) cm^2
   (b) Work out the volume
       of the cuboid in
       (i) m^3
       (ii) cm^3

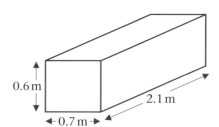

> $V = lwh$
> Volume of a cuboid was
> covered in Foundation
> Unit 3.

10.2 Area and circumference of circles

(◦) **26** Area of a circle

- Area of a circle $= \pi r^2 = \pi \times r \times r$
- Circumference of a circle $= 2\pi r$
  $$= 2 \times \pi \times r \text{ or } \pi \times d$$

> r is the radius
> d is the diameter

Example 3

Find **(a)** the circumference and **(b)** the area of a circle with diameter 17 cm.

(a) Circumference $= \pi d = \pi \times 17 = 53.4$ cm (to 1 d.p.)

(b) Area $= \pi r^2$ ● ────────────────── You need to find the radius.

Radius $=$ diameter $\div\ 2 = 17 \div 2 = 8.5$ cm

Area $= \pi \times (8.5)^2 = 227$ cm^2 (to the nearest whole number)

Example 4

The area of a circular table top is 1.2 m^2.

Work out the circumference. ● ──────────────── To work out the circumference you need to know the radius.

Area $= 1.2$ m$^2 = \pi r^2$

So $r^2 = \dfrac{1.2}{\pi}$

$r = \sqrt{\dfrac{1.2}{\pi}}$

Circumference $= 2 \times \pi \times \sqrt{\dfrac{1.2}{\pi}}$

$= 3.88$ cm (to 2 d.p.)

Example 5

Work out **(a)** the area and **(b)** the perimeter of this pond.

The pond is a semicircle.

Give your answer for the perimeter

(i) in terms of π **(ii)** numerically.

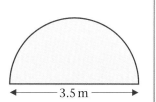

←──── 3.5 m ────→

$r = \dfrac{3.5}{2} = 1.75$ m

Area of a semicircle is half the area of the circle.

(a) Area of pond $= \frac{1}{2} \times \pi r^2$

$= \frac{1}{2} \times \pi \times 1.75 \times 1.75$

$= 4.81$ m^2 (to 2 d.p.)

(b) Perimeter of pond $=$ diameter $+$ half circumference of circle

$= d + \frac{1}{2}\pi d$

$= 3.5 + \frac{1}{2} \times \pi \times 3.5$

(i) Perimeter $= (3.5 + 1.75\pi)$ m

(ii) Perimeter $= 9$ m (to the nearest whole number)

Using a calculator.

Example 6

The shape is made from an equilateral triangle with side 8 cm and a semicircle with diameter 8 cm.
Work out the perimeter of the shape.
Give your answer in terms of π.

The length of the arc of the semicircle is
$\frac{1}{2} \times$ circumference of circle $= \frac{1}{2} \times \pi \times 8 = 4\pi$
Perimeter of shape $= 8 + 8 + 4\pi = (16 + 4\pi)$ cm

Example 7

Work out the perimeter and area of this quarter circle.
Give your answer in terms of π.

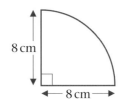

Area of circle $= \pi r^2 = \pi \times 8^2 = 64\pi$ cm^2
Area of quarter circle $= \frac{1}{4} \times 64\pi = 16\pi$ cm^2
Perimeter of quarter circle $= 8 + 8 +$ arc length
$$= 16 + \frac{1}{4} \times \pi \times \text{diameter}$$
$$= 16 + \frac{1}{4} \times \pi \times 8 \times 2$$
$$= (16 + 4\pi) \text{ cm}$$

Exercise 10B

1 Work out the circumference and area of these circles
   (a) radius 6 cm   (b) radius 14 cm
   (c) radius 8.3 cm   (d) radius 0.74 m
   (e) diameter 11.3 cm   (f) diameter 13.9 mm
   (g) diameter 1.6 m

2 The cross-section of a cable is a circle with diameter 2.5 cm.
   Work out the cross-sectional area.

3 The circumference of a circular pond is 25 metres.
   Work out its diameter and area.

4 A circle has a radius of 32 cm.
   Work out the circumference of the circle to the nearest cm.   [E]

5 Work out the area and circumference of these circles.
Give your answers
    (i) in terms of π **(ii)** numerically.

(a)

radius 16 cm

(b)
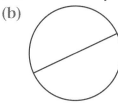
diameter 24 mm

(c)
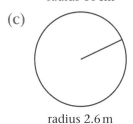
radius 2.6 m

(d)
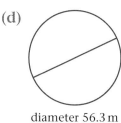
diameter 56.3 m

6 The diameter of a bicycle wheel is 800 mm.
Work out how far it travels in
(a) 1 revolution
(b) 50 revolutions.

7 A circus ring has radius 17 m.
Work out its area and circumference.

8 The circumference of a circular pond is 83 metres.
Work out its diameter.

9 Work out the area and perimeter of these semicircles.
Give your answers
    (i) in terms of π
    (ii) numerically.

(a)
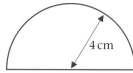
4 cm

(b)
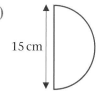
15 cm

(c)

radius 3.6 cm

(d)
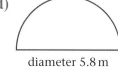
diameter 5.8 m

10 A semicircular pond has a radius of 2.5 m.
Work out the area and perimeter of the pond.

11 A semicircular pipe has a cross-sectional area of 14.1 cm².
   Work out the radius of the pipe.

12 The diagram shows the cross-section of a greenhouse.
   The roof is a semicircle and
   the sides are quarter circles.

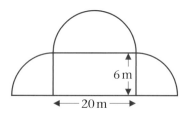

   (a) Work out the area of the
       cross-section.
   (b) Work out the perimeter of
       the cross-section.

13 An arch-shaped door has a
   curved top.
   The curve is a quarter circle
   with radius 3 m.
   Work out the area of the door.
   Give your answer in terms of π.

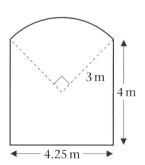

14 The cross-section of a door catch is a
   rectangle measuring 4 mm by 6 mm
   with a quarter circle with radius 4 mm.
   Work out the perimeter.
   Give your answer in terms of π.

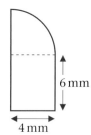

15 Work out the area and perimeter of these shapes.
   The shapes are made up of rectangles and semicircles.

   (a) 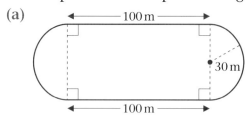   (b)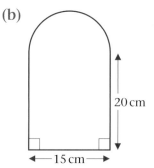

16 A circular piece of card has a square hole
   cut from it, as shown.
   The radius of the circle is 5 cm.
   The side of the square is 1.5 cm.
   Work out the area of the remaining card.

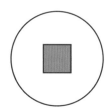

10.3 Areas of parallelograms and triangles

The area of a triangle is half the area of a rectangle that encloses it, so:

- Area of a triangle
    $= \frac{1}{2} \times$ base $\times$ vertical height
    $= \frac{1}{2} \times b \times h$

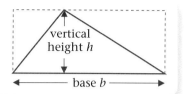

You can cut a corner off a rectangle and replace it on the other side to make a parallelogram, so:

- Area of a parallelogram = base $\times$ vertical height
    $= b \times h$

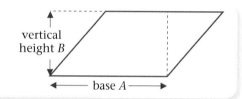

Example 8

ABRT and *PQRS* are parallelograms.

Angle *BQR* = 90°

PST is a straight line.

Show that *ABRT* and *PQRS* have the same area.

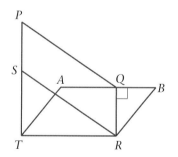

PQRS is a parallelogram.
So *PS* = *QR*.
Label these lengths *l*.

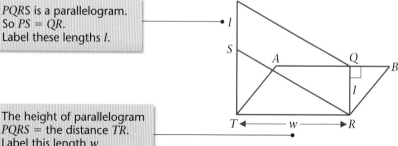

The height of parallelogram *PQRS* = the distance *TR*.
Label this length *w*.

From the diagram:
Area of *PQRS* = $l \times w$
Area of *ABRT* = $w \times l$ = Area of *PQRS*

Exercise 10C

1 Find the areas of these shapes.

(a)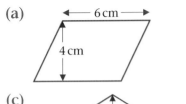

(b)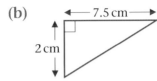

(c)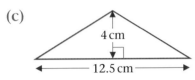

(d)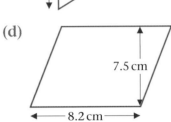

2 A metal badge is made by cutting a rectangle from a triangle as shown.
Find the area of metal in the badge.

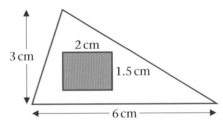

> Write an expression for the area of each triangle.

3 *ABCD* is a rectangle with length *l* and width *w*.

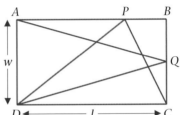

Show that area of triangle *AQD* = area of triangle *DPC*.

4 *AB* is parallel to *PXQY*.
ABXP and *ABYQ* are parallelograms.
Show that they have the same area.

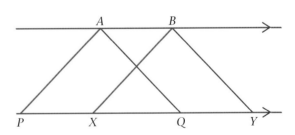

5 *ABCD* is a rectangle.
AYBX is a parallelogram.
Show that they have the same area.

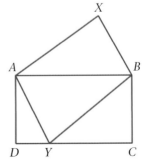

6 *ABCD* is a rectangle.
CPQD is a parallelogram.
QDM is a straight line.
QD = DM
Show that *ABCD* and *CPQD*
have the same area.

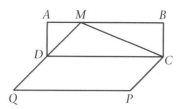

10.4 Volumes and surface areas of prisms

- A **prism** is a 3-D shape with the same cross-section all along its length.
- Volume of a prism = area of cross-section × length
- The total surface area of a prism is the sum of the areas of its faces.

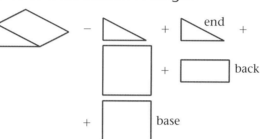

Example 9

Find the volume of the length of gutter shown.

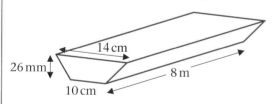

26 mm = 2.6 cm, 8 m = 800 cm.   　Convert all the measurements to the same units.

Area of cross-section (a trapezium) = $\frac{1}{2}(14 + 10) \times 2.6$

$$\text{Volume} = 800 \times \frac{1}{2}(14 + 10) \times 2.6$$
$$= 24\,960 \text{ cm}^3$$

Area of trapezium
$= \frac{1}{2}(a + b)h$

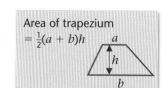

Area of a trapezium was covered in Foundation Unit 3.

Example 10

Find the surface area of this triangular prism.

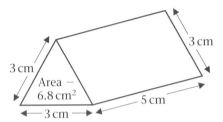

The prism has two triangular faces and three rectangular faces.

Surface area = $\triangle_{5.8}$ + $\triangle_{5.8}$ + $\boxed{3 \times 5}$ + $\boxed{3 \times 5}$ + $\boxed{3 \times 5}$

$\qquad\quad = 13.6 + 15 + 15 + 15$

$\qquad\quad = 58.6 \, \text{cm}^2$

Exercise 10D

In questions **1–5**, work out the **(a)** total surface area and **(b)** the volume.

1

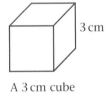

A 3 cm cube

2

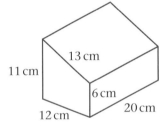

3

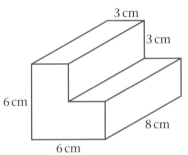

4

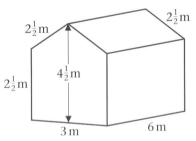

5

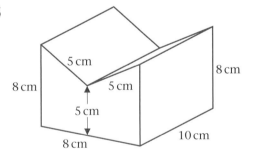

In questions **6–9**, work out the volumes of the shapes shown.

6

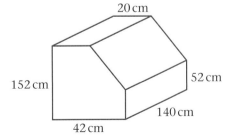

7

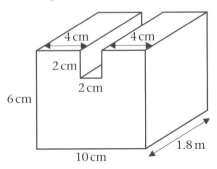

8

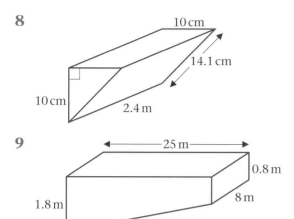

9

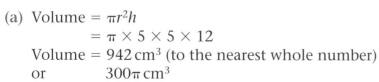

10 Find the surface area of the shapes in questions **8** and **9**.

10.5 Surface area and volume of cylinders

- The curved surface area of a cylinder is $2\pi rh$.
- The total surface area of a cylinder is $2\pi rh + 2\pi r^2$.

A cylinder is a special prism where the cross-section is a circle.

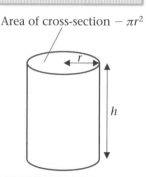

- The volume of a cylinder is
  area of cross-section × height = $\pi r^2 h$.

Area of cross-section $-\pi r^2$

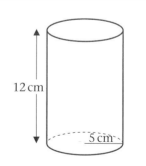

Example 11

Calculate (a) the volume
      (b) the total surface area
of a cylinder radius 5 cm and height 12 cm.
Give your answers both numerically and in terms of π.

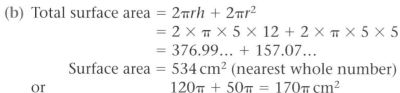

(a) Volume = $\pi r^2 h$
       = $\pi \times 5 \times 5 \times 12$
   Volume = 942 cm^3 (to the nearest whole number)
   or $300\pi \text{ cm}^3$

(b) Total surface area = $2\pi rh + 2\pi r^2$
         = $2 \times \pi \times 5 \times 12 + 2 \times \pi \times 5 \times 5$
         = $376.99... + 157.07...$
   Surface area = 534 cm^2 (nearest whole number)
   or $120\pi + 50\pi = 170\pi \text{ cm}^2$

Give your answers to 3 significant figures unless instructed otherwise.

Example 12

A cylindrical water butt holds 600 litres of water.
The height of the butt is 1.4 metres.
Calculate the radius of the water butt.

The volume of water = 600 litres
$\qquad\qquad\qquad = 600 \times 1000\,\text{cm}^3$
$\qquad\qquad\qquad = 600\,000\,\text{cm}^3$

Remember:
1 litre = 1000 cm³

The volume (V) of the water butt = $\pi r^2 h$
So $600\,000 = \pi \times r^2 \times 140$

Remember:
1.4 m = 140 cm

So $\dfrac{600\,000}{\pi \times 140} = r^2$

$\qquad r^2 = \sqrt{1364.1\ldots}$

$\qquad\ \ r = 36.9\,\text{cm}$ (to 1 d.p.)

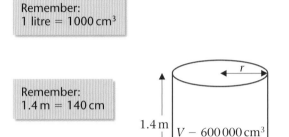

1.4 m $V - 600\,000\,\text{cm}^3$

Exercise 10E

1 Calculate the volumes and total surface areas of these cylinders.
   Give your answers numerically and in terms of π.

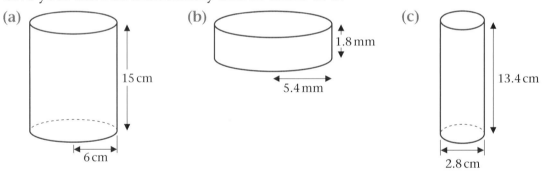

(a) 15 cm, 6 cm

(b) 1.8 mm, 5.4 mm

(c) 13.4 cm, 2.8 cm

2 A cylindrical water butt holds 1000 litres of water.
   The diameter of the water butt is 1 m.
   Calculate the height of the water butt in metres correct to 2 d.p.

3 An iron ingot is in the shape of a cuboid 5 cm by 20 cm by 30 cm. It is to be melted down and recast into cylinders.
   The cylinders are to have a diameter of 10 cm and height 18 cm.
   (a) Calculate the maximum number of cylinders that can be made from the iron.
   (b) What volume of iron is wasted?

4 A café has tumblers in the shape of a cylinder.
The tumblers have height 18 cm and diameter 6 cm.
How many tumblers can be filled from a 2 litre bottle of
lemonade?

5 Work out the area of the curved surface of a cylinder with
radius 5 cm and length 12 cm.

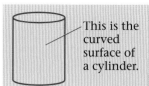

This is the curved surface of a cylinder.

6 For each of the following cylinders, work out
     (i)   the curved surface area
     (ii) the total surface area
     (iii) the volume.

  (a) radius 4.5 cm, length 225 cm
  (b) radius 12 mm, length 2 m
  (c) diameter 15 mm, length 6 cm
  (d) diameter 3 cm, length 4 mm

10.6 Using Pythagoras' theorem to find the hypotenuse

25 Introduction to Pythagoras' theorem
25 Pythagoras' theorem calculator
26 Pythagoras' theorem tool

• **Pythagoras' theorem** states that in a right-angled triangle
the square on the hypotenuse is equal to the sum of the
squares on the other two sides.
$$c^2 = a^2 + b^2 \quad \text{or} \quad a^2 + b^2 = c^2$$

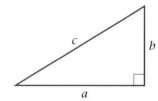

Example 13

Calculate the length of the side f.

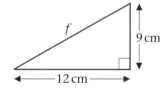

Using Pythagoras' theorem $c^2 = a^2 + b^2$
$$f^2 = 12^2 + 9^2$$
$$= 144 + 81$$
$$= 225$$
So $f = \sqrt{225} = 15$ cm

Example 14

The diagram represents a ladder of length l resting against the wall of a house. The foot of the ladder is 2 m from the wall. The top of the ladder is 7.6 m from the base of the wall.

Calculate the length of the ladder.

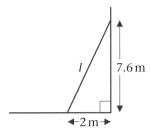

Using Pythagoras' theorem $c^2 = a^2 + b^2$

$$l^2 = 2^2 + 7.6^2$$
$$= 4 + 57.76$$
$$= 61.76$$

So length $l = \sqrt{61.76} = 7.858\ldots$
$$= 7.86 \text{ m (to 2 d.p.)}$$

Example 15

Find the distance between $A(1, 4)$ and $B(3, -2)$.

First draw a diagram.

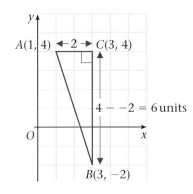

Draw a right-angled triangle with AB as the hypotenuse.

ACB is a right-angled triangle.

$$AB^2 = AC^2 + CB^2$$
$$= 2^2 + 6^2$$
$$AB^2 = 40$$
$$AB = \sqrt{40} = 6.32 \text{ (to 2 d.p.)}$$

Exercise 10F

1 Calculate the lengths marked with letters in these triangles.

(a)

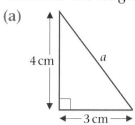

4 cm

a

3 cm

(b)

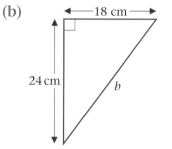

18 cm

24 cm

b

(c)

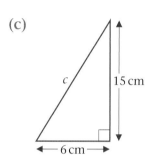

c

15 cm

6 cm

(d)

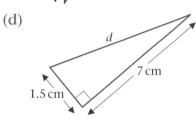

d

7 cm

1.5 cm

2 Calculate the lengths marked with letters in these triangles.

(a)

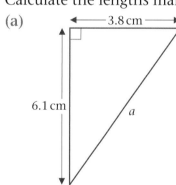

3.8 cm

6.1 cm

a

(b)

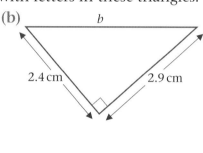

b

2.4 cm

2.9 cm

(c)

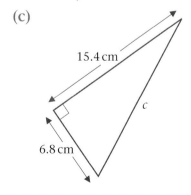

15.4 cm

c

6.8 cm

(d)

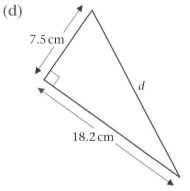

7.5 cm

d

18.2 cm

3 A rectangle is 24 cm long and 15 cm wide.
Calculate the length of the diagonal of the rectangle.

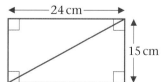

24 cm

15 cm

4 A balloon is held to the ground by a cable at point P.
The balloon is 10 m horizontally from P.
The height of the balloon is 50 m.
How long is the cable?

5 Calculate the distance AD in this trapezium.

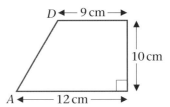

6 Find the distance between
  (a) $A(2, 3)$ and $B(5, 7)$ (b) $C(0, 4)$ and $D(5, 16)$
  (c) $E(-1, 3)$ and $F(3, 4)$ (d) $G(1, -2)$ and $H(6, 5)$
  (e) $J(-2, -3)$ and $K(-6, 4)$ (f) $L(-3, 2)$ and $M(2, -5)$

10.7 Using Pythagoras' theorem to find one of the shorter sides of a triangle

• Pythagoras' theorem states that in any right-angled triangle
$$a^2 = c^2 - b^2 \quad \text{or} \quad b^2 = c^2 - a^2$$

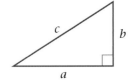

Example 16

In triangle ABC, calculate the length AB.

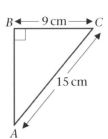

Using Pythagoras' theorem $a^2 = c^2 - b^2$
$$AB^2 = AC^2 - BC^2$$
$$= 15^2 - 9^2$$
$$= 225 - 81$$
$$AB^2 = 144$$
So $AB = \sqrt{144} = 12$ cm

Example 17

An isosceles triangle *DEF* has *DF* = *EF* = 12.6 cm and
DE = 8.5 cm.
Calculate the vertical height of the triangle to 3 s.f.

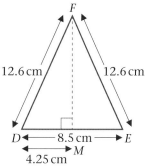

First draw a diagram.
The vertical height is *FM*.
M is the midpoint of *DE*.

Using Pythagoras' theorem $a^2 = c^2 - b^2$

$$FM^2 = 12.6^2 - 4.25^2$$
$$= 158.76 - 18.0625$$
$$FM^2 = 140.6...$$
$$\text{So } FM = \sqrt{140.6...}$$
$$= 11.86... = 11.9 \text{ cm (to 1 d.p.)}$$

Example 18

A square has a diagonal of 10 cm.
Calculate the length of each side to 3 s.f.

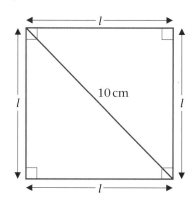

First draw a diagram.
Remember a square has
four equal sides and each
of its angles is a right
angle.

Let *l* be the length of a side. The diagonal is then the
hypotenuse of a right-angled triangle with two shorter sides *l*.
Using Pythagoras' theorem $a^2 + b^2 = c^2$

$$l^2 + l^2 = 10^2$$
$$2l^2 = 100$$
$$l^2 = 50 \qquad \text{Divide both sides by 2.}$$
$$\text{So} \quad l = \sqrt{50} = 7.07 \text{ cm (to 2 d.p.)}$$

Exercise 10G

1 Calculate the lengths of the sides labelled x in these right-angled triangles.

(a)

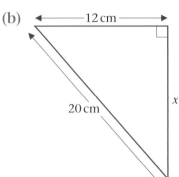

(b)

(c)

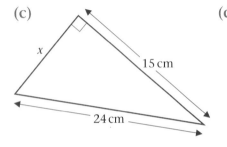

(d)

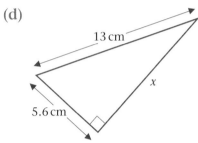

2 Calculate the lengths marked with letters.
Give your answers correct to 1 d.p.

(a)

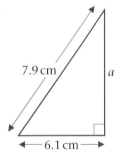

(b)

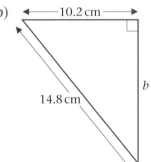

(c)

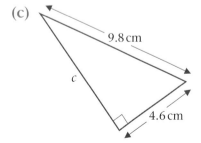

(d)

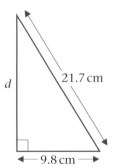

3 Calculate the heights of these isosceles triangles.

(a)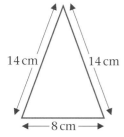

14 cm   14 cm

8 cm

(b)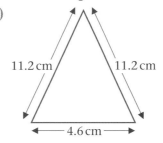

11.2 cm   11.2 cm

4.6 cm

4 Calculate the length of one side of a square with diagonal 12 cm.

5 The foot of an 8 m ladder is placed 2 m from a vertical wall. How far up the wall does the ladder reach?

6 A ramp is made of a piece of wood 2 m long. It gives access to a building whose step is 25 cm high. How far is the edge of the ramp from the building?

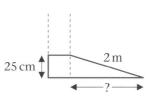

25 cm   2 m   ?

Mixed exercise 10

1 Work out the number of
(a) cm^2 in $7 m^2$
(b) m^2 in $5000 cm^2$
(c) mm^3 in $6 cm^3$
(d) m^3 in $32\,500 cm^3$
(e) cm^2 in $7800 mm^2$
(f) cm^2 in $307 m^2$
(g) cm^3 in $9500 mm^3$
(h) m^3 in $5\,000\,000 cm^3$

2 Work out the area and circumference of these shapes.

(a)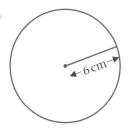

6 cm

(b)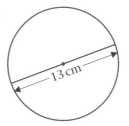

13 cm

(c)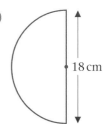

18 cm

3 Work out the length of the marked side.

(a)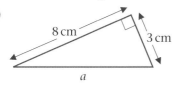

8 cm   3 cm

a

(b)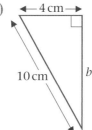

4 cm

10 cm b

(c)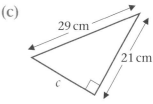

29 cm   21 cm

c

4 Brighton station is 17 km east of Worthing station. Brighton station is also 14 km south of Burgess Hill station. Work out the straight line distance between Worthing station and Burgess Hill station.

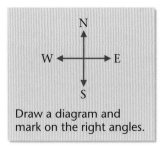

Draw a diagram and mark on the right angles.

5 Calculate the length of *BC*. Give your answer correct to 1 decimal place.

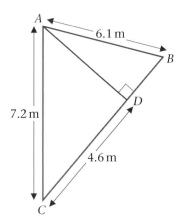

6 Find the volume and surface area of each of these solids.

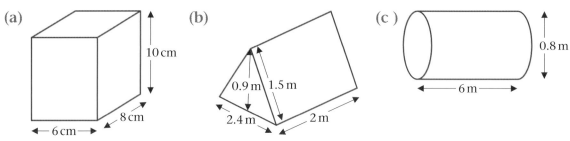

(a) 10 cm, 8 cm, 6 cm

(b) 0.9 m, 1.5 m, 2.4 m, 2 m

(c) 0.8 m, 6 m

7 This is the cross-section of a ramp. It is 1 metre wide. Work out the volume of the ramp.

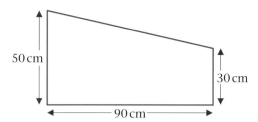

50 cm, 30 cm, 90 cm

8 A cylindrical can has a diameter of 8 cm and height 15 cm.
   (a) Calculate the volume of the can.
   (b) Work out the total surface area of the can.

9 A bicycle wheel has a diameter of 70 cm. Calculate the distance the bicycle wheel covers in 50 revolutions.

10 A copper pipe has a circular cross-section with diameter
12 mm. It is filled with water. The volume of the water is
measured as 423 cm³ by completely draining the pipe.
Work out the length of the pipe.

11 The volume of a container is 9000 litres.
The container is a cuboid with height 2 metres and width
1.5 metres. How long is the container?

12 A machine makes circular washers which are 0.8 mm thick.
Each washer is a circular disc with a circular hole in the
centre. The external diameter is 2.2 cm and the internal
diameter is 1.4 cm.
Work out, in cm³, the volume of 1500 washers.

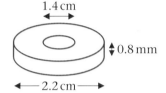

13 A cuboid has
     a volume of 40 cm³
     a length of 5 cm
     a width of 2 cm.

(a) Work out the height of the cuboid.

(b)

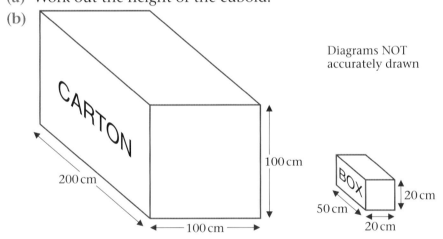

Diagrams NOT
accurately drawn

A carton measures 200 cm by 100 cm by 100 cm.
The carton is to be completely filled with boxes.
Each box measures 50 cm by 20 cm by 20 cm.
Work out the number of boxes which can completely fill the carton.   [E]

Summary of key points

1 Area
  ○ $1\,m^2 = 100 \times 100\,cm^2 = 10\,000\,cm^2$
  ○ $1\,cm^2 = 10 \times 10\,mm^2 = 100\,mm^2$

2 Volume
  ○ $1\,m^3 = 100 \times 100 \times 100\,cm^3 = 1\,000\,000\,cm^3$
  ○ $1\,cm^3 = 10 \times 10 \times 10\,mm^3 = 1000\,mm^3$

3 Area of a circle $= \pi r^2 = \pi \times r \times r$

4 Circumference of a circle
  $= 2\pi r = 2 \times \pi \times r$ or $\pi \times d$

5 Area of a triangle
  $= \frac{1}{2} \times$ base $\times$ vertical height
  $= \frac{1}{2} \times b \times h$

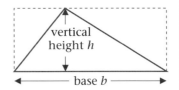

6 Area of a parallelogram $=$ base $\times$ vertical height
  $= b \times h$

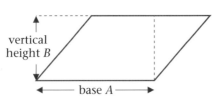

7 A **prism** is a 3-D shape with the same cross-section all along its length.

8 Volume of a prism $=$ area of cross-section $\times$ length

9 The total surface area of a prism is the sum of the areas of its faces.

10 The curved surface area of a cylinder is $2\pi rh$.

Area of cross-section $- \pi r^2$

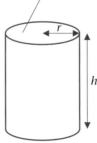

11 The total surface area of a cylinder is $2\pi rh + 2\pi r^2$.

12 The volume of a cylinder is
  area of cross-section $\times$ height $= \pi r^2 h$.

13 Pythagoras' theorem states that in a right-angled triangle the square on the hypotenuse is equal to the sum of the squares on the other two sides.

- $c^2 = a^2 + b^2$ or $a^2 + b^2 = c^2$
- $a^2 = c^2 - b^2$ or $b^2 = c^2 - a^2$

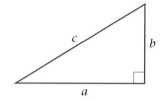

Examination practice paper

Section A (calculator)

1 On centimetre squared paper draw a rectangle
that has length 6 cm and width 4 cm. **(2 marks)**

2 (a) Work out 25% of £12. **(1 mark)**

  (b) Write 20% as a fraction. **(1 mark)**

Shaun has 9 sweets.
He shares them with his sister.
For each sweet he gives his sister, Shaun eats 2.

  (c) How many sweets does he give to his sister? **(2 marks)**

3 Bags of crisps cost 45p each.
Chantelle has £5 to spend on crisps.

  (a) What is the greatest number of bags of crisps
    that Chantelle could buy for £5? **(2 marks)**

  (b) How much change should she get? **(1 mark)**

4 Jade uses the formula $P = 3r$ to find
the perimeter of an equilateral triangle.

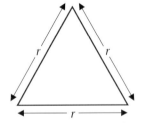

  (a) Work out the perimeter P when $r = 5$ cm. **(1 mark)**

  (b) Work out the value of r when $P = 30$ cm. **(1 mark)**

5 Here is part of Sharon's gas bill.

GAS BILL

New reading	34 823 units
Old reading	33 095 units

Price per unit 35p

Work out how much Sharon has to pay for the
units of gas she used. **(4 marks)**

6 Draw a sketch of

  (a) a cylinder   **(1 mark)**

  (b) a triangular prism.   **(1 mark)**

7 (a) (i)   **(ii)**

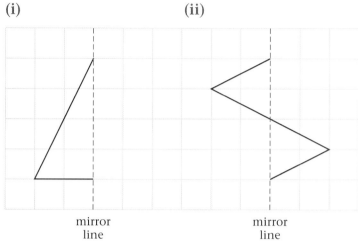

On a copy of the grid, reflect the shapes in the mirror line.
                                                        (2 marks)

  (b) Draw in any lines of symmetry on these shapes.

  (i)   **(ii)**

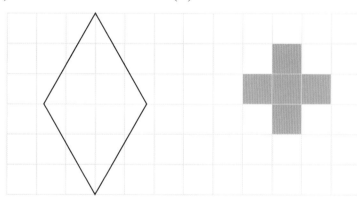

                                                        (3 marks)

  (c) Write down the order of rotational symmetry for these shapes.

  (i)   **(ii)**

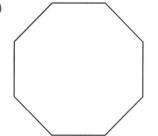 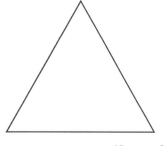

                                                        (2 marks)

8 Here is the sketch of a triangle.
Make an accurate drawing of
the triangle.

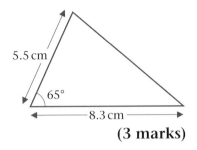

5.5 cm

65°

8.3 cm

(3 marks)

9 William uses this word formulae to work out the mileage
cost of hiring a van.

Mileage cost = mileage rate × no. of miles travelled

The mileage rate was 15p per mile.
William travelled 200 miles.

(a) Work out the mileage cost   **(2 marks)**

mileage cost = m
mileage rate = r
no. of miles travelled = n

(b) Write down the rule as an algebraic formula   **(1 mark)**

10 Work out

  (a)   **(i)** $3 - 4$

      (ii) 5×-2

      (iii) $-12 \div -4$ **(3 marks)**

  (b) Find the value of

      (i) $5^3 \times 5^2$

      (ii) $\dfrac{4^5}{4^2}$ **(2 marks)**

11 Jim bought an MP3 player for £40.
He sold it and made a 20% profit.
At what price did Jim sell the MP3 player?   **(3 marks)**

12 Solve the equations.

  (a) $5p + 7 = 22$ **(2 marks)**

  (b) $5q - 4 = 3q + 7$ **(2 marks)**

  (c) $5r + 7 = 2(2r - 4)$ **(2 marks)**

13 Rajid uses the formula $v = u + 5t$ to find the
speed v of a ball dropped off a cliff.

  (a) Find the value of v when $u = 0$ and $t = 3$ **(1 mark)**

  (b) Find the value of v when $u = 10$ and $t = 6$ **(1 mark)**

  (c) Find the value of t when $u = 10$ and $v = 20$ **(2 marks)**

  (d) Make t the subject of the formula.   **(2 marks)**

14 Nesta buys a new washing machine for £160 plus VAT at $17\frac{1}{2}$%.
Work out the total cost of the washing machine.

(3 marks)

15 The equation $x^3 + 2x = 16$
has a solution between 2 and 3.

Use a trial and improvement method to find this solution.
Give your answer correct to 1 decimal place.
You **must** show **all** your working.　　　　　**(4 marks)**

16 *ABC* is a right-angled triangle.

$AB = 12$ cm
$BC = 12$ cm

Work out the length of *AC*.
Give your answer correct to
2 decimal places.

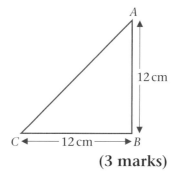

(3 marks)

Total for Section A: 60 marks

Section B (non-calculator)

1 Write down the answer to

(a) 5×0.3

(b) $5 \div 100$ **(2 marks)**

2

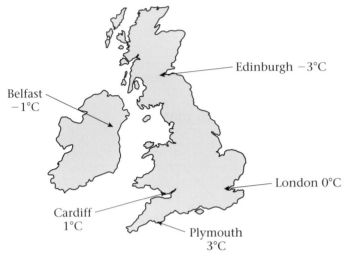

The map shows the temperature in 5 cities, at midnight, one night last year.

(a) Arrange the temperatures in order.
Start with the lowest. **(2 marks)**

(b) Write down the city that has a temperature that is

(i) 2 degrees lower than Belfast.

(ii) 2 degrees higher than Cardiff. **(2 marks)**

3

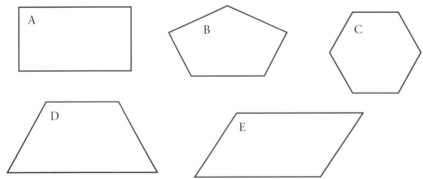

Two of these shapes have only **one** line of symmetry.

(a) Write down the letters of these **two** shapes. **(2 marks)**

Two of these shapes have rotational symmetry of order 2.

(b) Write down the letters of these **two** shapes. **(2 marks)**

4 Write down the names of these 3-D shapes.

(a)

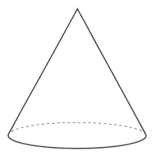

(b)

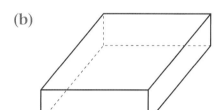

(2 marks)

5 Mary uses the formula | Pay = hours worked × rate of pay |
to work out her pay.

Work out Mary's pay when her hours worked are
8 and her rate of pay is £4. **(2 marks)**

6 Solve the equations.
(a) $p + 4 = 7$ **(1 mark)**
(b) $3t = 15$ **(1 mark)**

7 (a) Draw a line 9 cm long. **(1 mark)**
(b) Mark with a cross (X) a point halfway along
the line you have drawn. **(1 mark)**
(c) Draw a circle with a diameter of 9 cm. **(2 marks)**

8 Gary goes shopping.

He buys a magazine for £3.75
2 bags of sweets at £1.25 each
3 bars of chocolate at 80p each.

He pays with a £10 note.
How much change should he receive? **(4 marks)**

9 Work out
(a) $\frac{1}{4}$ of 20 **(1 mark)**
(b) $\frac{2}{3}$ of £45 **(2 marks)**

10 Here is a mileage chart.

It gives information on distance between these places.

York

24	Leeds			
71	44	Manchester		
96	69	35	Preston	
133	120	166	154	Birmingham

(a) Write down the distance from Leeds to Preston.

(1 mark)

Susie travelled from
York to Leeds then from
Leeds to Manchester then from
Manchester to Birmingham.
She then travelled home to York from Birmingham.

(b) Work out the total distance she travelled. **(3 marks)**

11

(a) What type of triangle is Triangle A? **(1 mark)**

(b) Which **two** of these triangles are congruent
to Triangle A?

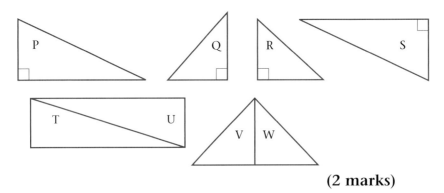

(2 marks)

12 Work out

(a) $\frac{1}{4} + \frac{3}{8}$ **(2 marks)**

(b) $\frac{1}{4} \times \frac{2}{3}$ **(2 marks)**

13 Simone is thinking about buying a new TV on a credit agreement.
The cash price is £1200.
The deposit on the credit agreement is £120 followed by 15 payments of £100.
Work out how much extra the TV would cost Simone if she bought the TV using the credit agreement rather than paying the cash price.

(3 marks)

14 Here is triangle *PQR*.

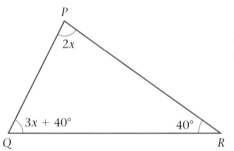

Diagram NOT accurately drawn

Angle $P = 2x$
Angle $Q = 3x + 40°$
Angle $R = 40°$
Work out the value of x. **(3 marks)**

15

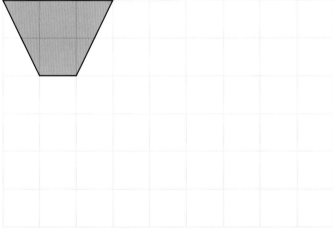

The diagram shows a trapezium drawn on a grid of centimetre squares.

On a copy of the grid, show how this trapezium tessellates.
You should draw at least 5 trapeziums. **(2 marks)**

16 Using ruler and compasses, draw an equilateral triangle with a side length of 6 cm. **(2 marks)**

17 Amy, Beth and Colin share 27 sweets in the ratio $2:3:4$. Work out the number of sweets that each of them receives. **(3 marks)**

18 n is an integer.
   (a) Write down all the values for n in the inequality $-3 \leqslant n < 2$ **(2 marks)**
   (b) Solve the inequality $5x + 3 > 2$ **(2 marks)**

19 Dennis sails his boat from a port P to a lighthouse L.
   (a) Measure and write down the bearing of the lighthouse L from the port P.

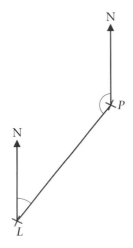

Scale: 1 cm represents 5 km   (1 mark)

From the lighthouse L, Dennis sails on a bearing of 300°. He sails for 40 km on this bearing to a port Q.

   (b) Copy the diagram. Mark port Q with a cross (X) and label it Q.
      Use the scale of 1 cm to represent 5 km. **(2 marks)**

20 Change 3.5 m² into cm². **(2 marks)**

Total for Section B: 60 marks

Formulae sheet

Area of trapezium $= \frac{1}{2}(a + b)h$

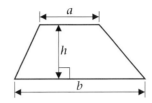

Volume of prism = area of cross-section × length

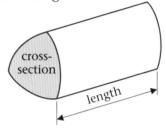

Answers

Exercise 1A

1. (a) 7566 (b) 29283 (c) 17723
   (d) 15164 (e) 45648 (f) 31218
   (g) 7675 (h) 16180 (i) 53308
2. (a) 24 remainder 2 (b) 56
   (c) 46 (d) 43
   (e) 35 remainder 12 (f) 23
   (g) 69 remainder 2 (h) 46 remainder 2
   (i) 38

Exercise 1B

1. (a) −7 (b) 4 (c) 10 (d) 9
   (e) −1 (f) 2 (g) −2 (h) −10
2. (a) 24 (b) −15 (c) −8 (d) 3
   (e) −40 (f) −6 (g) −30 (h) 2
3. 11 metres
4. −18°C
5. (a)

	1st number		
×	−3	5	−8
2nd	2	−6	10	−16
number	−7	21	−35	56
	4	−12	20	−32

(b)

	1st number		
−	3	−5	7
2nd	−2	5	−3	9
number	4	−1	−9	3
	−3	6	−2	10

(c)

	1st number		
+	−1	−3	6
2nd	4	3	1	10
number	7	6	4	13
	−2	−3	−5	4

(d)

	1st number		
÷	8	−16	−24
2nd	−2	−4	8	12
number	4	2	−4	−6
	−8	−1	2	3

Exercise 1C

1	6.2	2	5.45	3	0.8	4	20.02
5	2.953	6	3.24	7	17.97	8	39.38
9	9.427	10	158.88	11	106.2	12	8.68
13	3.3	14	388.555				

Exercise 1D

1. (a) 34.4 (b) 7.98 (c) 0.0798
   (d) 20.1 (e) 0.1692 (f) 1.692
   (g) 0.1692 (h) 0.0632 (i) 11.31
2. (a) £16.38 (b) £7.80
   (c) £2.03 (d) £13.05
3. (a) 38.4 pints (b) 62.4 pints (c) 134.4 pints
4. (a) £92.15 (b) £160.05 (c) £315.25
5. (a) £71.40 (b) £166.60 (c) £220.15
6. (a) 38.25 l (b) 63.75 l (c) 140.25 l

Exercise 1E

1. 1.8   2. 3.7   3. 0.825
4. 3.356   5. 25.4   6. 4.65
7. £12.50
8. 13 cans (with half a can left over)
9. (a) 3 (b) 4.2 (c) 7.9
   (d) 47 (e) 5.23 (f) 2.8
10. £62.50

Exercise 1F

1. 1500 m
2. (a) 150 miles (b) 400 miles
3. (a) 10 h (b) 16 h (c) 7 h
4. (a) 4 s (b) 7 s (c) 50 s
5. 250 ml 6. 3.6 kg   7. 9 m
8. 4 mm   9. 15 cm   10. 36 l
11. $5\frac{1}{2}$ ft   12. 90 kg
13. 320 km
14. 48 km per hour

Exercise 1G

1. (a) 4^3 (b) 2^6
   (c) $5^3 \times 7^2$ (d) $3 \times 5^2 \times 11^3$
2. (a) 27 (b) 648 (c) 49 (d) 16
3. (a) $x = 4$ (b) $n = 7$ (c) $m = 0$
4. (a) 6^6 (b) 5^6 (c) 7^9 (d) 10^3
   (e) 8^3 (f) 10^2 (g) 4^2 (h) 3^3
   (i) 2^9 (j) 5^9 (k) 3^4 (l) 4^2
   (m) 3^3 (n) 5^{10} (o) 7 (p) $2^0 = 1$
   (q) x^7 (r) z^2 (s) c^5 (t) y^3
   (u) 4^6 (v) 3^6

Exercise 1H

1. (a) $\frac{1}{6}$ (b) $\frac{1}{3}$ (c) $\frac{1}{2}$
   (d) $\frac{1}{7}$ (e) $\frac{1}{9}$ (f) $\frac{1}{20}$
2. (a) 10 (b) 2 (c) 4
   (d) $\frac{5}{2}$ or $2\frac{1}{2}$ (e) $\frac{10}{3}$ or $3\frac{1}{3}$ (f) 8
3. (a) $1\frac{2}{3}$ (b) $3\frac{1}{2}$ (c) 4
   (d) 8 (e) $5\frac{1}{3}$ (f) $1\frac{3}{5}$
4. (a) $\frac{1}{m}$ (b) $\frac{1}{y}$ (c) x (d) $\frac{1}{y^3}$

Mixed exercise 1

1 (a) 10 591   (b) 23 646   (c) 31   (d) 53
2 (a) -9 (b) 10   (c) 4   (d) 2
3 (a) -16 (b) 2   (c) -2 (d) 35
4 (a) 12.5   (b) 12.3   (c) 93.7   (d) 10.63
5 £26.50
6 (a) 39.36   (b) 21.45   (c) 0.75   (d) 89
7 106.7 miles
8 (a) (i) 7°C   (ii) -10°C
   (b) (i) 6°C   (ii) 8°C
   (c) -7°C
9 (a) £458.40   (b) £14.50
10 (a) £34.10   (b) €782.26
11 (a) (i) 280 km   (ii) 700 km
   (b) (i) 3 hours   (ii) $5\frac{1}{2}$ hours
12 6 cm
13 5 kg
14 (a) 3^3 (b) 5^4
   (c) $5^2 \times 7^2 \times 9$ (d) $3^2 \times 5^2$
15 (a) 343   (b) 1296   (c) 1
   (d) 432   (e) 72   (f) 343
16 (a) 3   (b) 5   (c) 4
17 (a) 2^9 (b) 5^9 (c) 3^5 (d) 7
   (e) 9^3 (f) 7^2 (g) 4^3 (h) $3^0 = 1$
18 (a) $\frac{1}{9}$ (b) $\frac{1}{6}$ (c) 2   (d) 1.6
   (e) $\frac{5}{4}$ (f) $\frac{7}{3}$ or $2\frac{1}{3}$ (g) $\frac{1}{x}$ (h) y
19 Large tub, 1.9p per gram
   Regular tub, 2p per gram
   The large tub is better value.

Exercise 2A

1 (a) $\frac{3}{10}$ (b) $\frac{1}{7}$ (c) $\frac{1}{7}$ (d) $\frac{3}{35}$
   (e) $\frac{4}{15}$ (f) $\frac{3}{32}$ (g) $\frac{5}{36}$ (h) $\frac{1}{11}$
   (i) $\frac{5}{12}$ (j) $\frac{2}{15}$
2 (a) $2\frac{2}{3}$ (b) $1\frac{1}{5}$ (c) $3\frac{3}{4}$ (d) $3\frac{1}{2}$
   (e) $1\frac{1}{7}$ (f) $1\frac{1}{2}$ (g) $1\frac{1}{5}$ (h) $2\frac{2}{7}$
3 $3\frac{1}{2}$ inches   **4** $4\frac{1}{5}$ litres
5 $3\frac{1}{3}$ litres   **6** $2\frac{1}{4}$ hours

Exercise 2B

1 (a) 9   (b) 4   (c) 10   (d) 20
   (e) 12   (f) 8   (g) 20   (h) 40
   (i) £13.50   (j) 4.5 m   (k) 90 p   (l) 16 kg
2 50 g   **3** 18 houses   **4** 40 matches
5 £24   **6** 21   **7** £625

Exercise 2C

1 (a) 0.5   (b) 0.25   (c) 0.75   (d) 0.6
   (e) 0.7   (f) 0.55   (g) 0.625   (h) 0.17
   (i) 0.875   (j) 0.8
2 (a) $\frac{3}{10}$ (b) $\frac{3}{5}$ (c) $\frac{21}{100}$ (d) $\frac{9}{25}$
   (e) $\frac{789}{1000}$ (f) $\frac{623}{1000}$ (g) $\frac{1}{50}$ (h) $\frac{31}{1000}$
   (i) $\frac{1}{125}$ (j) $\frac{203}{1000}$

Exercise 2D

1 (a) $\frac{8}{15}$ (b) $\frac{7}{15}$
2 (a) 0   (b) $\frac{1}{2}$ (c) $\frac{1}{8}$
3 (a) $\frac{1}{12}$ (b) $\frac{5}{36}$ (c) $\frac{1}{3}$ (d) $\frac{4}{9}$

4 $\frac{3}{5}$ **5** $\frac{3}{10}$ **7** $\frac{5}{7}$
7 (a) $\frac{3}{5}$ (b) $\frac{2}{5}$
8 $\frac{1}{5}$ **9** $\frac{19}{20}$
10 (a) $\frac{2}{5}$ (b) $\frac{12}{25}$ (c) $\frac{3}{25}$

Exercise 2E

1 (a) 1   (b) $\frac{6}{7}$ (c) $\frac{2}{3}$ (d) $\frac{1}{4}$ (e) $\frac{2}{5}$
   (f) $\frac{1}{3}$ (g) $1\frac{1}{5}$ (h) $1\frac{2}{3}$ (i) $1\frac{1}{5}$ (j) 1
2 (a) $1\frac{1}{4}$ (b) $1\frac{3}{8}$ (c) $1\frac{1}{2}$
   (d) $\frac{1}{4}$ (e) $\frac{1}{2}$ (f) $\frac{1}{4}$
   (g) $\frac{11}{12}$ (h) $1\frac{3}{20}$ (i) $\frac{23}{24}$
   (j) $\frac{5}{12}$ (k) $\frac{2}{15}$ (l) $\frac{27}{40}$
   (m) $\frac{41}{60}$ (n) $\frac{69}{77}$ (o) $1\frac{31}{52}$
   (p) $\frac{26}{63}$ (q) $\frac{14}{65}$ (r) $\frac{7}{60}$
3 (a) 4   (b) $5\frac{4}{5}$ (c) $5\frac{5}{7}$
   (d) $3\frac{1}{4}$ (e) $3\frac{1}{2}$ (f) $1\frac{1}{4}$
   (g) $6\frac{3}{4}$ (h) $3\frac{7}{10}$ (i) $1\frac{3}{8}$
   (j) $3\frac{1}{15}$ (k) $3\frac{26}{35}$ (l) $4\frac{20}{21}$
   (m) $2\frac{4}{21}$ (n) $3\frac{19}{40}$
4 $1\frac{1}{4}$ kg   **5** $\frac{7}{12}$ hour
6 (a) $\frac{17}{30}$ (b) $\frac{13}{30}$
7 $1\frac{1}{8}$ kg   **8** $2\frac{1}{8}$ m
9 3 hours   **10** $2\frac{1}{4}$ m

Exercise 2F

1 (a) $\frac{1}{5}$ (b) $\frac{2}{7}$ (c) $\frac{5}{16}$ (d) $\frac{1}{14}$ (e) $\frac{3}{20}$
   (f) $\frac{4}{15}$ (g) $\frac{7}{96}$ (h) $\frac{9}{40}$ (i) $\frac{1}{27}$ (j) $\frac{1}{14}$
2 $\frac{3}{20}$ **3** $\frac{1}{4}$ kg
4 $\frac{1}{4}$ hour   **5** $\frac{5}{8}$ yards

Exercise 2G

1 $\frac{2}{5}$ **2** $\frac{2}{5}$ **3** $\frac{1}{4}$
4 $\frac{3}{25}$ **5** $\frac{3}{7}$ **6** $\frac{3}{7}$
7 $\frac{4}{9}$ **8** $\frac{1}{2}$ **9** $\frac{2}{15}$
10 $\frac{2}{11}$ **11** $\frac{2}{25}$ **12** $\frac{3}{19}$

Exercise 2H

1 (a) $\frac{2}{15}$ (b) $\frac{1}{2}$ (c) $\frac{3}{10}$ (d) $\frac{1}{2}$ (e) $\frac{5}{6}$
   (f) $4\frac{8}{9}$ (g) $\frac{4}{11}$ (h) $\frac{1}{9}$ (i) $1\frac{1}{5}$ (j) $1\frac{1}{4}$
2 (a) $1\frac{1}{8}$ (b) $2\frac{3}{4}$ (c) $5\frac{5}{18}$ (d) $16\frac{1}{5}$
   (e) $3\frac{1}{4}$ (f) $10\frac{4}{5}$ (g) $3\frac{3}{4}$ (h) $\frac{3}{4}$
3 (a) $1\frac{1}{11}$ (b) $1\frac{11}{13}$ (c) $1\frac{9}{11}$ (d) $1\frac{13}{17}$
   (e) $3\frac{1}{7}$ (f) $8\frac{1}{6}$ (g) 12   (h) $13\frac{1}{3}$
4 8   **5** $7\frac{1}{8}$ kg
6 $1\frac{1}{2}$ hours   **7** $3\frac{1}{14}$

Mixed exercise 2

1 (a) $\frac{6}{35}$ (b) $\frac{8}{45}$ (c) $\frac{15}{28}$
2 (a) $1\frac{4}{11}$ (b) $1\frac{5}{7}$ (c) 4

3 3 hours

4 (a) 24   (b) 9   (c) 18

5 36

6 (a) 0.75   (b) 0.125   (c) 0.3

   (d) 0.65   (e) 0.8   (f) 0.27

7 (a) $\frac{7}{10}$ (b) $\frac{381}{1000}$ (c) $\frac{27}{100}$

   (d) $\frac{3}{100}$ (e) $\frac{9}{250}$ (f) $\frac{1}{500}$

8 (a) $\frac{1}{5}$ (b) $\frac{4}{5}$

9 (a) $\frac{12}{25}$ (b) $\frac{8}{25}$

10 (a) $\frac{5}{7}$ (b) $\frac{3}{11}$ (c) $1\frac{1}{2}$ (d) $\frac{1}{3}$

11 (a) $1\frac{7}{15}$ (b) $\frac{7}{20}$ (c) $\frac{3}{8}$ (d) $1\frac{1}{10}$

12 (a) $5\frac{5}{8}$ (b) $3\frac{11}{20}$ (c) $3\frac{9}{10}$ (d) $2\frac{7}{30}$

13 $\frac{5}{12}$

14 $3\frac{3}{4}$ kg

15 $1\frac{1}{8}$ yards

16 (a) $\frac{2}{9}$ (b) $\frac{2}{5}$ (c) $\frac{7}{32}$ (d) $\frac{2}{15}$

17 $\frac{5}{24}$

18 (a) $\frac{1}{2}$ (b) $\frac{2}{3}$ (c) $\frac{5}{48}$ (d) $\frac{1}{2}$

19 $2\frac{1}{2}$ kg

20 $\frac{3}{4}$ hour

21 (a) $\frac{1}{2}$ (b) $\frac{4}{5}$ (c) $3\frac{3}{4}$

   (d) $\frac{2}{7}$ (e) $2\frac{10}{27}$ (f) $4\frac{2}{5}$

22 6 lessons

23 $6\frac{1}{8}$ pints

24 (a) 170 minutes

   (b) (i) 80   (ii) 300   (iii) 420 men

   (c) 40%

Exercise 3A

1 (a) $\frac{1}{5}$ (b) $\frac{1}{2}$ (c) $\frac{1}{4}$ (d) $\frac{3}{4}$

   (e) $\frac{8}{25}$ (f) $\frac{16}{25}$ (g) $\frac{3}{8}$ (h) $\frac{5}{8}$

2 (a) 0.3   (b) 0.7   (c) 0.45   (d) 0.85

   (e) 0.32   (f) 0.51   (g) 0.185   (h) 0.725

3 (a) 24%   (b) 30%   (c) 55%   (d) 60%

   (e) 37%   (f) $23\frac{1}{2}$%   (g) $17\frac{1}{2}$%   (h) $42\frac{1}{2}$%

4 (a) 90%   (b) 30%   (c) 60%   (d) 20%

   (e) $57\frac{1}{2}$%   (f) 16%   (g) 34%   (h) 37%

5 (a) Tim

   (b) $\frac{4}{5}$ is 80% which is more than 75%.

6 (a) £570   (b) 37.5%

7 90 out of 120 is 75%.

   24 out of 30 is 80%.

   24 out of 30 is better.

Exercise 3B

1 (a) £30   (b) £5.70

   (c) £6.13 (to nearest p)   (d) £30

   (e) £7920   (f) £4.63 (to nearest penny)

2 (a) £780   (b) £16 380

3 £16 740

4 Sofa £315, Bed £139.30, Coffee table £21.35

5 (a) £16.71   (b) £3.14   (c) £1373.75

6 £206.25

7 €8

8 (a) £0.93   (b) £52.43

9 £113.70

10 (a) £19 440   (b) £188

   (c) £17 560   (d) £4051.20

11 (a) $\frac{7}{100}$ (b) 0.18   (c) 40 families

Exercise 3C

1 (a) £31.50   (b) £51

2 £470   **3** £44 800

4 £297   **5** £254.40

6 £11 480   **7** £18 962.50

8 £270.25

9 (a) £350   (b) £131.25

   (c) £196.88 (nearest penny)

10 (a) £14 040   (b) £17 992   (c) £25 688

11 Ladder £96.35, tin of paint £7.05, electric drill £44.06

12 (a) 440 g   (b) 1.65 g   (c) 247.5 g

13 (a) £678 950   (b) £1 322 750

   (c) £2 127 500   (d) £334 800

14 £3055.50

Exercise 3D

1 90%   **2** 80%

3 (a) 26%   (b) 38.4%   (c) 35.6%

4 (a) $66\frac{2}{3}$%   (b) $33\frac{1}{3}$%

5 20%   **6** 17.5%   **7** 25%

8 20%   **9** 37.5%   **10** 22%

Exercise 3E

1 (a) 2:1   (b) 3:1   (c) 3:1

   (d) 3:2   (e) 5:3   (f) 3:2

   (g) 5:3   (h) 10:3   (i) 3:2

   (j) 2:1   (k) 4:2:1   (l) 5:4:1

   (m) 5:3:1

2 2:3   **3** 1:3   **4** 9:4

5 5:21   **6** 3:10   **7** 4:3:2

Exercise 3F

1 150 g   **2** 300 ml

3 30 l   **4** 125 cups of coffee

5 3000 g (3 kg)   **6** 4000 cm = 40 m

7 160 cm

8 (a) 1150 m   (b) 675 m

Exercise 3G

1 (a) $x = 3$ (b) $x = 4$ (c) $x = 2$ (d) $x = 2$

   (e) $x = 3$ (f) $x = 18$ (g) $x = 12$ (h) $x = 40$

2 9 men   **3** 2 turns   **4** 28 cm

5 30 cashews   **6** 9.6 cm   **7** £216.80

8 (a) 4:1   (b) 25 A3 sheets

Exercise 3H

1 (a) £6   (b) £18

2 (a) £4   (b) £32

3 (a) £1.20   (b) £4

4 500 g flour, 250 g sugar, 125 g butter

5 (a) €404.15   (b) £194.85

6 (a) £250   (b) £187.50

7 4 days

8 5 days

9 6 hours

Exercise 3I

1 (a) 100 km (b) 250 km (c) 25 km
2 (a) 3 hours (b) 5 hours 50 minutes
   (c) 2 hours 20 minutes
3 (a) £1.50 (b) £19.50
4 (a) £3.74 (b) £41.14
5 (a) 6000 words (b) 333 words (to nearest word)
   (c) 1667 words (to nearest word)
6 9 minutes 22.5 seconds
7 3.75 m
8 (a) 8.78 volts (3 s.f.) (b) 5.70 amperes (3 s.f.)
9 (a) 161.3 miles (1 d.p.) (b) 5.58 litres
10 12 oz flour, 6 oz butter, 3 oz sugar
11 1250 g potatoes, 500 g tomatoes, 125 g flour and
    $37\frac{1}{2}$ g butter

Exercise 3J

1 (a) 15 and 10
   (b) 70 and 30
   (c) £24 and £6
   (d) £14.35 and £10.25
   (e) 200, 100 and 50
   (f) 90 cm, 30 cm and 30 cm
   (g) £120, £90 and £30
   (h) £20.50, £12.30 and £4.10
2 Juan gets £96, Gabrielle gets £64 and Kwame gets £40
3 800 women
4 $\frac{4}{7}$ 5 17.5 cm   6 1 : 4   7 3 : 5

Mixed exercise 3

1 (i) (a) $\frac{3}{10}$ (b) $\frac{9}{10}$ (c) $\frac{7}{20}$ (d) $\frac{17}{20}$
       (e) $\frac{9}{50}$ (f) $\frac{16}{25}$ (g) $\frac{7}{40}$ (h) $\frac{17}{40}$
   (ii) (a) 0.3 (b) 0.9 (c) 0.35 (d) 0.85
        (e) 0.18 (f) 0.64 (g) 0.175 (h) 0.425
2 (a) 50% (b) 20% (c) 80% (d) 65%
   (e) 65% (f) 56% (g) $27\frac{1}{2}$% (h) $27\frac{1}{2}$%
3 Lucy saved the most since $\frac{3}{4}$ = 75% is less than 76%
4 (a) £29.38 (b) £58.74 (c) £10 293
5 (a) €4.50 (b) €3.75 (c) €2.48
6 (a) 68 (b) 12
7 £37.40   8 80%
9 £900   10 £3.75
11 65%   12 No, the increase is 12.5%
13 10 : 5 : 4
14 (a) 2 m (b) 1.8 cm
15 (a) x = 8 (b) x = 4
16 5 cm   17 Pamela receives £70
18 3 : 2
19 (a) 12 days (b) $4\frac{1}{2}$ days
20 £4.80
21 7.5 m
22 990 g (3 s.f.)
23 35.6 cm (3 s.f.)
24 (a) $\frac{1}{4}$ (b) $\frac{11}{20}$
25 £105
26 (a) (i) £1250 (ii) $\frac{1}{25}$
    (b) 12 : 5
27 (a) 8 days (b) £75.20

Exercise 4A

1 (a) Equation (b) Equation (c) Expression
   (d) Formula (e) Formula (f) Expression
   (g) Identity (h) Identity

2 (a) Formula (b) Identity (c) Expression
   (d) Equation (e) Formula (f) Expression

Exercise 4B

1 (a) 8 (b) 0 (c) 5 (d) 30
   (e) 9 (f) 66 (g) 40 (h) 18
   (i) 9 (j) 26 (k) 9 (l) 54
   (m) 64 (n) 1
2 (a) 1 (b) $3\frac{1}{2}$ (c) $1\frac{1}{2}$ (d) $\frac{1}{2}$
   (e) $\frac{5}{16}$ (f) $1\frac{1}{16}$ (g) 0 (h) 0
   (i) $\frac{9}{16}$ (j) 10 (k) 4 (l) $\frac{3}{32}$
   (m) 1
3 (a) 1 (b) 11 (c) 13.5 (d) 9.5
   (e) 9.75 (f) −8.5 (g) 12.5 (h) 7
   (i) 1.25 (j) 27 (k) 27 (l) 9.25
   (m) −1.828 125

Exercise 4C

1 1   2 −11   3 11
4 −3   5 8   6 −1
7 −8   8 −2   9 2
10 0   11 28   12 −30
13 5   14 −36   15 2
16 −18   17 −30   18 54
19 30   20 −6   21 −15
22 −20   23 18   24 −2
25 25   26 6   27 97
28 14   29 65   30 16
31 1   32 1   33 49
34 9   35 432   36 −375
37 −48   38 32   39 −11
40 −27   41 0.25   42 20.25

Exercise 4D

1 (a) x^6 (b) $3x^5$
2 (a) x^9 (b) x^9 (c) x^{11} (d) x^{13}
   (e) x^3 (f) x^6 (g) x^5 (h) x^2
   (i) x^{10} (j) x^{36} (k) x^{35} (l) x^{32}
3 (a) x^{18} (b) x^{13} (c) x^5
4 (a) $14x^8$ (b) $30x^{10}$ (c) $40x^9$ (d) $30x^{13}$
   (e) $6x^3$ (f) $3x^4$ (g) $7x^6$ (h) $5x^5$
   (i) x^6 (j) x^{15} (k) x^{24} (l) x^{20}
5 (a) x^{10} (b) x^7 (c) x^8 (d) $7x^5$
   (e) $40x^6$ (f) $24x^8$ (g) $5x^3$ (h) $3x^7$
   (i) $6x^9$ (j) x (k) x (l) $5x$
   (m) $7x$

Mixed exercise 4

1 $P = 2ab$ formula, $2ab + 3c$ expression,
   $2(x^2 + 3x) = 2x^2 + 6x$ identity, $3 (x + 1) = 9$ equation,
   πr^2 expression
2 (a) 11 (b) 21 (c) 0 (d) 56
   (e) 26 (f) 14 (g) 24 (h) 0
   (i) 98 (j) 81 (k) 64 (l) 27
   (m) 4 (n) 0.0625 (o) 7
3 (a) 1 (b) 7 (c) 2 (d) −6
   (e) 4 (f) 24 (g) −4 (h) 0
   (i) −12 (j) 12 (k) −18 (l) −128
   (m) $\frac{1}{4}$ (n) 4 (o) 5

4 (a) x^9 (b) x^3 (c) x^{15} (d) x
   (e) x^5 (f) x^{12} (g) 1 (h) x^6
   (i) x^{11} (j) x^9 (k) x^3 (l) x
5 (a) $4x^8$ (b) $15x^8$ (c) $21x^5$ (d) $4x^4$
   (e) $8x^5$ (f) $9x$ (g) x^{10} (h) x^9
6 (a) a^7 (b) $15x^3y^4$

Exercise 5A

1 $x - 7 = 9$ **2** $x + 3 = 11$
3 $8x = 32$ **4** $9 + x = 20$
5 $7x - 3 = 32$ **6** $3x = 21$
7 $3(x + 1) = 24$ **8** $4x + 5 = 13$
9 $2(5 + x) = 16$ **10** $7 + 5x = 27$
11 (a) $x + 7 = 11$ (b) 4
12 (a) $5x = 45$ (b) 9
13 (a) $4(x + 2) = 36$ (b) 7
14 (a) $2x - 5 = 12$ (b) 8.5
15 (a) $6x + 7 = 31$ (b) 4
16 (a) $x - 8 = 7$ (b) 15
17 (a) $8x = 56$ (b) 7
18 (a) $6(x + 2) = 42$ (b) 5
19 (a) $5x - 1 = 29$ (b) 6
20 (a) $9(x - 4) = 54$ (b) 10

Exercise 5B

1 $p = 3$ **2** $a = 5$ **3** $h = 9$
4 $c = 11$ **5** $n = 0$ **6** $g = 5$
7 $t = 9$ **8** $n = 8$ **9** $x = 14$
10 $v = 11$ **11** $d = 8$ **12** $c = 5$
13 $q = 7$ **14** $f = 7$ **15** $k = 0$
16 $y = 10$ **17** $r = 42$ **18** $g = 45$
19 $b = 48$ **20** $m = 0$

Exercise 5C

1 $y = 4$ **2** $a = 5$ **3** $h = 3$
4 $e = 3$ **5** $d = 2$ **6** $c = 1$
7 $u = 0$ **8** $v = 3\frac{1}{2}$ **9** $x = -1$
10 $p = 1\frac{3}{4}$ **11** $q = 2\frac{3}{5}$ **12** $k = 2\frac{3}{8}$
13 $f = 1\frac{1}{2}$ **14** $n = 3\frac{2}{5}$ **15** $e = 2\frac{1}{2}$

Exercise 5D

1 $a = -4$ **2** $c = 5$ **3** $p = 6$
4 $b = 1$ **5** $q = 3$ **6** $x = 3$
7 $d = 5$ **8** $y = 3$ **9** $n = 7$
10 $k = 0$ **11** $u = 2\frac{1}{2}$ **12** $r = 2\frac{2}{5}$
13 $v = 4\frac{2}{3}$ **14** $t = \frac{4}{5}$ **15** $m = 2\frac{1}{2}$
16 $g = \frac{5}{6}$ **17** $b = \frac{1}{2}$ **18** $h = 1\frac{1}{3}$
19 $e = 4\frac{1}{2}$ **20** $f = \frac{2}{3}$
21 (a) $x = 3$ (b) $y = 6$

Exercise 5E

1 $a = 19$ **2** $b = 5$ **3** $c = 24$
4 $d = 10$ **5** $e = 6$ **6** $f = 16$
7 $g = 6$ **8** $h = 21$ **9** $m = 7$
10 $n = 15$ **11** $p = \frac{1}{3}$ **12** $q = 0$
13 $t = -4$ **14** $v = \frac{4}{5}$ **15** $x = -6$
16 $y = 1\frac{2}{3}$ **17** $a = -1$ **18** $b = 4\frac{1}{2}$
19 $c = \frac{2}{3}$ **20** $d = -2$ **21** $x = -2\frac{1}{3}$

Exercise 5F

1 $x = 2$ **2** $x = 4$ **3** $x = 13$
4 $x = 2$ **5** $x = 1$ **6** $x = 3$
7 $x = 1$ **8** $x = 4$ **9** $x = 8$
10 $x = 2$ **11** $x = 1$ **12** $x = 4$
13 $x = -3$ **14** $x = 0$ **15** $x = 2\frac{1}{2}$
16 $x = \frac{3}{5}$ **17** $x = -1$ **18** $x = 1\frac{2}{3}$
19 $x = -2$ **20** $x = -\frac{2}{3}$

Exercise 5G

1 8 **2** $a = 40°$, largest angle is $80°$
3 12 **4** $130°, 80°, 150°$
5 $8\,\text{cm}, 9\,\text{cm}, 7\,\text{cm}$ **6** 11
7 $y = 7$ **8** 52
9 $15\,\text{cm}$ **10** $x = 6$ $y = 4$

Exercise 5H

1 $x = \pm 7$ **2** $x = \pm 8$ **3** $x = \pm 5$
4 $x = \pm 3$ **5** $x = \pm 6$ **6** $x = \pm 3$
7 $x = \pm 2$ **8** $x = \pm\frac{3}{8}$ **9** $x = \pm\frac{5}{2}$
10 $x = \pm\frac{1}{2}$ **11** $x = \pm\frac{3}{7}$ **12** $x = \pm\frac{6}{5}$
13 $x = \pm\frac{1}{4}$ **14** $x = \pm\frac{9}{2}$ **15** $x = \pm 2$

Exercise 5I

1 $x = 1.83$ **2** $x = 4.02$ **3** $x = 4.4$
4 $x = 9.9$ **5** $x = 3.11$ **6** $x = 2.81$
7 $x = 3.3$

Exercise 5J

1 (a)

(b)

(c)

(d)

(e)

(f)

(g)

(h)

(i)

(j)

2 (a) $4 < 7$ (b) $-15 < -9$
   (c) $3 > -11$ (d) $-23 > -27$
   (e) $(2 + 3) > (5 - 1)$ (f) $(-2 + 3) > (2 - 3)$
   (g) $(15 - 4) > (3 - 14)$ (h) $(0 - 6) > (0 - 15)$

3 (a) $x > -2$ (b) $x \leqslant 1$
   (c) $x < -1$ (d) $x \geqslant 1$

4 (a)

   (b)

   (c)

   (d)

5 (a) $-3 \leqslant x \leqslant 1$ (b) $-4 < x \leqslant -2$ (c) $0 < x < 4$

Exercise 5K

1 $x < 4$ **2** $x \geqslant 6$ **3** $x \leqslant 6$
4 $x > 6$ **5** $x < 9$ **6** $x > 4$
7 $x \geqslant 0$ **8** $x \leqslant 5$ **9** $x \geqslant 3$
10 $x < 2$ **11** $x > 3$ **12** $x \geqslant 1$
13 $x > 2\frac{3}{4}$

14 $x \leqslant \frac{1}{2}$

15 $x \geqslant -2$

16 $x > \frac{5}{4}$

17 $x < -1\frac{1}{2}$

18 $x \leqslant \frac{3}{4}$

19 2, 3, 4
20 $-3, -2, -1, 0, 1$
21 $-2, -1, 0, 1$
22 0, 1, 2, 3
23 $-3, -2, -1, 0$
24 1, 2, 3
25 $-1, 0, 1, 2, 3$
26 $-2, -1, 0, 1, 2$
27 $-3, -2, -1$
28 $x < 2\frac{1}{2}$ **29** $x \geqslant \frac{3}{4}$ **30** $x > -3$
31 $x \geqslant -2\frac{2}{3}$ **32** $x > -8$ **33** $x > 3\frac{1}{2}$
34 $x \geqslant 2\frac{3}{4}$ **35** $x \leqslant -\frac{2}{3}$ **36** $x > \frac{7}{8}$
37 $x > 1$ **38** $x \geqslant 2$ **39** $x \leqslant -1$

40 $x > -1\frac{2}{3}$ **41** $x < 2\frac{1}{2}$ **42** $x \leqslant 3$
43 $x \geqslant 7$ **44** $x > 0$ **45** $x < 3$
46 $x \geqslant 6$ **47** $x < 2$ **48** $x > -\frac{4}{5}$
49 $x \leqslant 1$ **50** $x \leqslant 3$ **51** $x < 2\frac{1}{5}$
52 $x \geqslant 2$ **53** $x \geqslant \frac{1}{2}$ **54** $x < -3$
55 $x > -4\frac{2}{3}$, smallest integer satisfying inequality is -4
56 $x \leqslant -\frac{3}{5}$, largest integer satisfying inequality is -1

Mixed exercise 5

1 (a) $a = 5$ (b) $c = 10$ (c) $p = 7$
   (d) $d = 12$ (e) $x = 3$ (f) $b = 4$
   (g) $r = 3$ (h) $x = 5$ (i) $c = 5$
   (j) $b = \frac{1}{2}$ (k) $d = 1\frac{2}{3}$ (l) $y = \frac{4}{5}$
   (m) $t = 2\frac{1}{3}$ (n) $w = 2\frac{1}{2}$

2 (a) $a = -4$ (b) $b = -6$ (c) $c = -1$
   (d) $e = -5\frac{1}{2}$ (e) $h = -2$ (f) $m = -\frac{3}{4}$
   (g) $p = -2\frac{5}{6}$ (h) $q = -\frac{2}{3}$ (i) $u = -3$
   (j) $w = -6\frac{1}{2}$ (k) $y = -2\frac{1}{2}$

3 (a) $a = 3$ (b) $b = 7$ (c) $c = 5$
   (d) $d = 7$ (e) $e = 6$ (f) $f = 3\frac{3}{7}$
   (g) $m = 1$ (h) $t = 3\frac{1}{4}$ (i) $a = 3$
   (j) $b = 4$ (k) $d = \frac{1}{2}$ (l) $g = -\frac{2}{3}$
   (m) $p = -4\frac{2}{3}$

4 48 cm

5 (a) $x = 2$ (b) $y = \frac{1}{2}$
6 (a) $x = 4$ (b) $y = 3\frac{1}{2}$ (c) $2t + 23$
7 $x = -1\frac{1}{2}$
8 (a) $4x + 10$ (b) $x = 6$
9 (a) $a = \pm3$ (b) $b = \pm2$
   (c) $b = \pm\frac{8}{3}$ (d) $d = \pm5$
10 (a) $x = 2.35$ (b) $x = 4.55$ (c) $x = 4.27$
   (d) $x = 3.76$ (e) $x = 2.4$ (f) $x = 1.77$
11 $x = 1.7$
12 (a) 55.9
   (b) Yousef is correct. The answer lies between 3.65 and 3.7.

13 (a)

   (b)

   (c)

   (d)

   (e)

   (f)

   (g)

14 (a) $x \leqslant -1$ (b) $x > 3$ (c) $0 \leqslant x < 2$
    (d) $-3 < x < 3$ (e) $-2 < x \leqslant 0$ (f) $-1 \leqslant x \leqslant 3$

15 (a) $-3, -2, -1, 0$ (b) $1, 2, 3$
    (c) $-2, -1, 0, 1, 2, 3, 4$ (d) $-3, -2$

16 (a) $x > 10$ (b) $x \leqslant 5$
    (c) $x \leqslant 4\frac{1}{2}$ (d) $x \leqslant -2$
    (e) $x \geqslant -1\frac{1}{2}$ (f) $x < 0$
    (g) $x > -\frac{1}{2}$ (h) $x < 6\frac{1}{2}$
    (i) $x \geqslant -2$

17 (a) $x < 2\frac{1}{2}$

    (b) $x \geqslant -\frac{1}{2}$

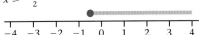

    (c) $x > 1\frac{2}{3}$

    (d) $x \leqslant -1$

    (e) $x < 2$

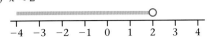

    (f) $x > 0$

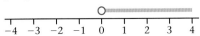

18 (a) $x < 3\frac{1}{2}$ (b) $y^2 + 7y + 12$
19 (a) $x = \frac{3}{5}$ (b) $-2, -1, 0, 1, 2, 3$
20 (a) $x = 3$ (b) $y = 6$

Exercise 6A

1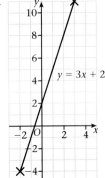

2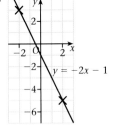

3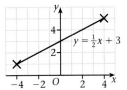

Exercise 6B

1 (a) Gradient $= 2$, y-intercept $= -3$
    (b) Gradient $= -1$, y-intercept $= 5$
    (c) Gradient $= 3$, y-intercept $= -6$
    (d) Gradient $= \frac{1}{2}$, y-intercept $= 2$

2 (a) (i) and (iii), (ii) and (iv)
    (b) (i), (ii) and (iv)
    (c) (i) and (ii)

3 (ii), (iii) and (vi)

4 (i), (ii), (iii), (iv) and (vi)

5 $y = -x + 5$

Exercise 6C

1 $x = 2, y = 5$
2 $x = 4, y = 5$
3 $x = 6, y = -1$
4 (a) $x = 5, y = 1$
    (b) $x = -1, y = 4$
    (c) $x = -4, y = -2$

5 (a)

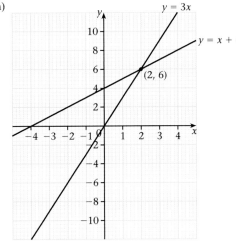

    (b)

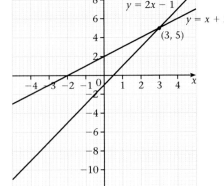

(c)

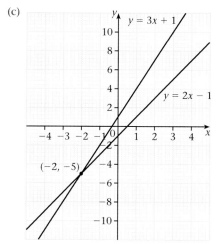

(d)

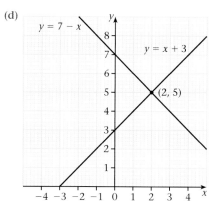

(e)

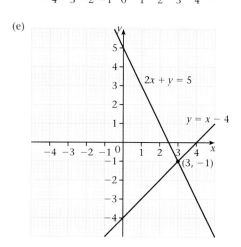

(f)

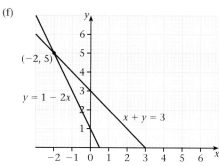

Exercise 6D

The equations in parts (c) will vary depending on the chosen lines of best fit.

1 (a)
(b)

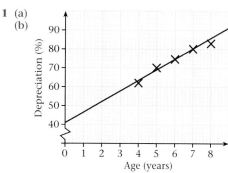

(c) $D = 5.6A + 41$

2 (a)
(b)

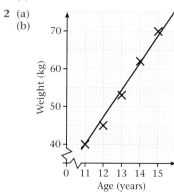

(c) $w = 7.25A - 40$

3 (a)
(b)

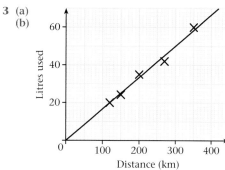

(c) $L = 0.17D$

4 (a)
(b)

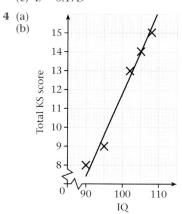

(c) $S = 0.41I - 29$

5 (a) (b)

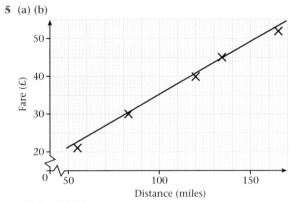

(c) $F = 0.28D + 7$

Exercise 6E

1 (a) (i) 120 SF   **(ii)** 30 SF   **(iii)** 90 SF   **(iv)** 210 SF
   (b) (i) £42   **(ii)** £54   **(iii)** £87   **(iv)** £77

2 (a)

Kilograms (kg)	0	10	20	30	40	50
Pounds (lb)	0	22	44	66	88	110

(b)

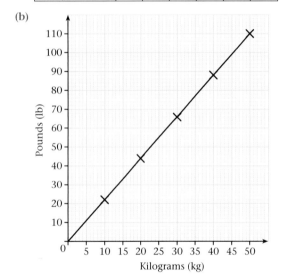

(c) (i) 73 lb   **(ii)** 19 kg

3 (a) 45 miles   **(b)** 11:00   **(c)** 30 min
   (d) (i) 45 mph   **(ii)** 36 mph   **(iii)** 36 mph

4 (a)

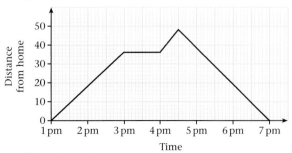

(b) 16 km per hour

5 (a) 1 min   **(b)** The first stage   **(c)** 10.85 km/h

Exercise 6F

1 (a)   **(b)**

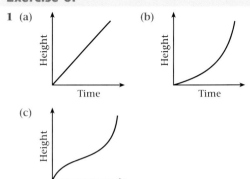

(c)

2 (a) The car was travelling at a constant speed and then slowed down steadily to travel at a slower speed.
   (b) The car was travelling along, then suddenly stopped, stood at rest for a short while, then started moving again, speeding up suddenly to the speed it was originally travelling at.

3

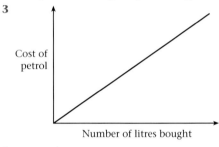

4

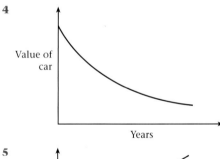

5

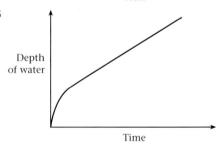

6 Ben earns a certain amount each week before overtime. He earns extra money in proportion to the number of overtime hours he works.

7

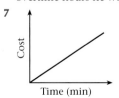

8 Lester started from rest, accelerated for the first 2 seconds to reach his maximum speed. He sprinted at this constant speed for about 6 seconds. He slowed down slightly for the last 2 seconds of the sprint, probably due to tiredness.

9 (a) 60 m (b) 10 m (c) 6.8 m

10 (a) £80 (b) 125 miles

Exercise 6G

1 (a)

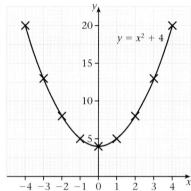

(b)

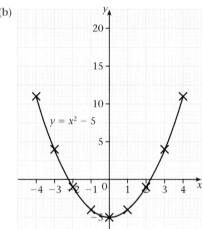

(c)

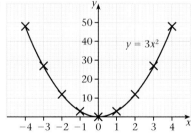

(d)

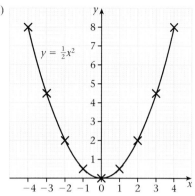

(e)

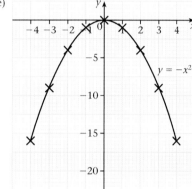

(f)

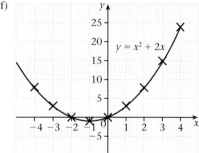

(g)

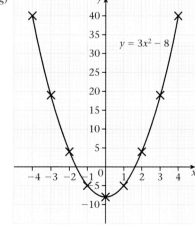

(h)

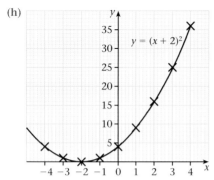

$y = (x + 2)^2$

2 (a)

x	−4	−3	−2	−1	0	1	2
y	2	−1	−2	−1	2	7	14

(b)

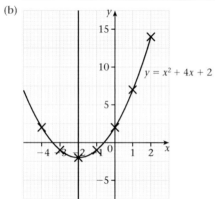

$y = x^2 + 4x + 2$

(c) $x = -2$

3 (a)

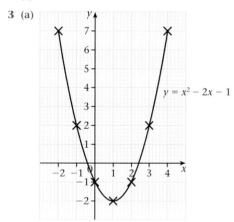

$y = x^2 - 2x - 1$

(b) Min. value of $y = -2$ and occurs at $x = 1$

4 (a)

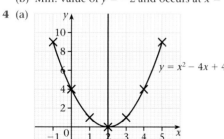

$y = x^2 - 4x + 4$

(b) $x = 2$
(c) Min. value of $y = 0$ and occurs at $x = 2$

5 (a)

x	−4	−3	−2	−1	0	1	2
y	11	1	−5	−7	−5	1	11

(b)

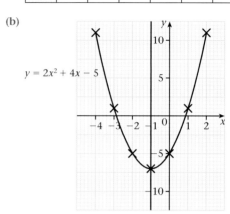

$y = 2x^2 + 4x - 5$

(c) $x = -1$
(d) Min. value of $y = -7$ and occurs at $x = -1$

6 (a)

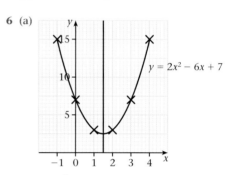

$y = 2x^2 - 6x + 7$

(b) $x = 1\frac{1}{2}$

7 (a)

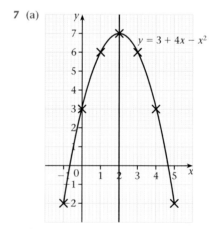

$y = 3 + 4x - x^2$

(b) $x = 2$
(c) Max. value of $y = 7$ and occurs at $x = 2$

Exercise 6H

1

x	-2	-1	0	1	2	3	4
y	6	1	-2	-3	-2	1	6

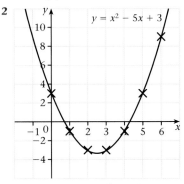

(a) (i) $x = -0.7$ and $x = 2.7$
    (ii) $x = -1.4$ and $x = 3.4$ (iii) $x = 1$
(b) $(1, -3)$
(c) Any $y < -3$

2

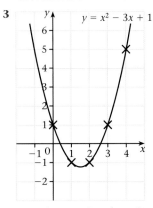

$y = -1$: $x = 1$ and $x = 4$
$y = 4$: $x = -0.2$ and $x = 5.2$
$y = 8$: $x = -0.9$ and $x = 5.9$
Coordinates of minimum value, $(2.5, -3.25)$

3

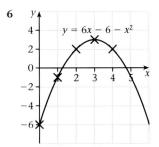

$y = -1$: $x = 1$ and $x = 2$
$y = 0$: $x = 0.4$ and $x = 2.6$
$y = 3$: $x = -0.6$ and $x = 3.6$
Coordinates of minimum value, $(1.5, -1.25)$

4

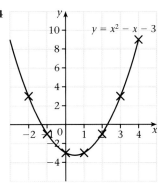

$y = -1$: $x = -1$ and $x = 2$
$y = 0$: $x = -1.3$ and $x = 2.3$
$y = 5$: $x = -2.4$ and $x = 3.4$
Coordinates at minimum value, $(0.5, -3.25)$

5

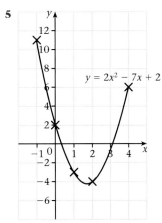

$y = -1$: $x = 0.5$ and $x = 3$
$y = 0$: $x = 0.3$ and $x = 3.2$
$y = 6$: $x = -0.5$ and $x = 4$
Coordinates at minimum value, $(1.75, -4.125)$

6

$y = 1$: $x = 1.6$ and $x = 4.4$
$y = 0$: $x = 1.3$ and $x = 4.7$
$y = -5$: $x = 0.2$ and $x = 5.8$
Coordinates at maximum value, $(3, 3)$

7

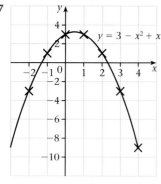

$y = 1$: $x = -1$ and $x = 2$
$y = 0$: $x = -1.3$ and $x = 2.3$
$y = -5$: $x = -2.4$ and $x = 3.4$
Coordinates at maximum value, (0.5, 3.25)

8 (a)

x	-3	-2	-1	0	1	2	3
y	18	8	2	0	2	8	18

(b)

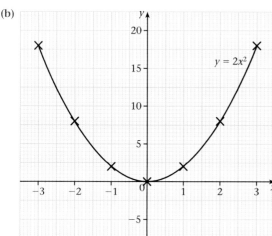

(c) (i) $y = 12.5$ (ii) $x = -2.45$ and $x = 2.45$

Mixed exercise 6

1 $x = 3$, $y = 2$

2 (a)

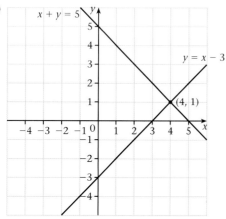

(b)

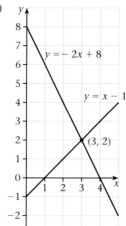

(c)

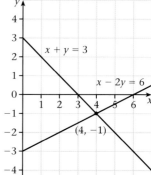

3 (a) (b)

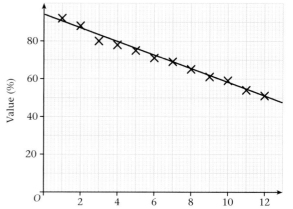

(c) $y = -3.6x + 94$

4 (a)

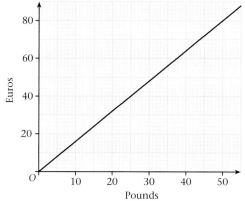

(b) (i) 70 euros   **(ii)** £23

5 (a)

Weight (lb)	Time (min)
5	90
10	165
15	240
20	315

(b)

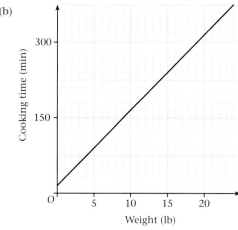

(c) (i) 270 min   **(ii)** 11 lb

6 (a) Kate starts to fill the bath at a steady rate. She turns off the taps for a short time then tops up the bath quickly. She turns off the taps and enjoys her bath. Finally she pulls out the plug and the water leaves the bath at a steady rate.
(b) While Kate first fills the bath the water temperature remains constant. When she turns off the taps the temperature falls. When she tops up the bath the temperature rises. The water temperature then falls steadily, continuing to fall when Kate empties the bath.

7 (a)   **(b)**

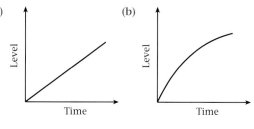

8 (a)

x	-3	-2	-1	0	1	2	3
y	1	-2	-3	-2	1	6	13

(b) (c)

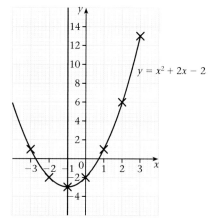

line of symmetry is $x = -1$

(d) $x = -2.7$ and $x = 0.7$

9 (a)

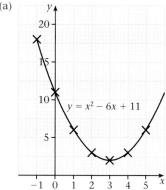

(b) Min. value of $y = 2$ and occurs at $x = 3$

10 (a)

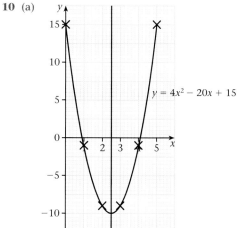

(b) $x = 2\frac{1}{2}$

(c) $x = 0.9$ and $x = 4.1$

11 (a) 15 min **(b)** 14.6 km

(c)

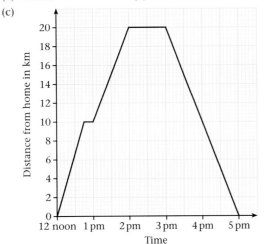

12 (a)

x	-2	-1	0	1	2	3	4
y	11	5	1	-1	-1	1	5

(b)

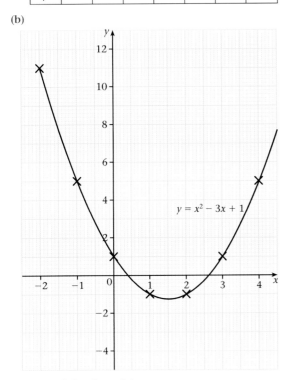

$y = x^2 - 3x + 1$

(c) $x = -0.6$ and $x = 3.6$

Exercise 7A

1 Perimeter = 35 cm
2 Wage = £185
3 Perimeter = 22 cm
4 Total bill = £19.20
5 Area = 40 cm²
6 (a) Total cost = number of stamps × cost of 1 stamp
 (b) Total cost = £5.04
7 (a) Number left = starting number − number sold
 (b) Number left = 29

8 Take-home pay = £184
9 (a) Number per person = number of sweets ÷ number of people
 = 21 sweets
 (b) Number of people = number of slices ÷ number of slices received
 = 12
10 Average speed = 43 mph
11 Angle sum = 900°
12 Exterior angle = 45°
13 Area = 50 cm² (to nearest whole number)

Exercise 7B

1 Length of each side = 7 cm
2 Number of hours worked = 33 hours
3 Width = 7 cm
4 Monthly charge = £9.90
5 Total distance travelled = 159 miles
6 Number of hours worked = 18 hours
7 Height = 3 cm
8 Time = $2\frac{1}{2}$ hours
9 Weight = 5 lb
10 Vertical height = 4 cm

Exercise 7C

1 $P = 6l$
 (a) $P = 18$ **(b)** $P = 42$
 (c) $P = 174$ **(d)** $P = 51.6$
2 (a) $A = 21$ **(b)** $A = 63$
 (c) $A = 22.2$ **(d)** $A = 37.8$
3 (a) $C = 6$ **(b)** $C = 16$
 (c) $C = 12$ **(d)** $C = 29$
 (all to nearest whole number)
4 (a) $E = 12$ **(b)** $E = 23$
5 (a) $y = 11$ **(b)** $y = 15$
 (c) $y = 23$ **(d)** $y = 18$
6 $P = 4a + b$
 (a) $P = 28$ **(b)** $P = 55$
 (c) $P = 24.6$ **(d)** $P = 27.3$
7 (a) $F = 50$ **(b)** $F = 212$
 (c) $F = -22$ **(d)** $F = 32$
8 (a) $V = 40$ **(b)** $V = 140$
 (c) $V = 240$ **(d)** $V = 199.206$
9 (a) $v = 20$ **(b)** $v = 20$
 (c) $v = 20$ **(d)** $v = 59$
10 (a) $T = 90$ **(b)** $T = 135$
 (c) $T = 195$ **(d)** $T = 285$
11 (a) $P = 70n$
 (b) (i) £2.80 **(ii)** £4.20 **(iii)** £8.40
12 (a) $V = 20$ **(b)** $V = 480.2$
 (c) $V = 26.875$

Exercise 7D

1 (a) $l = 4$ **(b)** $l = 9$
 (c) $l = 23$ **(d)** $l = 5.9$
2 (a) (i) $h = 9$ **(ii)** $h = 18$
 (b) (i) $b = 5$ **(ii)** $b = 15$
3 (a) (i) $F = 6$ **(ii)** $F = 14$
 (b) (i) $V = 7$ **(ii)** $V = 20$
4 (a) $x = 6$ **(b)** $x = 12$
 (b) $x = -6\frac{1}{2}$ **(c)** $x = -3$
5 (a) (i) $b = 3$ **(ii)** $b = 14$
 (b) (i) $a = 3$ **(ii)** $a = 5\frac{1}{2}$
6 (a) $x = 2$ **(b)** $x = -6\frac{1}{2}$
 (b) $x = 20$ **(c)** $x = -\frac{1}{4}$

7 (a) $h = 4$ (b) $h = 5$ (c) $h = 4$
8 (a) (i) $u = 5$ (ii) $u = 7$
   (b) $a = 6$ (c) $t = 4$
9 (a) $x = 20$ (b) $x = 85$
   (b) $x = 37$ (c) $x = 0$
10 (a) $d = 15$ (b) $d = -72$
   (b) $d = 45$ (c) $d = -58.24$

Exercise 7E

1 $d = \frac{P}{5}$ 2 $I = \frac{P}{V}$ 3 $w = \frac{A}{l}$

4 $d = \frac{C}{\pi}$ 5 $h = \frac{V}{lw}$ 6 $r = \frac{A}{\pi l}$

7 $x = \frac{y + 3}{4}$ 8 $n = \frac{t - 5}{3}$ 9 $y = P - 2x$

10 $m = \frac{y - c}{x}$ 11 $u = v + gt$ 12 $t = \frac{u - v}{g}$

13 $b = \frac{2A}{h}$ 14 $T = \frac{100I}{PR}$ 15 $V = \frac{D}{T}$

16 $V = \frac{kT}{P}$ 17 $T = \frac{PV}{k}$ 18 $v = \frac{I}{m} + u$

19 $b = \frac{2A}{h} - a$ 20 $x = 3(y + 2)$ 21 $x = \frac{1}{2}y + 1$

22 $y = \frac{1}{3}x - 2$ 23 $A = 2(17 - H)$ 24 $x = \frac{2y + 6}{3}$

25 $y = \frac{3x - 6}{2}$ 26 $q = P + 12$ 27 $x = \frac{y^2 + 12y}{2}$

Mixed exercise 7

1 (a) Total cost = £2000
  (b) Fixed costs = £700
  (c) Number of miles travelled = 7200 miles
2 (a) $v = 15$ (b) $u = 28$
3 (a) $A = l^2$ (b) $A = 81$
4 (a) $P = 2(l + w)$
  (b) (i) $P = 26$ (ii) $P = 20.2$
5 (a) $d = 31$ (b) $b = 28$
6 (a) (i) 68 °F (ii) 113 °F (iii) 158 °F
  (b) (i) 100 °C (ii) 50 °C (iii) 25 °C
7 9 trees
8 (a) $P = 4x + 8$ (b) length = 15.5 cm
9 $P = 5x + 2y$
10 (a) 57.6 (b) −133.95 (c) −594
11 (a) 300 cm² (b) 195 cm²
   (c) 10.585 cm² (d) 1.495 cm²
12 (a) 261.8 cm³ (b) 769.7 cm³
   (c) 203.9 cm³
13 (a) 56 (b) −52 (c) −124
14 20
15 (a) $S = 7$ (b) $m = 5$
16 (a) $v = 80$ (b) $v = 29.5$
17 (a) −5 (b) 73
18 $b = \frac{P - 2a}{2}$ 19 $x = \frac{1}{2}(P - y)$
20 $a = 2s - b - c$ 21 $D = TV$
22 $h = \frac{2A}{a + b}$ 23 $x = 5 - 2y$

Exercise 8A

1 (a)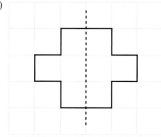

(b)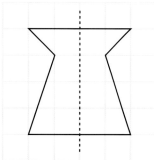

(c)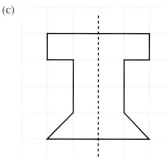

2 (a)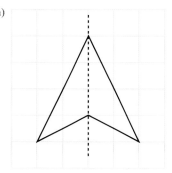

(b)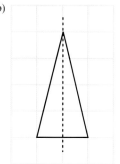

(c)

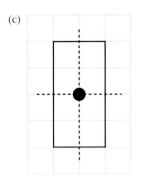

(d)

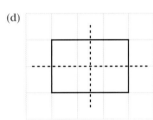

(e)

(f)

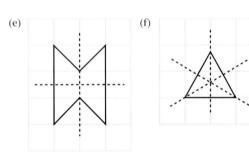

3

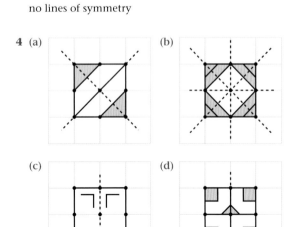

no lines of symmetry

4 (a)   (b)

(c)   (d)

(e)   (f)

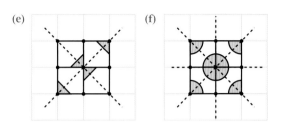

Exercise 8B

1 (a) 4   (b) no rotational symmetry
  (c) 2   (d) 5
  (e) no rotation symmetry
  (f) 4
2 (a) 7   (b) 10   (c) 8   (d) 12

Exercise 8C

1 (a)

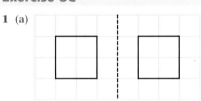

(b)

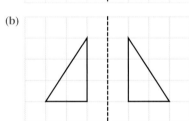

(c)

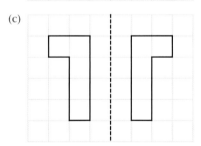

(d)

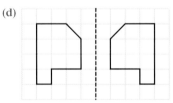

(e)

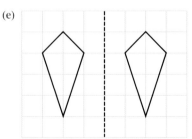

(f)

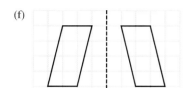

(g)

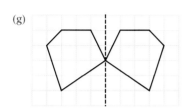

(h)

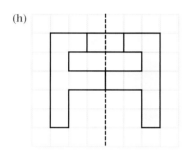

(i)

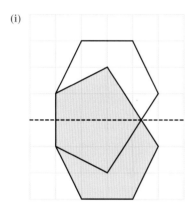

(j)

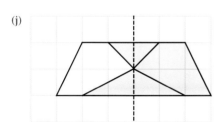

2

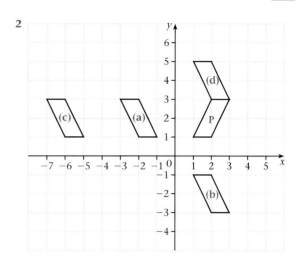

3

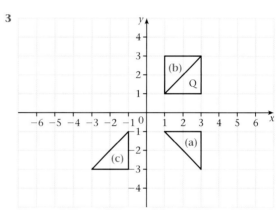

4 (a) $x = 0$ (b) $x = 3\frac{1}{2}$
   (c) $y = 0$ (d) $y = -x$

Exercise 8D

1 (a)

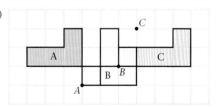

(b)

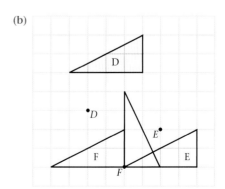

(c)

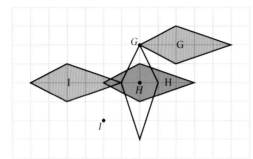

(d)

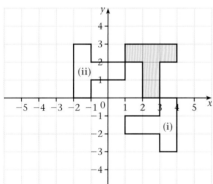

2 B rotation of 90° anticlockwise, centre origin
  C rotation 180°, centre origin
  D rotation of 90° clockwise, centre origin

3 (a)

(b)

1 (a)   (b)

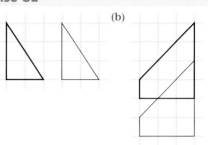

(c)   (d)

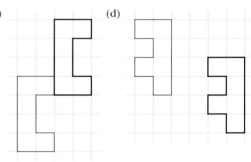

(e)

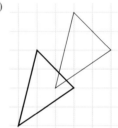

(f)

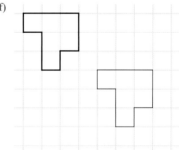

(g)

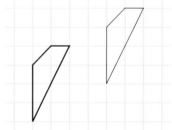

2 (a) (i)

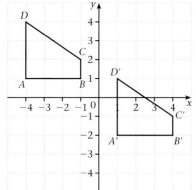

(ii) Translation by 5 units in the *x*-direction and
−3 units in the *y*-direction, or by $\begin{pmatrix} 5 \\ -3 \end{pmatrix}$.

(b) (i)

(ii) Translation by 2 units in the *y*-direction,
or by $\begin{pmatrix} 0 \\ 2 \end{pmatrix}$.

(c) (i)

(ii) Translation by 2 units in the *x*-direction and
−3 units in the *y*-direction, or by $\begin{pmatrix} 2 \\ -3 \end{pmatrix}$.

(d) (i)

(ii) Translation by −1 units in the *y*-direction, or
by $\begin{pmatrix} 0 \\ -1 \end{pmatrix}$.

3 (a) 1 square right and 3 squares down
(b) 1 square right and 5 squares up
(c) 2 squares left and 3 squares up
(d) 2 squares left and 5 squares down
(e) 2 squares right and 4 squares up
(f) 2 squares left and 5 squares up

Exercise 8F

1 (a)

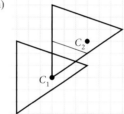

(b)

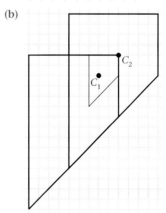

(c) **(d)**

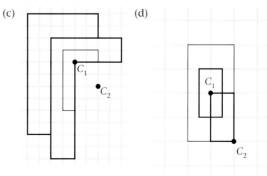

2 (c) Perimeter of shape 16 units.
  Perimeter of enlargements 32 units.
  (d) Perimeter of shape 12 units.
  Perimeter of enlargements 6 units.

3 (c) Area of shape 7 squares.
  Area of enlargements 28 squares.
  (d) Area of shape 8 squares.
  Area of enlargements 2 squares.

4 (a) Centre (0, 0), scale factor 2
  (b) Centre (0, 0), scale factor 3
  (c) Centre (0, 0), scale factor 2

5 Corresponding angle pairs:
  A and *P*, *B* and *Q*, *C* and *R*

6 (a) Scale factor 2
  (b) Scale factor 3
  (c) Scale factor 2

7
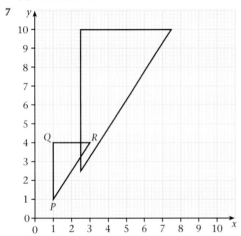

8 (a) 2 times
  (b) 4 times
  (c) 8 times

9 All squares are similar.

10 Rectangles are not all similar. For example
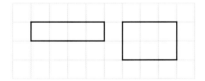

Exercise 8G

1 (a)
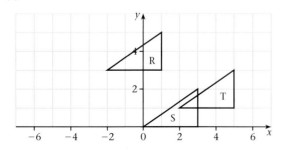

  (b) Translation by $\begin{pmatrix} -2 \\ -1 \end{pmatrix}$

2 (a) (b)
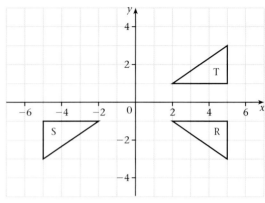

  (c) 180° rotation, centre (0, 0)
  (d) 180° rotation, centre (0, 0)

3 (a) (b)
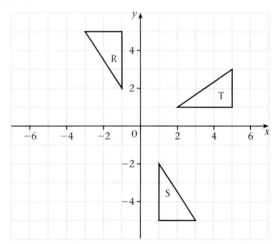

  (c) anticlockwise 90° rotation, centre (0, 0)
  (d) clockwise 90° rotation, centre (0, 0)

4 (a) (b)
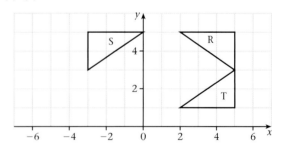

  (c) 180° rotation, centre (1, 3)
  (d) 180° rotation, centre (1, 3)

5 (a) (b)

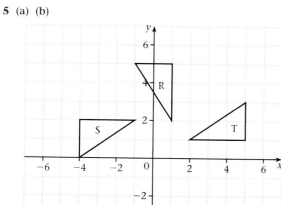

(c) 180° rotation, centre (0.5, 1.5)
(d) 180° rotation, centre (0.5, 1.5)

Exercise 8H

1 (a) (b)

(c) (d)

2 (a) (b)

3 (a) (b)

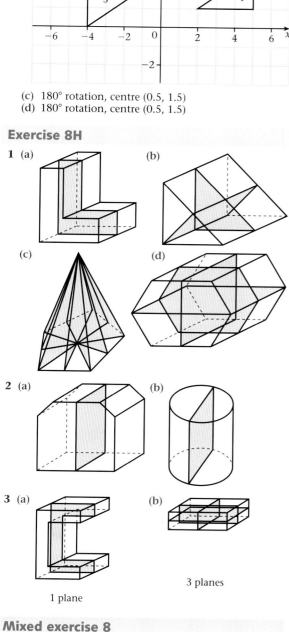

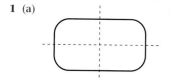
1 plane

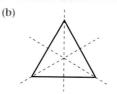
3 planes

Mixed exercise 8

1 (a) (b)

(c)

no lines of symmetry

(d)

no lines of symmetry

2 (a) 2   (b) 3   (c) 2   (d) 8

3 (a)

(b)

Other planes are possible.

4

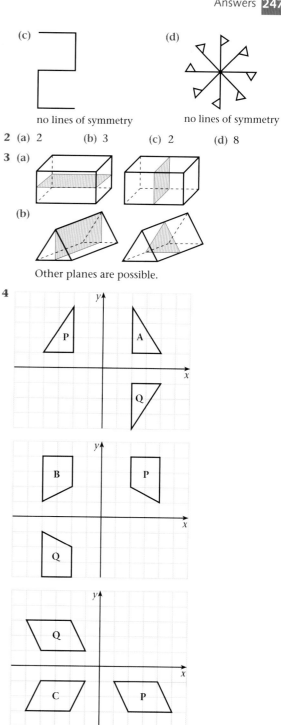

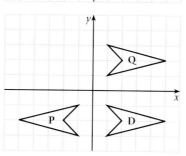

5

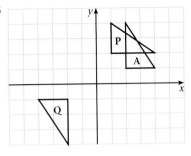

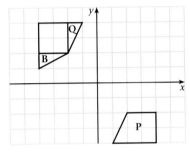

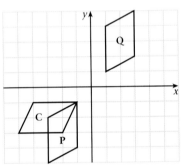

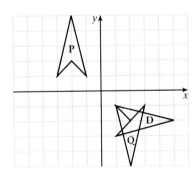

6

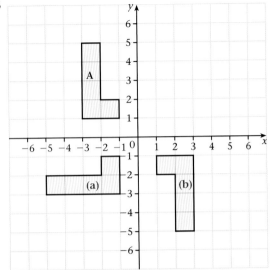

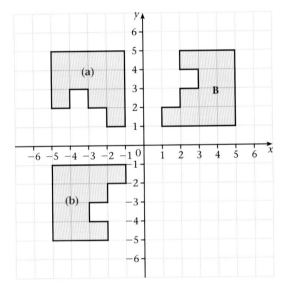

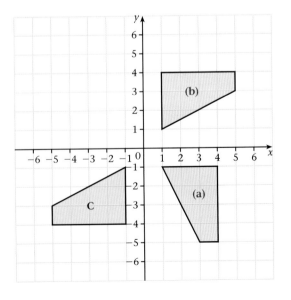

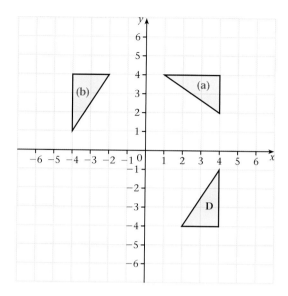

7 (a) Rotation of 90° anticlockwise, around the origin.
   (b) Rotation of 180°, around the origin.
   (c) Rotation of 90° clockwise, around the origin.

8

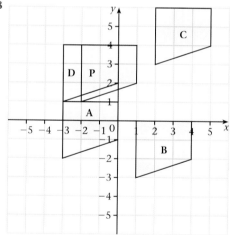

9 $\begin{pmatrix} 1 \\ -6 \end{pmatrix}$ translates **T** onto **A**

   $\begin{pmatrix} 7 \\ 0 \end{pmatrix}$ translates **T** onto **B**

   $\begin{pmatrix} 5 \\ -4 \end{pmatrix}$ translates **T** onto **C**

   $\begin{pmatrix} -2 \\ -2 \end{pmatrix}$ translates **T** onto **D**

10

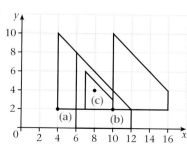

11

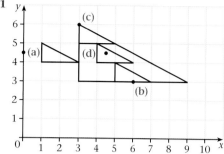

12 (a) (i)   Scale factor of enlargement **A** → **B** = $1\frac{1}{2}$
       (ii) Scale factor of enlargement **B** → **A** = $\frac{2}{3}$
       (iii) Centre $(-2, 0)$
    (b) (i)   Scale factor of enlargement **A** → **B** = $\frac{1}{2}$
       (ii) Scale factor of enlargement **B** → **A** = 2
       (iii) Centre $(9, 0)$

13 (a)

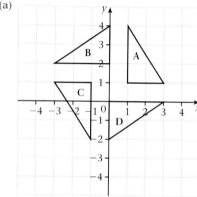

   (b) 180° rotation about $(0, 1)$

Exercise 9A

1 (a) 35°   (b) 110°   (c) 40°
   (d) 120°   (e) 245°   (f) 50°

2 (a)

   (b)

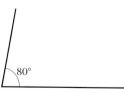

   (c)

(d)

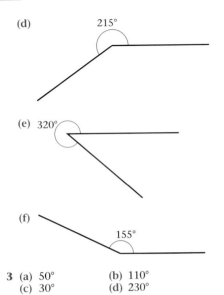

(e) 320°

(f)

155°

3 (a) 50°   (b) 110°
(c) 30°   (d) 230°
(e) 90°

Exercise 9B

1 (a) 50 mm
(b) 30 mm
(c) 65 mm
(d) 28 mm
(e) 83 mm

2 (a)   32 mm

(b)   57 mm

(c)   44 mm

(d)   61 mm

(e)   87 mm

3 (a)

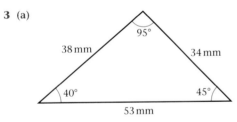

(b)

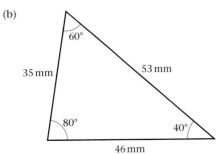

(c)

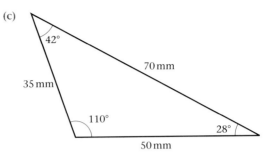

(d)

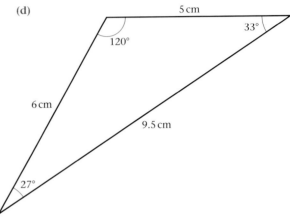

(e)

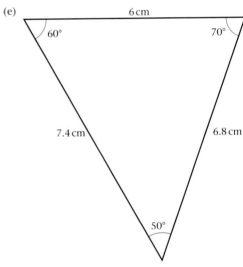

(f)

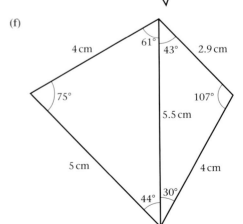

Exercise 9C

1 (a) 058° (b) 238°

2 (a) 034° (b) 124°
(c) 256° (d) 076°

3 (a) 091° (b) 058°
(c) 036° (d) 196°
(e) 271° (f) 294°
(g) 130° (h) 164°

4 (a) 051° (b) 056°
(c) 232° (d) 246°
(e) 289° (f) 286°
(g) 232° (h) 179°

5 (a) 024° (b) 072°
(c) 204° (d) 317°

Exercise 9D

1 (a) 12 km (b) 8 km
(c) 10 km (d) 5 km
(e) 8.5 km

2

	Ramsey	Castletown	Douglas
Castletown	32		
Douglas	18.8	14.4	
Peel	22.4	16.4	15.6

(Distances in kilometres)

3 45 km

4

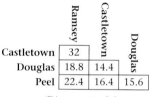

5

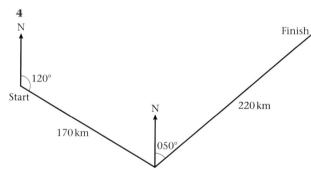

Less than actual size

6 (a) Actual size is 25 m by 32.5 m
(b) Measurements on map are 4 mm wide and 5 cm long

7 Real distances: Brownsea island is 2 km by 1.25 km
Bournemouth pier is 225 m long

Exercise 9E

All constructions are shown at less than actual size.

1 (a)

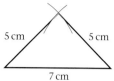

(b)

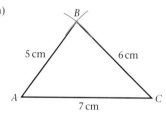

(c)

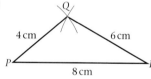

2 (a)

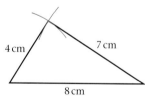

(b)

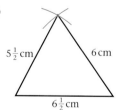

(c)

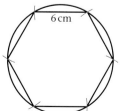

(d)

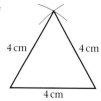

3

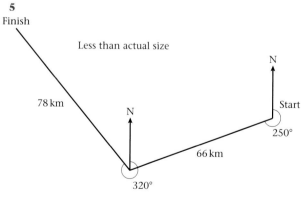

4

Exercise 9F

All constructions are half actual size.

1 (a)

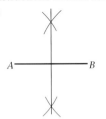

(b)

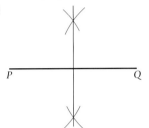

(c)

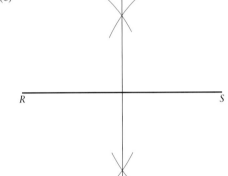

2

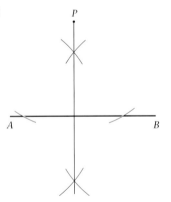

3 (a)

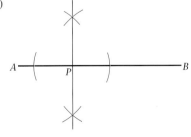

(b)

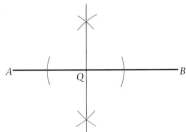

(c)

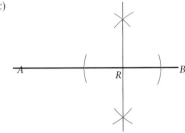

4 (a)

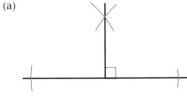

(b)

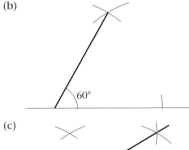

(c)

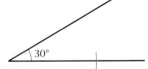

(d) (e)

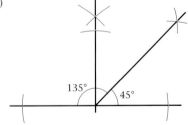

Exercise 9G

1 (a) Half size:

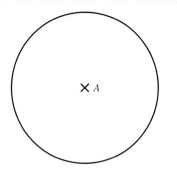

(b)

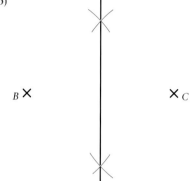

(c)

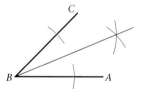

(d) Half size:

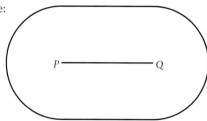

2

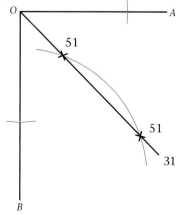

3 (a), (b), (c), (d)
Half size:

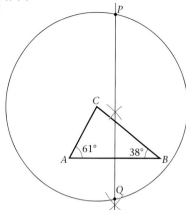

4 Half size:

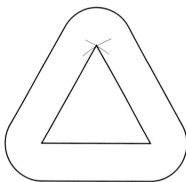

5 Half size:

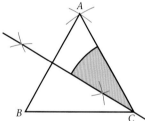

6 Half size:

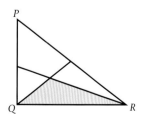

7 Half size:

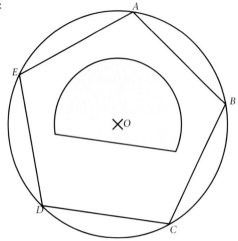

8 Half size:

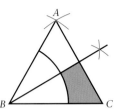

Exercise 9H

Constructions are shown half size.

1 (a)

(b)

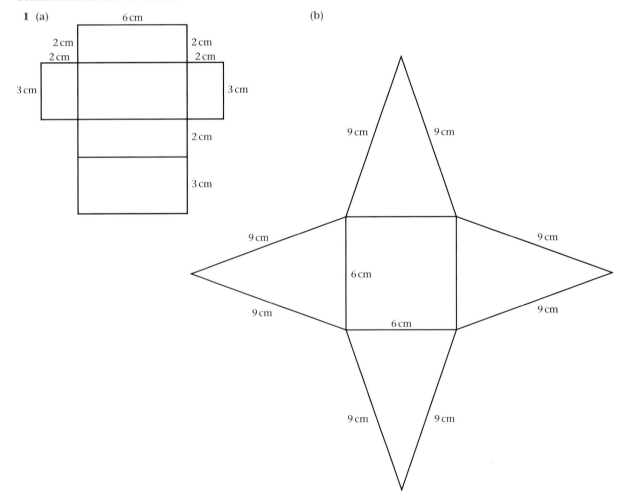

2

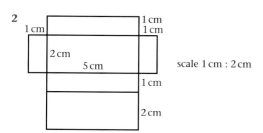

scale 1 cm : 2 cm

3

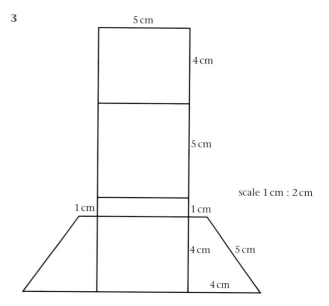

scale 1 cm : 2 cm

4

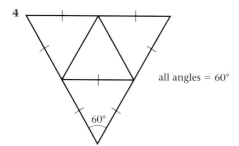

all angles = 60°

5

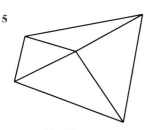

pyramid with trapezium as base

6 Yes, since the length of the rectangle is the same as the 'length' of the semi-circle.

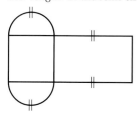

7 (a), (c), (e) and (f)

8 Possible answer:

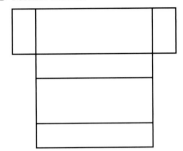

9

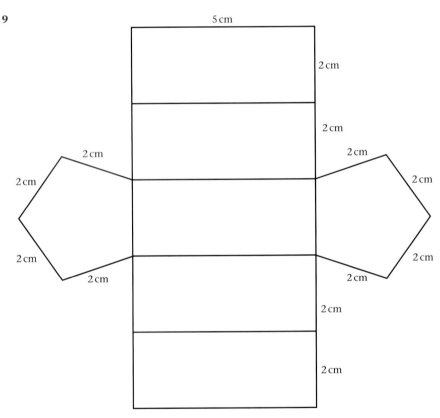

10 (a)

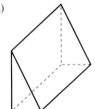

(b)

11

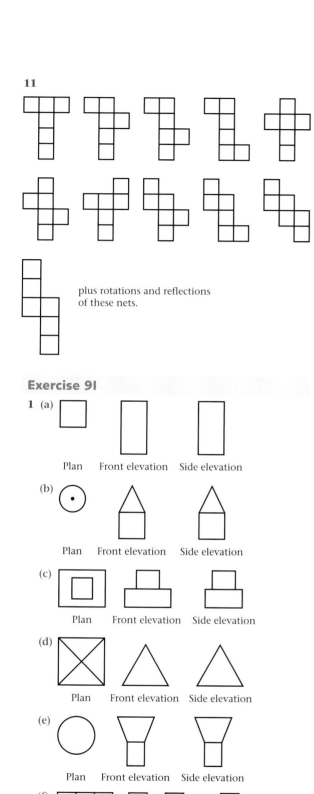

plus rotations and reflections of these nets.

Exercise 9I

1 (a)

Plan   Front elevation   Side elevation

(b)

Plan   Front elevation   Side elevation

(c)

Plan   Front elevation   Side elevation

(d)

Plan   Front elevation   Side elevation

(e)

Plan   Front elevation   Side elevation

(f)

Plan   Front elevation   Side elevation

(g)

Plan   Front elevation   Side elevation

(h)

Plan   Front elevation   Side elevation

2 (a)   (b)   (c)

(d)

(e)   (f)   (g)

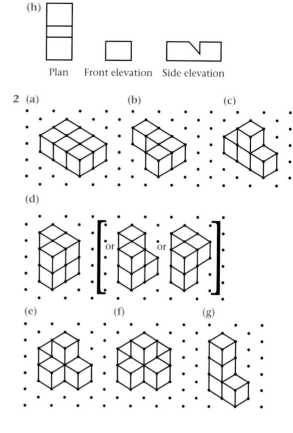

Exercise 9J

1 A and C are congruent
2 A and C are congruent
3 A and C are congruent
4 B and D are congruent
5 A and C are congruent
6 F and G are congruent,
J and L are congruent

Exercise 9K

1 30°
2 ∠BCD = 130°, ∠BAD = 100°
3 ∠BCD = 100°, ∠BAD = 160°
4 x = 36°

Exercise 9L

1 (a) 40°   (b) 140°
2 (a) 60°   (b) 120°
3 12 sides
4 (a) 18°   (b) 20 sides
5 (a) 150°   (b) 135°   (c) 147°

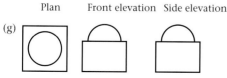

1 (a)

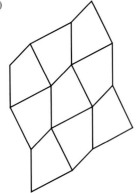

(b)

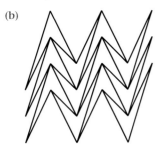

(c)

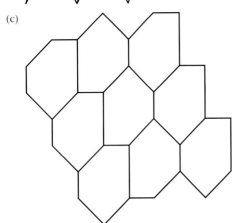

2

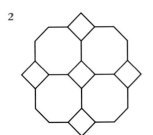

3 e.g.

Mixed exercise 9

1 (a) Half size:

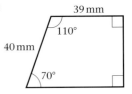

(b) Half size:

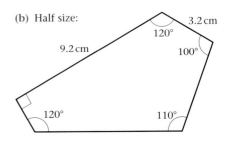

2 The trapezium on the RHS does not 'meet' the sides of the 2 triangles and the rectangle, to close up to make the 5th side.

3 (b)

4 (a) 40
(b) 6840°

5 (a) $a = 100°$
(b) $x = 130°$

6 (a) 070°
(b) 250°
(c) 090°
(d) 270°

7 (a), (b) Half size:

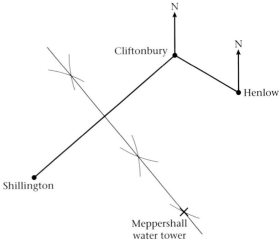

8 (a), (b)

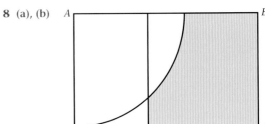

9 (a), (b)

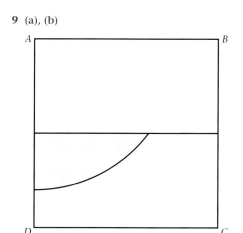

10 Half size:

11 (a) (b) (c)

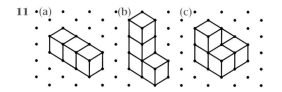

12 (a) Half size:

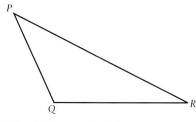

(b) $PR = 10.6\,\text{cm}$, $\angle Q = 26°$

13

150°

14

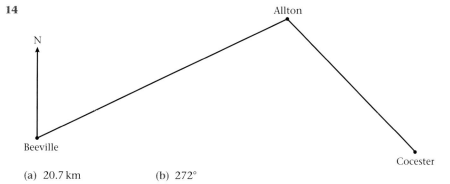

(a) 20.7 km (b) 272°

15

Plan   Front elevation   Side elevation

(a)

(b)

(c)

(d)

16

17 $b = 94°$

18 (a) $5x + 120 = 360$ (b) $58°$

19 Half size:

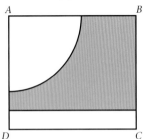

20 Half size:

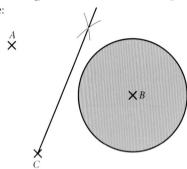

21 (a)

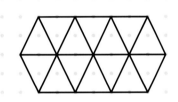

(b)

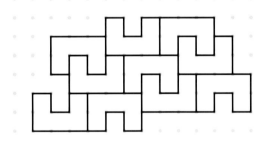

(c)

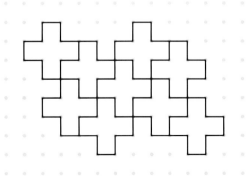

Exercise 10A

1 (a) 50 000   (b) 280 000
   (c) 12 000   (d) 1 050 000
   (e) 2.6   (f) 0.34
   (g) 800   (h) 2200
   (i) 24   (j) 362

2 (a) 2 300 000   (b) 40 000
   (c) 304 000   (d) 7
   (e) 0.53   (f) 0.0265
   (g) 4000   (h) 13 050
   (i) 8.4   (j) 0.43

3 (a) (i) 6.3 m^2 (ii) $63\,000 \text{ cm}^2$
   (b) (i) 0.882 m^3 (ii) $882\,000 \text{ cm}^3$

Exercise 10B

1 (a) Circumference = 37.7 cm, area = 113 cm^2 (3 s.f.)
   (b) $C = 88.0$ cm, $A = 616 \text{ cm}^2$ (3 s.f.)
   (c) $C = 52.2$ cm, $A = 216 \text{ cm}^2$ (3 s.f.)
   (d) $C = 4.65$ m, $A = 1.72 \text{ m}^2$ (3 s.f.)
   (e) $C = 35.5$ cm, $A = 100 \text{ cm}^2$ (3 s.f.)
   (f) $C = 43.7$ mm, $A = 152 \text{ mm}^2$ (3 s.f.)
   (g) $C = 5.03$ m, $A = 2.01 \text{ m}^2$ (3 s.f.)

2 4.91 cm^2 (3 s.f.)

3 Diameter = 7.96 m (3 s.f.), area = 49.7 m^2 (3 s.f.)

4 201 cm

5 (i) (a) Area = $256\pi \text{ cm}^2$, circumference = 32π cm
     (b) Area = $144\pi \text{ mm}^2$, circumference = 24π mm
     (c) Area = $6.76\pi \text{ m}^2$, circumference = 5.2π m
     (d) Area = $792.42\pi \text{ m}^2$, circumference = 56.3π m
   (ii) (a) Area = 804.25 cm^2 (2 d.p.)
       circumference = 100.53 cm (2 d.p.)
     (b) Area = 452.39 mm^2 (2 d.p.)
       circumference = 75.40 mm (2 d.p.)
     (c) Area = 21.24 m^2 (2 d.p.)
       circumference = 16.34 m (2 d.p.)
     (d) Area = 2489.46 m^2 (2 d.p.)
       circumference = 176.87 m (2 d.p.)

6 (a) 2513 mm (4 s.f.)
   (b) 125.66 m (2 d.p.)

7 Area = 907.9 m^2 (1 d.p.),
   circumference = 106.8 m (1 d.p.)

8 Diameter = 26.42 m (2 d.p.)

9 (i) (a) Area = $8\pi \text{ cm}^2$, perimeter = $(8 + 4\pi)$ cm
     (b) Area = $28.125\pi \text{ cm}^2$, perimeter $(15 + 7.5\pi)$ cm
     (c) Area = $6.48\pi \text{ cm}^2$, perimeter = $(7.2 + 3.6\pi)$ cm
     (d) Area = $4.205\pi \text{ m}^2$, perimeter = $(5.8 + 2.9\pi)$ m
   (ii) (a) Area = 25.13 cm^2 (2 d.p.)
       perimeter = 20.57 cm (2 d.p.)
     (b) Area = 88.36 cm^2 (2 d.p.)
       perimeter = 38.56 cm (2 d.p.)
     (c) Area = 20.36 cm^2 (2 d.p.)
       perimeter = 18.51 cm (2 d.p.)
     (d) Area = 13.21 m^2 (2 d.p.)
       perimeter = 14.91 m (2 d.p.)

10 Area = 9.82 m^2 (2 d.p.), perimeter = 12.85 m (2 d.p.)

11 3.00 cm (2 d.p.)

12 (a) 333.6 m^2 (1 d.p.)
   (b) 82.3 m (1 d.p.)

13 $(12.5 + 2.25\pi) \text{ m}^2$

14 $(20 + 2\pi)$ mm

15 (a) Area = 8827.43 m^2 (2 d.p.),
     perimeter = 388.50 m (2 d.p.)
   (b) Area = 388.36 m^2 (2 d.p.),
     perimeter = 78.56 m (2 d.p.)

16 76.3 cm^2 (1 d.p.)

Exercise 10C

1. (a) 24 cm²   (b) 7.5 cm²
   (c) 25 cm²   (d) 61.5 cm²
2. 6 cm²
3. Area of $\triangle AQD = \frac{1}{2}w \times l = \frac{1}{2}lw$

   Area of $\triangle DPC = \frac{1}{2}l \times w = \frac{1}{2}lw$ = area of $\triangle AQD$
4. Let d be the distance between AB and $PXQY$.
   Area of $ABXP = d \times AB$
   Area of $ABYQ = d \times AB$ = area of $ABXP$
5. Area of $AYBX = 2 \times$ area of $\triangle ABY = AB \times AD$
   Area of $ABCD = AB \times AD$ = area of $AYBX$
6. Extend AD to meet QP at H.
   AB, DC and QP are parallel. (Sides of rectangle and parallelogram)
   $\angle AMD = \angle DQH$ (alternate angles)
   $\angle ADM = \angle QDH$ (vertically opposite angles)
   $MD = QD$
   So AMD is congruent with HQD (ASA)
   and $AD = DH$
   Area of $CPQD = DC \times DH = DC \times AD$ = area of $ABCD$

Exercise 10D

1. (a) 54 cm²   (b) 27 cm³
2. (a) 1044 cm²   (b) 2040 cm³
3. (a) 246 cm²   (b) 216 cm³
4. (a) 99 cm²   (b) 63 cm³
5. (a) 444 cm²   (b) 520 cm³
6. 739 760 cm³   7. 10 080 cm³
8. 12 000 cm³   9. 260 m³

Exercise 10E

1. (a) V: 1700 cm³, 540π cm³
       A: 792 cm², 252π cm²
   (b) V: 165 mm³, 52.488π mm³
       A: 224 mm², 77.76π mm²
   (c) V: 82.5 cm³, 26.264π cm³ (Numerical answers to 3 s.f.)
       A: 130 cm², 41.44π cm²
2. 1.27 m
3. (a) 2 cylinders   (b) 173 cm³ (to 3 s.f.)
4. 3 full tumblers
5. 376.99 cm² (2 d.p.)
6. (a) (i)   6361.73 cm² (2 d.p.)
       (ii) 6488.96 cm² (2 d.p.)
       (iii) 14 313.88 cm³ (2 d.p.)
   (b) (i)   1507.96 cm² (2 d.p.)
       (ii) 1517.01 cm² (2 d.p.)
       (iii) 904.78 cm³ (2 d.p.)
   (c) (i)   2827.43 mm² (2 d.p.)
       (ii) 3180.86 mm² (2 d.p.)
       (iii) 10 602.88 mm³ (2 d.p.)
   (d) (i)   376.99 mm² (2 d.p.)
       (ii) 1790.71 mm² (2 d.p.)
       (iii) 2827.43 mm³ (2 d.p.)

Exercise 10F

1. (a) $a = 5$ cm   (b) $b = 30$ cm
   (c) $c = 16.16$ cm (2 d.p.)   (d) $d = 7.16$ cm (2 d.p.)
2. (a) $a = 7.19$ cm (2 d.p.)   (b) $b = 3.76$ cm (2 d.p.)
   (c) $c = 16.83$ cm (2 d.p.)   (d) $d = 19.68$ cm (2 d.p.)
3. Length of diagonal = 28.30 cm (2 d.p.)
4. Length of cable = 50.99 m (2 d.p.)
5. $AD = 10.44$ cm (2 d.p.)
6. (a) 5   (b) 13
   (c) 4.12 (2 d.p.)   (d) 8.60 (2 d.p.)
   (e) 8.06 (2 d.p.)   (f) 8.60 (2 d.p.)

Exercise 10G

1. (a) 12 cm   (b) 16 cm
   (c) 18.73 cm (2 d.p.)   (d) 11.73 cm (2 d.p.)
2. (a) $a = 5.0$ cm (1 d.p.)   (b) $b = 10.7$ cm (1 d.p.)
   (c) $c = 8.7$ cm (1 d.p.)   (d) $d = 19.4$ cm (1 d.p.)
3. (a) Height = 13.4 cm (3 s.f.)
   (b) Height = 11.0 cm (3 s.f.)
4. Length of side = 8.49 cm (3 s.f.)
5. Ladder reaches 7.75 m up the wall (3 s.f.)
6. Distance from edge of ramp to building
   = 1.98 m (3 s.f.)

Mixed exercise 10

1. (a) 70 000   (b) 0.5
   (c) 6000   (d) 0.0325
   (e) 78   (f) 3 070 000
   (g) 9.5   (h) 5
2. Answers to 1 d.p.
   (a) Area 113.1 cm², perimeter 37.7 cm
   (b) Area 132.7 cm², perimeter 40.8 cm
   (c) Area 127.2 cm², perimeter 46.3 cm
3. (a) $a = 8.5$ cm (1 d.p.)
   (b) $b = 9.2$ cm (1 d.p.)
   (c) $c = 20$ cm
4. 22 km (3 s.f.)
5. 7.2 m (1 d.p.)
6. (a) Volume 480 cm³, surface area 376 cm²
   (b) Volume 2.16 m³, surface area 12.96 m² (2 d.p.)
   (c) Volume 3.02 m³, surface area 16.08 m² (2 d.p.)
7. 360 000 cm³
8. (a) 754 cm³ (3 s.f.)
   (b) 478 cm² (3 s.f.)
9. 109.96 m (2 d.p.)
10. 374 cm (3 s.f.)
11. 3 m
12. 271 cm³ (3 s.f.)
13. (a) 4 cm
    (b) 100 boxes

Examination practice paper

Section A (calculator)

1.

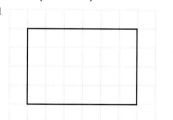

(not actual size)

2. (a) £3   (b) $\frac{1}{5}$ (c) 3 sweets
3. (a) 11 bags   (b) 5p
4. (a) 15 cm   (b) 10 cm
5. £604.80
6. (a)

   (b)

7 (a) (i)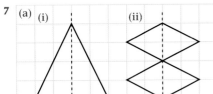

(ii)

(b) (i)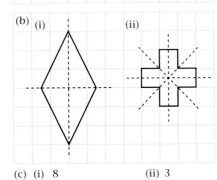

(ii)

(c) (i) 8 **(ii)** 3

8

5.5 cm

65°

8.3 cm

9 (a) £30
(b) $m = rn$
10 (a) (i) −1 **(ii)** −10 **(iii)** 3
(b) (i) 5^5 **(ii)** 4^3
11 £48
12 (a) $p = 3$ **(b)** $q = 5\frac{1}{2}$ **(c)** $r = -15$
13 (a) $v = 15$ **(b)** $v = 40$
(c) $t = 2$ **(d)** $t = \frac{1}{5}(v - u)$

14 £188
15 $x = 2.3$ (1 d.p.)
16 16.97 cm (2 d.p.)

Section B (non-calculator)

1 (a) 1.5 **(b)** 0.05
2 (a) −3°C, −1°C, 0°C, 1°C, 3°C
(b) (i) Edinburgh **(ii)** Plymouth
3 (a) B and D **(b)** A and E
4 (a) cone **(b)** cuboid
5 £32
6 (a) $p = 3$ **(b)** $t = 5$
7 (a) and (b)

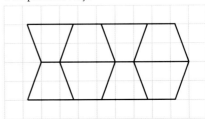

(c) Circle, diameter 9 cm
8 £1.35
9 (a) 5 **(b)** £30
10 (a) 69 miles **(b)** 367 miles
11 (a) A right-angled triangle **(b)** P and S
12 (a) $\frac{5}{8}$ **(b)** $\frac{1}{6}$
13 £420
14 $x = 20°$
15 One possible way:

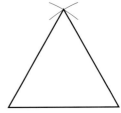

16 Half actual size:

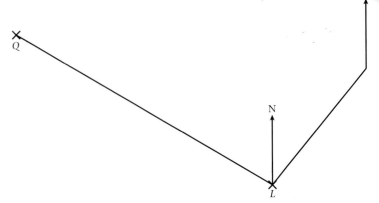

17 Amy 6 sweets, Beth 9 sweets, Colin 12 sweets
18 (a) −3, −2, −1, 0, 1 **(b)** $x > -\frac{1}{5}$
19 (a) 220°
(b)

20 35 000 cm²